AF903676

Systems of Control in International Adjudication and Arbitration

Systems of Control in International Adjudication and Arbitration

Breakdown and Repair

W. Michael Reisman

Duke University Press *Durham and London 1992*

© 1992 Duke University Press
All rights reserved
Printed in the United States of America
on acid-free paper ∞
Library of Congress Cataloging-in-Publication Data
appear on the last printed page of this book.

Quis custodiet ipsos custodes?

Contents

Preface

The invitation to deliver the Currie Lecture in 1989 happily coincided with the final phases of a research cycle. For the past five years, I had been examining control systems within a number of different types of international dispute resolution processes. The trend, in all of them, has been toward a breakdown of certain key practices and procedures that I believe perform a unique function in international dispute resolution. The implications should be a cause for concern, all the more when the need for effective modes of international dispute resolution is so widely perceived. The opportunity to address these issues in the lecture format was particularly timely for me, for, in contrast to a legal treatise which is essentially a specialist's user's manual that organizes every case in a complex mosaic, a lecture permits its composer to try to sketch and appraise broader trends and their implications for the larger community and thus to assist in the policy process by focusing on consequences and alternatives.

Control is a pervasive problem in international application. The selection of examples of international control systems could not be exhaustive. I selected examples that represent the broad categories of public international institutions, private commercial arrangements, and arrangements designed for mixed privity between public and private entities. Early in my research I decided not to examine the role of the International Court of Justice as a control of the administrative tribunals of the international civil service, for it appeared to be moving steadily toward an appeal function. The control system of the United States-Canadian Free Trade Agreement is, in contrast, very much akin to what I was studying. But as of the time this manuscript was completed, no cases had yet emerged.

In chapter 2 I have drawn on several short studies I published over the past five years which represented, at the time of their appearance, tentative appraisals. Equipped with a more comprehensive conception of control systems, I have, in some ways, revised my view of them here.

I had the good fortune to be involved in the review phases of the Klöckner and AMCO cases. Decisions in each have decisively shaped the control mechanisms of the World Bank's major arbitral initiative, the International Centre for the Settlement of Investment Disputes, or ICSID as it is commonly known. They are discussed in chapter 3. As will be clear, this second lecture is not concerned with those decisions on their merits, but only with the issue of their impacts on arbitral control mechanisms. Nonetheless, the reader should examine the pages dealing with them with the knowledge that, for some of the cases discussed, the author was a participant as well as an observer.

An earlier version of chapter 3 was published in the *Duke Law Journal.* After it appeared, three additional ICSID decisions pertinent to the problem considered were rendered. One of them appears to have addressed directly the issues raised in the *Duke Law Journal* article. Chapter 3 has been revised in their light.

Much of international arbitration is a folklore rather than a science, in the sense that it is not found in written form but is an oral tradition or *jurisprudence confidentielle*, known largely and, for the most part, exclusively to its practitioners. I am grateful to those who practice in this field or who engage in practice and scholarship, and who have shared their experience with me. Many people have helped me, but I am particularly grateful to Myres S. McDougal for comments on the materials in chapter 2, to Carolyn Lamm and W. Michael Tupman, for their comments and criticisms on some of the materials in chapter 3 and to Professor William Park for the ideas and criticisms he contributed to chapter 4. His influence on my thinking on this part of the problem will be apparent, and I am happy to acknowledge it.

I have had a number of discussions about the early phases of the Klöckner cycle with Jan A. Paulsson. He provided useful background and perspective in this and other areas of international commercial arbitration. In many discussions over the years, the late Paul Reuter was candid in describing and Cartesian in analyzing the role of the arbitrator. Andrew R. Willard read the entire manuscript, raised important and difficult questions, and made many useful suggestions. Dr. Edward Kwakwa helped in the research of chapters 3 and 4. The staff of the Yale Law School Library helped beyond the call of duty. Gene P. Coakley of the library staff rapidly found even the most obscure cases and doctrine. Tim Niedermann prepared the index. Cheryl A. DeFilippo typed the manuscript and supervised its final preparation with the efficiency and diplomatic skill for which she is so well-known at Yale.

I would not have been able to complete this book were it not for a fellowship at the Institute for Advanced Study in Berlin in 1990. Particular thanks are due to the very considerate and helpful library staff there.

Thanks for permission to reprint selections from previously published articles to: the University Press of America, for permission to print my "Termination of the United States Declaration Under Article 36(2) of the Statute of the International Court" which was originally published in *The United States and the Compulsory Jurisdiction of the International Court of Justice 71–106* (ed. A. C. Arend, 1986); the *American Journal of International Law* (AJIL), © The American Society of International Law, for selections from "Has the International Court Exceeded Its Jurisdiction?" in 80 AJIL pp. 128–134 (1986); selections from "The Other Shoe Falls: The Future of Article 36(1) Jurisdiction in the Light of Nicaragua" in 81 AJIL pp. 166–173 (1987); selections from "Respecting One's Own Jurisprudence: A Plea to the International Court of Justice" 83 AJIL pp. 312–317 (1989); *Yale Journal of International Law* (YJIL) for selections from "An International Farce: The Sad Case of the PLO Mission" 14:2 YJIL pp. 412–432 (1980); and *Duke Law Journal* for selections from "The Breakdown of the Control Mechanism in ICSID Arbitration" 4 *Duke Law Journal* pp. 739–807 (1990).

Michael Reisman
July 22, 1991

Systems of Control in International Adjudication and Arbitration

1 Introduction

Control Systems

Arbitration is a delegated and restricted power to make certain types of decisions in certain prescribed ways. Any restricted delegation of power must have some system of control. Controls are techniques or mechanisms in engineered artifacts, whether physical or social, whose function is to ensure that an artifact works the way it was designed to work. In social and legal arrangements in which a limited power is delegated, control systems are essential; without them the putative restrictions disappear and the limited power may become absolute. The impulse to establish control systems, one might add, is animated neither by cynicism nor by fear of initiative. It rests on a healthy grasp of reality, indeed, one on which the United States constitutional experiment is based. Nor should controls be conceived in a negative sense. Controls are necessary not only for efficient operation. Effective controls are the only assurance of limited government. In this sense controls are a sine qua non of liberty.

In sociolegal arrangements, controls may be internalized or externalized or combinations of both techniques may be used. Internal legal systems of control have ranged from devices such as reliance on supernatural intervention (for example, by the use of oaths or rituals), on the inculcation and demonstrable application of craft skills, on collegiate decision structures in which tasks and roles are distributed among a number of participants, on insistence on manifest reasoning, and on peer pressure.

External controls have included such devices as checks and balances exercised by coequal or coordinate decision entities or on complex hierarchical arrangements, each successive level providing some supervision and potential review and rectification of the work of the preceding. Hierarchical configurations of control are animated, in part, by the desire to control the preceding levels. Controls effected by balances may dispense with hierarchies; they depend, for their effectiveness, on power parities. For several centuries the international political system used this mechanism of "balance of power" as its control device. Although the language of mechanics and hydraulics is often used in these discussions, all legal controls, one should remember, must be effected by people.

Some control systems are genetic, in the sense that they are designed as part of the original conception of the process to whose operation they contribute. Others are added on, as experience reveals that the process is encountering factors or obstacles or operating in environments which had not been considered at the time of its creation. Hence new control arrangements—new fuses, new governors, another set of emergency brakes, an additional comptroller—are grafted on. The biological evolution of life on our planet has followed this trial-and-error approach. In social and legal arrangements, efforts are always made to plan controls, but subsequent corrections or additions are often required. In our constitutional scheme, for example, some control systems are built into the genetic constitution. Others, such as judicial review, were added on, by the initiative of some participants, when their appraisal persuaded them that additional controls were required.[1] Still others are fashioned after calamity generates the belief that recurrences can be avoided by additional controls.

When physical control systems break down—the brakes fail, the thermostat cuts out, or the governor pops—the system may simply stop functioning, go out of control, or destruct. When social and legal control arrangements break down, the decision process does not necessarily fail. But it certainly changes, as more power shifts to the now comparatively less-controlled decision-maker. This is particularly the case in arbitration. With controls it remains a delegated and restricted power. Without controls it becomes absolute. Thereafter, the arbitrator, like the Roman emperor, may be tempted to say "*quod voluit arbiter habet vigorem legis*": "whatever the arbitrator wants *is* the law." Hence the linkage between controls, limited power, and liberty.

Controls are a virtual prerequisite for international third-party decision. When we deal with optional international decision processes, that is those in which, for the most part, participation is voluntary and in which the expectation of the operation of the control mechanism may be an important factor in decisions opting to use a particular process, an actual or anticipated control breakdown such as this is likely to induce many actors henceforth to refrain from using the process. Thus controls in international adjudication and arbitration are not simply conditions of efficient operation. They are conditions of operation. Much as lawyers cannot practice law without clients, international tribunals cannot decide disputes without litigants. Litigants come on an entirely voluntary basis and have no reason to come to an uncontrolled process.

Yet breakdowns in legal controls in general are not necessarily calamitous. Depending on the values of the appraiser, some breakdowns may even be viewed as positive. If oligarchical controls break down, for example, those who have been freed from them may characterize the change as democratizing and liberating. When the breakdown concerns controls designed to restrain capital from creating concentrations which might reduce competition, the wealth elites who have been released may, similarly, characterize the change as liberating.

In international law one of the traditional controls on the exercise of power by states over investments there by nationals of other states was the insistence that applications of local law by the host state be subject to international review under a variety of criteria. When many of the developing states, in a movement called the New International Economic Order,[2] resolved that, henceforth, they could expropriate without international controls and control themselves, as it were, in their own courts, they characterized it as a liberation.[3] But the very foreign investors who were necessary both for their development and for the application of their domestic jurisdiction over them began to withdraw. When control systems break down and the result is a reduction in the overall effectiveness of the decision process of which they are a part, for example, by a reduction in participation, the breakdown must be characterized as a pathology. The point bears emphasis. While controls, from the perspective of some actors, may be viewed as unpleasant, unfair, or even intolerable restraints, the ultimate evaluation of their utility, if not indispensability, is their contribution to the effective operation of the system of which they are a part.

Because control systems affect the allocation of costs and benefits of the processes in which they operate, they are always highly political, often controversial, and frequently the subject of explicit policy consideration. When control systems cause changes which appear to have negative effects on the system to whose operation they are supposed to contribute, it becomes appropriate, if not urgent, to inquire about better alternatives.

Judicial Control Systems

In some domestic adjudication, a hierarchical judicial bureaucracy operates as the control system for state-sponsored dispute resolution. Successive levels of the bureaucracy appraise and reappraise the general workings of the system as well as the accuracy, consistency, and justice (the calculus of rectitude of the system and its environing culture) of particular applications, making adjustments where they seem appropriate. These levels are comprised of a permanent staff which is recruited to the bureaucracy, inculcated with organizational values and itself subjected to effective policing and disciplinary mechanisms. A distinct legislative bureaucracy provides an additional, contingent system of control, which can intervene when its own appraisals indicate that the performance of the judicial bureaucracy, for some of the tasks it has been assigned, is unsatisfactory.

"An ounce of prevention is worth a pound of cure." In terms of economy, the preferred control system is always internalized and prospective rather than externalized and retrospective. Judicial control is better accomplished, for example, within the court system than by the legislature, and better accomplished by the legislature than in extralegislative agitation. It is better that the system anticipate and obviate problems rather than repair them and whatever peripheral damage they will have caused *after* they erupt. Where control is vital for mission accomplishment and/or system survival and it is probable, following "Murphy's law," that some initial efforts at control will, as a matter of statistical probability, not succeed, back-up control systems are devised. Hence the common phenomenon of redundancy, multiple, sequential control levels, found in nature and human artifacts, is not necessarily a product of faulty planning or oversight.

All control systems involve costs. Judicial control systems have costs in terms of the funds needed to establish and maintain them and in terms of the time which must be expended in the successive levels of appeal before a dispute is finally resolved. It is arguable that the more hierarchical layers of protection a bureaucracy has, the more likely it is to get things right. But here, as elsewhere, there is no free lunch. The expenses of establishing and maintaining the vast control superstructure are "passed through" to users, raising the costs of justice, in terms of money and time, and, for some marginal actors, pricing them out of the very system which is supposed to offer them the opportunity to protect their rights. At the same time, other actors, calibrating the rising nuisance value provided by the sequential appeal options, may be encouraged to start dubious actions with the not implausible expectation that settlement, at an early stage, will appear more cost-effective to those they are harassing than a perforce lengthy and expensive vindication of their legal rights.

Added layers of control also increase time costs: the length of the interval between claim and disposition. The old adage "justice delayed is justice denied" is often true in the sense that a delayed victory may deprive the winner of substantial economic value. The costs generated by control systems are imposed on the parties who must pay, at many levels, to defend their positions and whose treasure may be immobilized pending final decision and on the community which must finance the control system and may, itself, be deprived, pending the final decision, of many of the benefits of the values frozen in dispute.

Considerations such as these generate a tension between two control system policies: justice and finality. The old Roman maxim said *interesse rei publicae ut sit finis litium*, "the public interest requires that there be an end to disputes," which imports a clear cutoff point, an arbitrary "enough-is-enough" point. Abraham Lincoln's statement that "nothing is final until it's right" rejects any arbitrary cutoff point. That statement may have been based as much on political realism as on moral conviction; for, right or wrong, diffused popular indignation can acquire a common vector and become political power. New arrangements to regain social stability may then be required. The interest in finality means that an arbitrary limit for control systems must be established. The interest in justice means simply that justice must be done, no matter what the cost nor how long it takes. Control systems perforce strike compromises between these interests. The compromises themselves will often reflect larger political configurations.

There is no such thing as an "ideal" control system, for each system is, like all legislation, an experiment in social control in which legal ingenuity and sometimes creativity try to adapt or invent institutional arrangements within the limits of available resources and political tolerances and in response to the special features of the context in which it operates. Because control systems are creatures of their contexts, it is no surprise that there are such striking differences between national and international control arrangements. In brief national systems are, for the most part, hierarchical and multilevel, while international control systems are, for the most part, nonhierarchical systemic adaptations.

Control Systems in International Arbitration

For a new and rapidly growing category of events which we often call, for lack of a better term, "transnational,"[4] international commercial arbitration, broadly understood, now performs many of the functions of domestic adjudication. But international arbitration lacks a set of bureaucratic institutions comparable to its domestic counterparts which might perform its control functions, and the international political environment has not been conducive to their creation. Hence international arbitration has approached the control problem in an entirely different way.

In international law the basic theory of arbitration is simple and rather elegant. Arbitral jurisdiction is entirely consensual. As in Roman law and the systems influenced by it, arbitration is a creature of contract. The arbitrator's powers are derived from the contract. Hence an arbitrator is not entitled to do anything not authorized by the parties: in its classical formula in the Digest of Justinian, *arbiter nihil extra compromissum facere potest.*[5] An arbitral award rendered within the framework of the common agreement of the parties is itself part of the contract and hence binding on them. But an award which is produced in ways inconsistent with the shared contractual expectations of the parties is something to which they had not agreed. The arbitrator has exceeded his power or committed what French law and international doctrine calls an *excès de pouvoir*. If an allegation of nullity can be sustained, the putative award is null and may be ignored by the "losing" party.

A theory like this is quite advantageous to parties, for it gives them an additional contractual option for resolving disputes without engaging the community's courts. It is also advantageous to the community. Private disputes are essentially diversions from productive activity. An arbitral control mechanism facilitates their economical resolution without more general disruption and without direct cost to the community. The doctrine of *excès de pouvoir* is supposed to function as a control mechanism in this theory. Without it, *whatever* an arbitrator did, no matter how inconsistent it might have been with his instructions, would have produced a binding award. The arbitrator would become an absolute decision-maker and arbitration would lose its character of restrictive delegation. *Excès de pouvoir* is the conceptual foundation of control for arbitration. It is not, however, without certain problems.

This kind of control mechanism can work well in an organized political-legal system, with a hierarchical control system equipped with an effective compulsory jurisdiction to review allegations of excessive jurisdiction and to decide impartially the alleged nullity of the award. But it is susceptible to abuse in a system, like the international one, in which there is no such permanent and effective hierarchical structure. In the absence of a reviewing authority, a party alleging that an arbitrator did something not authorized by the agreement to arbitrate is simultaneously prosecutor, judge, and jury *in sua causa*. The potential for abuse is obvious. Ironically, the very theory of nullity which serves, in domestic contexts, to police the arbitrator and thus encourages arbitration tends, in the international setting, to undermine it. But the alternative to the risk of unilateral abuse, no control, is also unacceptable.

As long as arbitration was infrequently used and parties could discount losing beforehand, this system, while hardly optimal, worked. But as modern transnational arbitration increased as a function of the expansion of transnational activity, the inadequacy of this control mechanism in this new context became more apparent. Arbitration was in danger of being undermined.

The apparent solutions were unsatisfactory.[6] Efforts to make awards binding without regard to their possible *excès de pouvoir*—in effect, abandoning all control systems—may well have discouraged resort to arbitration. Legal decision without control runs the danger of reducing predictability, and rational actors are unlikely to submit matters that are important to them to a voluntary dispute system that ranges from uncertain to capricious. Efforts to allow claims of nullity and to try to control them by making them precise have been countered by fears of abuse, for it has been assumed (and not unreasonably) that the more precise the grounds for nullifying, the more claims for nullification there will actually be. A leitmotiv of modern international arbitration has been the search for a way of breaking free of the unsatisfactory consequences of each of these alternatives by devising some sort of new institutional device that could provide responsible and predictable control, while minimizing the potential for abuse of claims of nullity.

The possibilities of solving this problem were quite limited in the absence of some sort of permanent or "standing" international institution or set of institutions. If such institutions could be created, even if they were not necessarily hierarchical, they would at least be *there* when the need arose. They could be authorized, preferably in advance of the dispute, to decide a claim that an international award was null for some *excès de pouvoir*. An unratified treaty between the United States and the United Kingdom signed on January 11, 1897, indicates the limits of a control scheme which depended, for its effectuation, on an institution that did not yet exist: if members of the tribunal were not unanimous with regard to claims exceeding £100,000, "either party may demand a review. . . . In such a case the matter in controversy shall be submitted to an Arbitral Tribunal, consisting of five jurists of repute."[7] But the establishment of this second tribunal required the agreement and cooperation of the parties, precisely the ingredient that would be absent at the stage in which it was most necessary.

Policy Considerations

Contemporary international arbitration must literally adopt or invent its own control system. In doing so it faces a number of intertwined practical and policy problems that are different from domestic adjudication and which tend to make a direct and unqualified co-optation of domestic control institutions counterproductive. A major incentive for international commercial arbitration is its promise of simplicity, economy, supranational neutrality, and speed. The fact that the parties can shape the tribunal and, if they so decide, individually appoint one of the arbitrators with the expectation that he or she will be sympathetic to their view certainly makes arbitration attractive, certainly more attractive than adjudication in an alien national court system. Many would say that properties such as these are arbitration's raison d'être.

But many of these same attractive features militate against an elaborate control mechanism; for, as in domestic practice, such a mechanism would temporally extend and raise the cost of dispute resolution. The desirable properties of international arbitration also militate against exclusive or heavy reliance on domestic courts as control institutions. Yet without these familiar control mechanisms, can one rely exclusively on the social controls inherent in face-to-face relationships, small groups, and "old boy networks?" The very scale and wide dispersal of transnational events reduces the efficacy of these social controls. National, legal, and general cultural heterogeneity, the larger number of actors and the increased randomness of arbitrator combinations, all of which are characteristic of contemporary international arbitration, make latent social controls such as peer pressure and common values of personal conscience more ephemeral and marginal and, on the whole, less effective than in more homogeneous national settings.

The diminished effect of all of these latent control devices could encourage violations and ultimately undermine resort to international arbitration. The absence of controls would leave the international arbitral system prey to "moral hazard,"[8] unable to correct those potentially serious injustices whose probability of occurrence is increased by the very absence of controls.

In national judicial bureaucracies, key parts of the control system may be lodged in the hierarchical network of courts hearing appeals. The fact that the same role may be assigned both review and control functions is confusing, but hardly unusual, especially in international law. There, the phenomenon of *dédoublement fonctionnel*,[9] the doubling of functions of particular actors, is the rule rather than the exception. But the consolidation of functions is not without problems.

The conflation of appeal and control should not lead students or actors to assume that the functions are identical. Appeal is a form of control, but it is not identical with it. Appeal, viewed from within the system, is concerned with rectifying any of a broad range of errors in order to put the decision in question in conformity with the key policies of the community. Control is concerned with the very existence of the community, its decision process, and its continuing efficient operation. In most general terms, discharge of the control function requires a broader macro-organizational perspective. Appeal is concerned with what is right for the parties. Control is concerned with the minimum conditions for the continuation of the process of decision itself.

The control and appeal functions may sometimes apply similar criteria and reach identical conclusions. But in many cases, issues of concern on appeal will not be relevant to the control function, in the sense that however the appeal may be decided, none of the concerns of control will be implicated. The point, which is elusive in a national setting because of the location of control functions in part of the judicial bureaucracy, is clearer in international arbitration. The comparatively limited grounds on which an award may be attacked in a review procedure, as opposed to the broader grounds on which an appeal may be lodged, signal different concerns. Indeed, a control system may enforce an award that would (indeed, should) be struck down had it been a judgment on appeal. Such an anomaly is characteristic of arbitral review.

The functional distinctions between and different responsibilities of appeal, review, and control raise acute problems in international commercial arbitration. Where there are widely differentiated institutions, as, for example, in the French municipal legal system, it might be possible to lodge these different functions in separate institutions. But internationally there are relatively few institutions with which to work. Some candidates, such as national courts, would impose costs on the functioning of international commercial arbitration that could price it out of the business.

For all of these reasons, modern international commercial arbitration, in its broad acceptance, continues to experiment with a number of types of unique control systems. Though each was devised at a different moment in the past, in a different institutional context, and with a different *Problematik*, they have interacted and interstimulated, for many of the problems are the same and the experience of one effort has been pertinent and of value to the other. Because most of the control systems are still in operation, they, together, constitute a type of living museum of comparative law and organization, its successes and its pathologies. For different reasons, most of the experiments are in crisis. Some of them are in danger of failing.

In this lecture, I propose to guide you through the museum. The museum has an international wing and, you will be surprised to discover, a very substantial national wing. The latter is inescapable. Even those who resist the idea of systemic controls for international commercial arbitration have appreciated that, in the final phases of the arbitral process, the assistance of national courts is necessary for enforcement and that the expectation of the probability of that enforcement is a key factor in "voluntary" compliance. Some of the exhibits are mixtures of both international institutional and national systems. National systems involve an interaction between international agreements expressing mandatory international control policies and national legislative instruments which operate in tandem with the international agreements, implementing them but, at the same time, incorporating potentially divergent national policies.

Behind each exhibit, whether international, national, or mixed, is the classic arbitral control device of the unilateral claim of *excès de pouvoir.* This particular control functions as a "failsafe," the final backup control device designed to kick into operation when all the others are exhausted. Failsafes are not an optimal control mechanism. Some failsafes—like Kubrick's "Doomsday Machine" or its contemporary reincarnation, "Mutual Assured Destruction"—are supposed to operate by destroying the system and all its participants.

Many people visit museums for diversion. My purpose in this lecture is not to provide a guided tour of curiosities and exotica for purposes of entertainment. Legal scholarship learns in order to improve. Its contribution in this field can be particularly important, for, to a remarkable extent, modern arbitration is less a creature of state initiative and more a creation of the academic and practicing bar. If there are problems in its current operation, they are ours to solve. Although I have tried to propose solutions in the three problem areas treated, my main objective has been to clarify the problem and to provoke others to invent solutions for other international institutions.

2 The International Court: The Atrophy of Informal Control Mechanisms

Some scholars still distinguish sharply between public international tribunals, supposedly operating only at the interstate level, and international commercial tribunals, which are established to resolve disputes of nonstate entities operating transnationally. The division may have been cogent in the past, but it has become obsolete and now obscures rather than clarifies important factual and policy issues. Many essentially commercial matters are heard in public international tribunals, such as the International Court of Justice. Conversely, the type of interstate matters that frequently appear on the docket of the International Court may also arise in international commercial tribunals. An institution such as the Iranian-U.S. Claims Tribunal processes both public and commercial international matters.[1]

The great public international tribunals have often served as models for private developments and vice versa. Thus, there has been a certain amount of interstimulation in which the experiences of one are shared and sometimes transferred to another. For all of these reasons, scholarly and policy purposes are served by beginning with an examination of the various control mechanisms of the International Court, the longest operating of currently extant international tribunals and one whose experiences have served as a touchstone for all subsequent international efforts, be they of public or private international law.

The Historical Background

Though we use the word "court" to describe both national and international phenomena, the institutions to which the single term refers indiscriminately are quite different. International courts historically were arbitral tribunals, created by state elites to resolve particular controversies. The individuals who were appointed to these tribunals understood that the institutions did not have a general jurisdiction *ratione materiae* or *ratione personae*. Their jurisdiction was limited to the particular issue submitted to them and to the particular parties submitting them. Once the issues assigned had been decided, the tribunal dissolved. Judicial exercises purporting to go beyond those limits were *excès de pouvoir* and were subject to nullification. In any case, they were sure to be ignored by the losing party.

But given the fact that only one question or, less frequently, one class of questions was submitted to the tribunal, the possibilities of excess were quite limited. Not surprisingly, the number of cases of noncompliance with awards on grounds of *excès de pouvoir* were very few. Scholarly discussion of the problem tended to be theoretical.

From 1899 on, efforts were mounted to establish more durable international courts. But from the standpoints of jurisdiction and political function, these experiments were still essentially of the classical type of international arbitration, with its distinctive control functions.

In 1920 a new tack was taken. A permanent tribunal, appropriately named the Permanent Court of International Justice (PCIJ), was established by the states that founded the League of Nations.[2] Rather than a tribunal created for a particular problem, the Permanent Court, as its name indicated, was to be continuous. In contrast with its predecessors, this court had a permanent registry and a permanent and imposing courthouse. Its judges were elected in a complex procedure by member-states of the League of Nations,[3] and they served for nine years[4] rather than, as in the past, for the duration of the case for which they were appointed.

The PCIJ could be used as a traditional arbitral tribunal: states that had agreed to arbitrate a dispute could decide to refer it to the Permanent Court rather than to an ad hoc tribunal, one which would be established by the parties only for that dispute and would dissolve on rendering its award. Article 29 of the 1926 Treaty of Commerce and Navigation Between Greece and the United Kingdom is typical of this sort of arbitral use of the PCIJ. Article 29 stated:

> The two Contracting Parties agree in principle that any dispute that may arise between them as to the proper interpretation or application of any of the provisions of the present Treaty shall, at the request of either party, be referred to arbitration.
>
> The court of arbitration to which disputes shall be referred shall be The Permanent Court of International Justice at The Hague.[5]

But the durability of the Permanent Court also permitted states so disposed to make longer-term commitments to submit all disputes or certain categories of disputes with regard to any other state seeking adjudication which had made a comparable commitment. Article 36 of the Statute of the Permanent Court provided:

> The Members of the League of Nations and the States mentioned in the Annex to the Covenant may, either when signing or ratifying the protocol to which the present Statute is adjoined, or at a later moment, declare that they recognize as compulsory ipso facto and without special agreement, in relation to any other Member of State accepting the same obligation, the jurisdiction of the Court in all or any of the classes of legal disputes concerning:
>
> (a) the interpretation of a treaty;
>
> (b) any question of international law;
>
> (c) the existence of any fact which, if established, would constitute a breach of an international obligation;
>
> (d) the nature or extent of the reparation to be made for the breach of an international obligation.

This optional system was fairly simple to describe and seemed to incorporate an intuitive equity. A state deposited a unilateral declaration with the secretary-general of the League of Nations (and later of the United Nations) stating that it was prepared to submit all or certain disputes it might have with any other state if that other state had made a comparable declaration. Thus, in a systematically incremental (and individually in an entirely optional) fashion, a type of general jurisdiction could begin to take shape, different from both the classic arbitral jurisdiction and the personal, territorial, and subject-matter jurisdiction enjoyed by, let us say, a federal court in the United States.

But the conception of jurisdiction that emerged was unique. Rather than a general jurisdiction over events taking place in or affecting a particular part of the planet or over particular types of issues or quanta of money, all deriving from the power of some organized political community, this was a filigree of unilateral and contingent jurisdictional commitments between such communities. Together, this filigree formed a gauzy, contingent fabric, extremely open-textured at the beginning, each warp and woof representing some commitment by a state to submit to the jurisdiction of the court the issues described in its commitment vis-à-vis some other state which, at some point in the past, had made a commitment that was, in its essentials, congruent.

Ideally, this process of unilateral commitments by states was to continue growing, weaving, interweaving, and becoming ever more dense, until a continuous fabric of international jurisdiction was created and covered the entire international community. Then all legal disputes would be resolved judicially. In the interim, before this judicial robe descended on the world, the court would be available for the vanguard, the "shock troops" of international adjudication—those states that had decided that they preferred to conduct all or designated parts of their foreign relations through international adjudication. And, of course, the court could also serve as a conventional arbitration tribunal to which states that had signed its statute without making special jurisdictional commitments could still submit themselves by an additional special agreement.

Restrictive Jurisdiction as an Internal Control Mechanism

This remarkable jurisdictional innovation was not accompanied by a corresponding innovation with regard to control. Nor was it certain if and to what extent the classical control mechanism of ad hoc arbitration—*excès de pouvoir*—still applied. It was arguable that a partial control was built into this system by its very optional character, for the statute contained neither a legal nor a moral obligation to adjudicate. After all, resort to adjudication in the international system was still entirely voluntary. From the standpoint of international law, a state might be obliged to seek to try to resolve peacefully its disputes with other states, but the modality of peaceful resolution to be selected was still a matter of its own discretion. So one might contend that *volenti non fit injuria*. But this could be called a control only in a rhetorical sense, for legal decision imports some procedural and substantive predictability. A state contemplating adjudication still counted on certain practices and procedures to be followed. Indeed, that expectation would have been one element in its decision to submit to adjudication, especially if the matter in dispute were important to it. Without a control system, a commitment to adjudicate would include a commitment to accept even capricious decisions inconsistent with procedural and substantive decisions.

Arguably, reciprocity provided another latent control. Because this system of submission to the court's jurisdiction was based upon reciprocity, no state could be obliged to adjudicate on more matters than the state seeking to invoke its declaration. By the same token, no state could ask more from another state than it had previously declared itself willing to accept. In theory, legal officers in different states could scan the declarations, which appeared annually in publications of the League and then the United Nations, to see which states had declarations roughly congruent with their own. Should disputes arise, a legal officer knew that his government had the option of either initiating adjudication in the court or, alternatively, being impleaded by the other state.

Neither of these features constituted a meaningful control system. To say that the voluntary character of adjudication here acted as a restraint simply talks around the problem. Arbitration, too, was voluntary, but no prudent government official would contemplate it were there not some controls available. Curiously enough, a regime which involved a much greater and ultimately unpredictable commitment than ad hoc arbitration had ever had—an open-ended commitment to submit to a court whose composition could change in unpredictable ways in a dispute concerning a state as yet unknown at a time of that state's choosing—did not incorporate an explicit and formal control system. To claim that reciprocity controlled the system begged the question which was whether mechanisms were in place to ensure that reciprocity was actually and properly applied.

Potentially drastic *external* controls were built into the enforcement phase of judgments rendered by the PCIJ's successor, the International Court of Justice. Article 60 of the statute of the court provides, in relevant part, "The judgment is final and without appeal." The obligation of the statute to comply with judgments is now reinforced in Article 94(1) of the UN Charter: "Each member of the United Nations undertakes to comply with the decision of the International Court of Justice in any case to which it is a party." The enforcement mechanism, in cases of noncompliance, is set out in Article 94(2) of the Charter: "If any party to a case fails to perform the obligations incumbent upon it under a judgment rendered by the Court, the other party may have recourse to the Security Council, which may, if it deems necessary, make recommendations or decide upon measures to be taken to give effect to the judgment."[6] Article 94 gives the Security Council rather broad discretion to ignore a noncompliance or to sanction it in some innocuous fashion: "The Security Council . . . may, if it deems necessary. . . ." "May" and "if it deems necessary" provide a redundancy of lawyers' "weasel words." Even if the Security Council chose to enforce a particular judgment, it was far from certain that the charter had really empowered it to accomplish the task. Should the council, under this scheme, elect to issue a recommendation, it would, by definition, have no compulsory force. Should the council decide to issue a decision, it would, presumably, be subject to the veto power of any of its Permanent Members. Even if a Permanent Member were a party to the dispute but did not participate in the council, the possibility of a veto was still high.[7]

Thus, the scheme allows for a measure of control through what amounts to a possibility of review and partial or total nullification, in effect, by the Security Council of a decision of the court. But in terms of the considerations of preferred control systems considered in the Introduction, this is a heavy-handed, externalized control mechanism. It does not allow for self-correction by the initial or even a proximate decision process. Nor can it operate without injury to the international adjudicative system. More moderate and informal controls, which can head off difficulties earlier, are preferable; some, such as a strict and restrictive theory of jurisdiction, were a legacy of general international arbitral law and were implicitly provided.

These sorts of informal internalized controls rested ultimately on the traditionally restricted conception of consensual jurisdiction. The Permanent Court was scrupulous in not asserting jurisdiction unless there were clear indications that the parties had agreed to it. The decisions and dicta on this point recur with regularity in the court's jurisprudence. In Mavromattis Palestine Concessions,[8] the court said: "Its jurisdiction is limited, . . . it is invariably based on the consent of the respondent and only exists insofar as this consent has been given." The court itself, the majority continued, "must satisfy itself that the suit before it, in the form in which it has been submitted and on the basis of the fact hitherto established, falls to be decided by application of the clauses [of the jurisdictional document]."[9] The judges who dissented in Mavromattis were in complete accord with the majority on the fundamental conception of jurisdiction. Thus John Bassett Moore, the American judge, in what is generally deemed to be a classic statement, said:

> Ever mindful of the fact that their judgments, if rendered in excess of power, may be treated as null, international tribunals have universally regarded the question of jurisdiction as fundamental. . . . The international judicial tribunals so far created have been tribunals of limited powers. Therefore no presumption in favor of their jurisdiction may be indulged. Their jurisdiction must always affirmatively appear on the face of the record.[10]

In the same case, Lord Finlay, dissenting, said: "The jurisdiction of the Permanent Court rests upon consent, and without consent, there is no jurisdiction over any state."[11]

The same approach was invoked by members of the International Court. In a dissenting opinion in the Ambatielos case, Judges McNair, Basdevant, Klaestad, and Read wrote in dissent: "Before declaring a State to be bound to submit a dispute to the decision of an international tribunal, the Permanent Court and the present Court have always considered it necessary to establish positively, and not merely on *prima facie* or provisional grounds, that the state in question had in some form given its consent to this process."[12]

As long as a doctrine such as this operated, neither the Permanent Court nor the International Court would implead a state which had not consented to jurisdiction. This was, at once, a control device and a practice that was necessary for getting judicial business. From the standpoint of any government's legal adviser, who had to determine whether or not to issue a document accepting jurisdiction for the future, the assurance that the restrictive theory of jurisdiction operated was indispensable. Without it, no document accepting jurisdiction could be responsibly issued.

The membership of the United Nations, at least in its first decade, seems to have wanted the institutions of international adjudication to retain this conception of jurisdiction as an informal control mechanism. The point was made dramatically in 1952 with regard to the question of the scope of competence to decide jurisdictional questions. Article 36(6) of the Statute of the International Court authorizes the court to make decisions in controversies about jurisdiction; the court is endowed with the competence to decide its own competence, the so-called *compétence de la compétence* or *Kompetenz Kompetenz*:[13]

> In the event of a dispute as to whether the court has jurisdiction, the matter shall be settled by the decision of the court.

This provision has frequently been claimed, particularly after the Nicaragua case, to mean that the International Court, as an international tribunal, is the final and absolute judge of its own jurisdiction. Were this the case, there would be no possibility of control over the frequently outcome-determinative decisions regarding jurisdiction. Given the relation of international judicial decision to the international political context, this interpretation does not seem plausible. Moreover, it is oblivious to the historical origin of the doctrine of *compétence de la compétence*.

In the nineteenth century, when this doctrine was not well established, it was reasonable to insist that an ad hoc tribunal which was uncertain of its jurisdiction and, without special authorization, not empowered to make law or decide by reference to equity, should suspend operations and refer the question back to the parties to determine whether or not jurisdiction was or should be available to decide a particular matter. After all, the tribunal's jurisdiction depended entirely on the consent of the parties. But this procedure, which would certainly avert an *excès de pouvoir*, would be cumbersome, inviting additional negotiations at the very moment when it had been acknowledged that further negotiations were fruitless, could be potentially disruptive of the arbitration, and could introduce long delays. Hence a doctrine assigning to the tribunal the competence to decide its jurisdiction gradually developed. But the notion that this competence was *absolute* and subject to no limitations was certainly not part of the understanding and would have had major implications for the control system. Even the claim of such a competence does not appear to have arisen during this period. As long as tribunals were ad hoc, created only for particular cases, the principle of the *compétence de la compétence* was unlikely to arise and even less likely to be abused.

Any possible doubt that might have lingered about contemporary international legal thinking on this matter was dispelled when the General Assembly of the United Nations reviewed the International Law Commission's "Draft Convention on Arbitral Procedure" in 1952.[14] The French version of Article 22, corresponding to Article 36(6) of the Statute of the International Court, had described the tribunal as "the *maître* of its own competence," and attributed to it "the widest powers to interpret the *compromis*." The assembly objected to the breadth of that ascription,[15] and the commission subsequently changed *maître de sa compétence* to *juge de sa compétence* and deleted the word "widest."[16] The implication, clearly, was that the competence to determine jurisdiction was subject to law and that the rigorous application of that law was still demanded.

In a national framework, the General Assembly's rebuke might have seemed like an infringement on judicial independence and a setback for law, without corresponding gains for control. Controls are supplied domestically through other arrangements. But internationally, the assembly's action was a reaffirmation of an indispensable control mechanism, without which third-party decision was less likely to be used. Rather than injuring international arbitration and adjudication, this clarification by both the commission and the General Assembly contributed to the effectiveness of international arbitration. For, as the commentary to the draft put it,

> It is not the fact alone that the *compromis* may provide that the award is binding on the parties which makes it so binding. The view of States that international law makes an arbitration award binding, the circumstance that the Tribunal faithfully had adhered to the fundamental principles of law governing its proceedings, these are the ultimate sources of the binding authority of an international arbitral award. States are required to take all necessary measures to carry into effect an award so rendered.[17]

Although the late Professor Scelle, the rapporteur of the *projet*, was rebuked for trying to change the law on this point, he was hardly insensitive to the problem of excess of jurisdiction. He included a provision and a procedure for it in the *projet*.[18] The commentary prepared by the secretariat observed:

> An international tribunal is not a court of general jurisdiction nor is it a court free from the established rules of law governing a judicial proceeding. The jurisdiction of the Tribunal is determined by the agreement of the parties; it may decide only the questions submitted to it. The Tribunal must decide under the rules of law applicable to it. It must

> conduct its proceedings in a judicial manner and with due observance of the fundamental rules of procedure.[19]

We find here a number of manifestations of the strong demand for limitations on international court jurisdiction. But the control system which emerges is not explicit or structured. It is implicit, and its operation depends on the court itself which is to be controlled. This would not appear to be the most satisfactory control arrangement, but, whether because of it or because of the probity of judges during the period of the life of the Permanent Court of International Justice and the early years of the International Court, no cases of abuse that would have kicked a control mechanism into operation arose.

The Demise of Restrictive Jurisdiction and the Rise of the "New" Jurisdiction

The Permanent Court's informal control mechanisms of restrictive jurisdiction worked reasonably well during the League of Nations and, with a few troubling exceptions, in the UN period. The case law on jurisdiction that developed in this period was, not surprisingly, influenced by the nineteenth-century practice of arbitral tribunals.

As in the past, the submission by the state parties to jurisdiction was viewed in contractual terms and was construed cautiously and conservatively. The basic style of judicial construction was restrictive rather than expansive and textual rather than teleological. In a large number of cases, in which a national court, securely embedded in an organized political system and hence confident of its own jurisdiction, might have moved unhesitatingly to adjudicate, the Permanent Court, and the International Court of Justice (ICJ) after it, held back and refused to assert jurisdiction.

A brief review of the practice of the ICJ until the watershed of November 1984 is a gallery of prudence. Of the forty cases brought (and not struck from the list) since 1945, nine rested in whole or in part on Article 36(2). Of these, the defendant states did not challenge jurisdiction in three of them, thereby assimilating them, to an extent, to special agreements or *forum prorogatum.* (The U.S. challenged and then withdrew objections in the Nationals in Morocco case,[20] but the French application there also rested on Article 36[1].) Of the remaining six, where jurisdiction was challenged directly or implicitly, the court found jurisdiction insufficient in three (Anglo-Iranian Oil Co.,[21] Norwegian Loans,[22] and Aerial Incident[23]) and achieved a comparable effect in a fourth by finding the claim inadmissible after having found jurisdiction (Nottebohm[24]). In short, from 1945 to 1984, the court affirmed a contested jurisdiction under Article 36(2) only twice (Rights of Passage[25] and Preah Vihear[26]). In the latter, a regional hegemon was plainly committed to seeing the defendant in court. In the former, a most problematic case, the defendant appeared and stayed. In any case, it was not certain that the applicant there sought a remedy requiring enforcement.

But there were some exceptions that, in retrospect, can be seen as the anticipation of a new trend. The first was Corfu Channel.[27] In October 1946 two British destroyers in transit through the Straits of Corfu struck mines which caused damage to the vessels and heavy loss of life. The United Kingdom took the matter to the Security Council.[28] Albania was not, at the time, a member of the United Nations but participated at the invitation of the Security Council. Under Article 32 of the charter, such invitations can be issued subject to conditions. The council had conditioned Albania's participation on its accepting the obligations of a member of the UN in a similar case.[29]

At the end of the deliberations, the council recommended that both parties refer the dispute to the International Court.[30] Britain promptly applied to the court, basing jurisdiction on the council's recommendation and the acceptance by the Albanian government of the council's conditions. Under those conditions, Britain argued, any member was obliged, in accordance with Article 25 of the charter, to accept and carry out the decisions of the Security Council. Albania appeared in court to challenge jurisdiction, claiming that it had not accepted the jurisdiction of the court and that Article 25 did not apply to "recommendations," but only to "decisions" taken under chapter 7 of the charter.

The court held that Albania, in its communication agreeing to appear before the court, had waived any objections. Hence it found jurisdiction.[31] Albania protested, but appeared in the Merits Phase, which it lost, whereupon it withdrew from the case and refused to accept the judgment of the court as to damages.

The court's *démarche* with regard to jurisdiction was certainly a radical departure from the principles that had governed it until that time. Exactly why the court proceeded in this direction is not clear. It is clear, however, that the repudiation of the court's jurisdiction by Albania shook the court's confidence. For the next two decades, the court reverted to a much more cautious and essentially classical approach in determining jurisdiction. In many cases in which the issue of jurisdiction was close, or it appeared clear that the protesting party would not comply, whatever the jurisdictional decision, the court found against jurisdiction.[32] In 1973, however, the court revived the approach it had taken in Corfu Channel and moved even more boldly to a much more expansive conception of its jurisdiction. This seemed to give proportionately more weight to the court's urgent interest in taking the case and less to the actual consent of the putative defendant.

When Australia and New Zealand proved unable to persuade France to terminate the atmospheric nuclear tests which France had been conducting at its proving ground in Muroroa, they each commenced a suit in the International Court of Justice against France. Each government sought to rely on two grounds: (i) the "General Act" of 1928, a general commitment to resolve disputes peacefully, which had been closely related to the League of Nations; and (ii) the optional declaration made by France in accord with Article 36 of the statute.[33]

There were difficulties with each purported base of jurisdiction. The General Act was effectively obsolete. Not only had it been replaced by a Revised General Act, but the secretary-general had not even been informing parties to the old act of changes in it, a lapse that strongly suggested desuetude. The French optional declaration also presented difficulties. While France had made a unilateral declaration accepting the jurisdiction of the International Court, it had explicitly excepted from that submission "disputes concerning activities connected with national defense."[34]

Nevertheless, the court issued an injunction against France based on a terse and essentially unreasoned statement on jurisdiction: "[T]he materials submitted to the Court lead it to the conclusion, at the present stage of the Proceedings, that the provisions invoked by the Applicant appear, *prima facie*, to afford a basis on which the jurisdiction of the Court might be founded."[35] The absence of any reasons was all the more troubling here, for the content of the injunction was essentially what the applicants were seeking from a final judgment. Hence, the court was provisionally granting the final judgment for the duration of the case, a matter that may have had significant security implications for the defendant.

France refused to appear in court and ignored the injunction. However, after a series of tests, France indicated, through political statements made by its highest officials, that future tests were not envisaged, as they were no longer necessary, and that France would, therefore, voluntarily abstain from tests in the atmosphere. In the second phase of the case, the court, over the protests of Australia and New Zealand, concluded that because France had agreed not to test in the atmosphere in the future, the case had become moot.[36]

The court had been shaken by the Albanian rebuff in Corfu Channel some two decades earlier, but that was now ancient history. A number of judges on the court viewed the Nuclear Tests cases as a substantial victory for the court's new role. They also viewed it as evidence that a new theory of jurisdiction and an expanded role for the court as an active negotiator in the settlement of international disputes were feasible.

In April 1984 it became clear that the theory of Nuclear Tests was not an exception to the doctrine of restrictive jurisdiction but had become the new orthodoxy. Nicaragua initiated a case against the United States concerning military and paramilitary activities in and against Nicaragua. It sought to base the jurisdiction of the court on interlocking declarations made by the United States and Nicaragua and on a jurisdictional clause in the Friendship, Commerce, and Navigation (FCN) Treaty between the two governments.[37]

At the jurisdictional phase, fourteen of the sixteen judges sitting in Nicaragua found that the court had: "[J]urisdiction to entertain the Application filed by the Republic of Nicaragua on 9 April 1984, insofar as that Application relates to a dispute concerning the interpretation or application of the Treaty of Friendship, Commerce and Navigation between the United States of America and the Republic of Nicaragua signed at Managua on 21 January 1956 on the basis of Article XXIV of that treaty."[38] Article 24(2) of the FCN Treaty provides: "Any dispute between the Parties as to the interpretation or application of the present Treaty, not satisfactorily adjusted by diplomacy, shall be submitted to the International Court of Justice, unless the Parties agree to settlement by some other specific means."[39] One of the judges who dissented from the court's holding on this ground found that there had been no negotiations.[40] The majority, for some reason not apparent on the face of the judgment, ignored Article 21(1)(d) of the treaty which provides: "The present treaty shall not preclude the application of measures: . . . (d) necessary to fulfill the obligations of the Party for the maintenance or restoration of international peace or security, *or necessary to protect its essential security interests*"[41] (emphasis added).

A smaller but still substantial majority of eleven judges concluded that the jurisdictional requirements of Article 36(2) of the Statute of the International Court of Justice were fulfilled by the interlocking and sufficiently congruent declarations of Nicaragua and the United States.[42] Nicaragua, in 1929, had submitted a communication which was the first step in making a unilateral declaration of unconditional submission to the jurisdiction of the court when it signed the Protocol, of which the Statute of the Permanent Court was a part. But it never submitted the requisite ratification of the Protocol, despite the fact that it had been duly notified that this deficiency rendered its effort at making a declaration nugatory.[43] Indeed, Nicaragua itself seems to have been aware of the problem, for it had not relied on that stillborn communication in its own adjudication with Honduras in the International Court in 1960, preferring instead a special agreement under statute Article 36(1).[44]

Yet, the Court found that the incomplete communication in 1929 had been completed, repaired, and transformed into a declaration by virtue of Article 36(5) of the Statute of the International Court.[45] Article 36(5) provides: "Declarations made under Article 36 of the Statute of the Permanent Court of International Justice and which are still in force shall be deemed, as between the parties to the present Statute, to be acceptances of the compulsory jurisdiction of the International Court of Justice for the period which they still have to run and in accordance with their terms." That provision had been designed to transfer to the new court declarations which had been made with regard to the Permanent Court of International Justice and which were still in force. The majority of eleven judges made Article 36(5) relevant to the case by characterizing the 1929 communication (which could not, under the terms of the instrument with regard to which it was submitted, be a Declaration) as a "Declaration."[46]

In the context of the statute, "Declaration" had been a term of art applied to communications which had met all of the criteria of Article 36 and were certified and circularized to that effect by the registrar of the court and the secretary-general of the United Nations. In this case, however, the court assigned a new meaning to the word "Declaration." It moved its reference backward, as it were, to phases of the communication process in which the legal requisites were still incomplete. It acknowledged the lack of legal effect of this earlier phase, now called a "Declaration," by introducing a new distinction which would reflect its ineffectiveness. The majority of the court found this "Declaration" was "valid" but not "binding." The majority then interpreted Article 36(5) as having been designed to transform and render binding such theretofore uncompleted and defective "Declarations."[47]

This clever device permitted the majority to use the word "Declaration" for something that had hitherto not been considered a "Declaration" with regard to Article 36, in particular, paragraph 5. The legislative history of the court's statute indicates that what the court was doing was not the intention of the transitional regime created in Article 36(5). The subcommittee of the Committee of Jurists, meeting in Washington in 1945, was quite explicit: "The subcommittee calls attention to the fact that many nations have heretofore *accepted* compulsory jurisdiction under the 'optional clause'." The subcommittee believes that a provision should be made at the San Francisco Conference for a special agreement for continuing these acceptances *in force* for the purpose of this Statute" (emphasis added).[48]

A majority of eleven on the court also found that the six-month clause present in the United States declaration (but absent in the now validated Nicaraguan one), bound the United States and defeated American efforts to terminate or modify its declaration with immediate effect.[49] As for the restriction in the United States declaration of matters coming under multilateral treaties, the court dismissed it on the ground that the claims of Nicaragua may have been based on the texts of conventions, but they now derived from customary and general international law.

The Friendship, Commerce, and Navigation Treaty, on which fourteen judges relied to find jurisdiction, had not been invoked by Nicaragua in its original application and was scarcely discussed during the oral proceedings. Indeed, Judge Oda, in his separate opinion, remarked that there was but a single reference to it by the agent of Nicaragua as "a subsidiary basis for the Court's jurisdiction."[50] The unduly short time allowed the judges to prepare and expand separate and dissenting opinions was also judicially noted. The unusual haste was particularly puzzling, as interim measures, largely accomplishing the basic remedy sought by the applicant, had already been ordered against the defendant and were in effect.[51]

In the 1986 Merits Phase of the case, the court returned to many of the jurisdictional issues. Nicaragua, it will be recalled, had belatedly invoked Article 24 of the 1956 Nicaragua-United States Treaty of Friendship, Commerce, and Navigation (the FCN Treaty).[52] Paragraph 2 of that provision provides: "Any dispute between the Parties as to the interpretation or application of the present Treaty, not satisfactorily adjusted by diplomacy, shall be submitted to the International Court of Justice, unless the Parties agree to settlement by some other pacific means."[53] In the 1984 phase, the court simply concluded that: "[T]here can be no doubt that, in the circumstances in which Nicaragua brought its Application to the Court, and on the basis of the facts there asserted, there is a dispute between the Parties, *inter alia*, as to the 'interpretation or application' of the [FCN] Treaty."[54] Article 21(1)(d) of the treaty removes virtually all the key items in Nicaragua's application from the jurisdiction of the court.[55] As will be recalled, it provides in relevant part: "The present Treaty shall not preclude the application of measures: . . . (d) necessary to fulfill the obligations of a Party for the maintenance or restoration of international peace and security, or necessary to protect its essential security interests."[56] Curiously, this provision was not even mentioned by the court in its Jurisdictional Judgment. Though Article 24(1), as well as customary international law, prescribe negotiation as a prerequisite to the unilateral initiation of adjudication, the court found that Nicaragua had discharged that requirement in substance, if not in form.[57]

In its Judgment on the Merits of June 27, 1986[58] (by which time the United States had withdrawn from the case in protest), the court made certain adjustments and retrofittings in its jurisdictional decision. It went through the motions of qualifying its theretofore rather superficial and dismissive treatment of the multilateral treaty reservation in the United States optional declaration.[59] But this was, in fact, a demarche in appearance only, as the court then proceeded to declare that the customary and conventional law invoked in the case were identical,[60] a factor which, whether correct or not, would not appear to be the point of a so-called multilateral treaty reservation.

The court also confirmed its holding of jurisdiction under Article 36(1) of the statute by virtue of the FCN Treaty. It brushed aside the manifest exclusions in Article 21(1)(d)[61] in a single superficial comparison between the text in the treaty and a comparable text in the General Agreement on Tariffs and Trade. Moreover, it substantially expanded the ambit of the jurisdictional clause of the FCN Treaty by interpreting the treaty broadly,[62] even reaching "implied" matters which also became subject to the treaty's jurisdictional clause.[63] In effect, virtually anything "unfriendly," even were it otherwise within the pale of lawful international action, was rendered unlawful because this was a treaty of "friendship."[64]

The Court Becomes Its Own Control

Not only had the implicit control system, based on a restrictive conception of jurisdiction, been discarded, but in its efforts to make its newly expanded conception of jurisdiction effective, the court sought to close a number of escape hatches. In doing so, it created a "Catch-22" for states that might contemplate using it. First, the court sought to make itself both the architect of its jurisdiction and its own control mechanism:

> Having taken part in the Proceedings to argue that the Court lacked jurisdiction, the United States thereby acknowledged that the Court had the power to make a finding on its own jurisdiction to rule upon the Merits. It is not possible to argue that the Court had jurisdiction only to declare that it lacked jurisdiction. In the normal course of events, for a party to appear before a court entails acceptance of the possibility of the Court's finding against that party. . . . Under Article 36, paragraph 6, of its Statute, the Court has jurisdiction to determine any dispute as to its own jurisdiction, and its judgment on that matter, as on the merits, is final and binding on the parties under Articles 59 and 60 of the Statute.[65]

Should a state decide that under these terms it had better not appear, lest its appearance be construed as a waiver of objections and an acceptance of jurisdiction, the court escalated the costs of resorting to that option. It revised the commonly accepted understanding of its statute so that party nonappearance would henceforth have certain default consequences.

Article 53 of the statute obliges the court to satisfy itself, in the absence of one of the parties, both that it has jurisdiction and that the claim of the other party is well-founded in fact and law. There is no default judgment procedure. In Nicaragua, however, the court said: "The Court cannot by its own enquiries entirely make up for the absence of one of the Parties; that absence, in a case of this kind involving extensive questions of fact, must necessarily limit the extent to which the Court is informed of the facts."[66] The court then proceeded to quote in a way quite contrary to its manifest intention (to which we will return), a dictum in the Corfu Channel Judgment. The court there said: "While Article 53 thus obliges the Court to consider the submissions of the Party which appears, it does not compel the Court to examine their accuracy in all their details."[67] In effect the court was now saying that not only was it for the court to determine jurisdiction, but that its substantive determinations, however they might depart from the expectations of the parties, were final and binding.

Henceforth, a party coming into court to contest jurisdiction would find itself caught in a double bind. On the one hand, it would run aground on the rocks of the court's Corfu doctrine: its very presence would be construed to confirm the court's claim to the competence to make a final binding decision on jurisdiction. But a party seeking to avoid the impassable shoals of Corfu by remaining aloof from proceedings could suffer a partial default judgment insofar as the court determined it unnecessary, as it now had entitled itself to do, to examine the accuracy of points in the plaintiff's case.

These changes are not accidental or careless. In effect the court has reconceived its role and function in international dispute resolution and, as a part of that, its approach to jurisdiction. Two years later, in the case concerning Border and Transborder Armed Actions between Nicaragua and Honduras,[68] the court again, this time unanimously, found jurisdiction. An interesting declaration appended to the judgment by Judge Manfred Lachs, the former president of the court and its most senior and experienced member, provides an insight into the thinking of a leader in the court's new approach to jurisdiction. After acknowledging that jurisdictional decisions seem legalistic, Judge Lachs stated that, "the mere opening of the door [of the court] may bring about a solution to a dispute." He added, "the parties retain their freedom of action, and full possibilities of finding solutions."[69]

The conception of the court's function implicit in these remarks is not one of a tribunal whose jurisdiction depends upon the agreement of the parties and whose confirmation in each particular case is the subject of a strict legal decision by the tribunal. Rather, it is of an institution performing an explicit political role, in which one of its legitimate functions is to move the parties toward diplomatic solutions. This is, to be sure, an important function and indeed has been assigned to different organs of the United Nations and the regional organizations. It is not one that was contemplated in the Statute or assigned to the International Court there and was not one which parties that signed on to Article 36 in the past had in mind. If the court were able to discharge it *along with* its own functions and to do it in ways that did not undermine its principal assignment, its initiative would be admirable. But if the court's diplomatic ambitions undermine the performance of its judicial functions, the court and the world community will be the worse for it.

Implications of the Demise of the Presumption of Confinement

The breakdown of this part of the control system of the International Court poses major challenges to states which seek a third-party instance for certain types of dispute resolution. The United States is a major consumer of Article 36(1)'s treaty-based jurisdiction; according to the 1985 ICJ Yearbook, Article 36(1) jurisdiction is incorporated in some thirty-five bilateral treaties to which the United States is party.[70] The United States also participates in a large number of multilateral treaties which incorporate Article 36(1) jurisdiction.[71] Even after the termination of Article 36(2) jurisdiction, the Department of State apparently continued to view Article 36(1) treaty jurisdiction as a desirable and important form of dispute resolution in treaties with commercial or other limited subject matter.

The doctrine of limited subject-matter jurisdiction in these treaties is an important feature of their attractiveness and is central to national decisions to use the International Court. The United States, like all other governments, views adjudication as only one of a number of facultative options available to states for the resolution of their disputes. Adjudication in international law is not mandatory. Some states lawfully refuse to adjudicate anything. Others may agree to selected matters. A state is entitled to refuse to agree in advance to either a treaty-based or special agreement invitation to adjudicate matters which it thinks would be better or, from its perspective, more sympathetically treated in other modes of dispute resolution. In much the same way that many declarations made under Article 36(2) carefully and lawfully circumscribe the matters which the declaring state wishes to submit to the jurisdiction of the court, clauses within treaties which establish jurisdiction under Article 36(1) are designed to operate only for those matters that the treaty parties are explicitly agreeing to submit. This "presumption of confinement," so to speak, is fundamental to the use of the treaty-based mode.

The presumption of confinement was a central and explicit consideration in U.S. decisions to use the International Court in the growing genre of FCN treaties. A State Department memorandum, prepared, it would appear, for

Congressional testimony long before the Nicaragua case, and dealing with the dispute settlement provisions of a particular FCN treaty, expresses the presumption unequivocally:

> The compromissory clause . . . is limited to questions of the interpretation or application of this treaty; i.e., it is a special not a general compromissory clause. It applies to a treaty on the negotiation of which there is a voluminous documentation indicating the intent of the parties. This treaty deals with subjects which are common to a large number of treaties, concluded over a long period of time by nearly all nations. Much of the general subject-matter—and in some cases almost identical language—has been adjudicated in the courts of this and other countries. The authorities for the interpretation of this treaty are, therefore, to a considerable extent established and well known. Furthermore, certain important subjects, notably immigration, traffic and military supplies, and the essential interests of the country in time of national emergency, are specifically excepted from the purview of the treaty.
>
> In view of the above, it is difficult to conceive how Article XXVII (the dispute resolution clause in the FCN treaty with China), [the treaty on which the memorandum is based] could result in this Government's being impleaded in the matter in which it might be embarrassed.[72]

Another State Department memorandum entitled "Department of State Memorandum on Provisions in Commercial Treaties Relating to the International Court of Justice" addressed the same issue:

> This paper . . . points out a number of features which in its view make the provision satisfactory. These include the fact that the provision is limited to differences arising immediately from the specific treaty concerned, that such treaties deal with familiar subject-matter and are fairly documented in the records of negotiation, that an established body of interpretation already exists for much of the subject-matter of such treaties, and that such purely domestic matters as immigration policy and military security are placed outside the scope of such treaties by specific exceptions.[73]

Both memoranda were pleaded to the court in the U.S.-Iranian Diplomatic Hostages case.

It is clear from these memoranda, and, indeed, consistent with the concerns of any government contemplating adjudication, that the incorporation of Article 36(1) jurisdiction in American FCN treaties was premised on the assumption that the jurisdiction with regard to those treaties would be confined to the explicit terms of the treaty. Certain subject-matter deemed to be of special national concern and, in particular, matters of military security, were not, in the U.S. view, any part of the jurisdictional bargain. Indeed, had the court in Nicaragua engaged in an international legal interpretation of the FCN Treaty even faintly approximating what is prescribed in Article 31 of the Vienna Convention on the Law of Treaties, it would have found it impossible to ignore this manifest expectation.

The court's judgment of June 27, 1986, shattered key elements of the presumption of confinement. The court reaffirmed its earlier decision under the FCN Treaty and then proceeded, as mentioned, to dispose of the restriction clause in the treaty in a single paragraph and in a procedure which hardly qualifies as a paragon of interpretation. The court conceded that the effect of Article 21 of the FCN Treaty was to reserve certain matters from the court's jurisdiction, but held that the determination of whether a matter was excluded was not within the unilateral competence of the state party. It was to be decided by the court. In making that determination, the court may, according to this theory, assume that the measures in question are related to the essential security interests of the state concerned, but even then it will determine whether the risk run by these "essential security interests" is reasonable, and secondly, whether the measures presented as being designed to protect these interests are not merely useful but "necessary."[74]

One key element in the presumption of confinement is thus terminated. While the United States may have thought that the insertion of words in Article 21 of the Nicaragua-U.S. Friendship, Commerce, and Navigation Treaty and comparable words in the other treaties of this genre effectively excluded military matters, it now learns that the court's new and retroactive theory of jurisdiction holds that these words are no more than an initial claim by the United States which will be tested by the court in terms of the court's own view of their contextual necessity and reasonableness.

A second element of the presumption of confinement concerns explicit subject-matter. The memoranda of the United States considered above indicate that it was assumed that only matters explicitly within the four corners of the treaty in question and which were not reserved were to be subject to the jurisdictional clause. The court, however, developed a theory of implication: "[T]here are certain activities of the United States which are such as to undermine the whole spirit of a bilateral agreement directed to sponsoring friendship between the two states parties to it."[75] The court extended this notion of implication in the following paragraph:

> A state is not bound to continue particular trade relations longer than it sees fit to do so, in the absence of a treaty commitment or other specific legal obligation; but where there exists such a commitment, of the kind

> *implied* in a treaty of friendship and commerce, such an abrupt act of termination of commercial intercourse as the general trade embargo of 1 May 1985 will normally constitute a violation of the obligation not to defeat the object and purpose of the treaty [emphasis supplied].[76]

Thus, a second part of the presumption of confinement on which the jurisdictional clauses of United States FCN treaties have rested crumbled.

Students of international law are inclined to study the problem of the jurisdiction of the International Court of Justice from a developmental perspective. More jurisdiction is better; decisions which enhance jurisdiction are the most worthy of applause. The consumers of international adjudication, governments and, more specifically, their international legal advisers, necessarily look at jurisdiction from a different angle. Because adjudication in international law is only one of a number of optional dispute resolution mechanisms, legal advisers must consider its appropriateness for their governments in terms of the nature of the dispute, the attitude of the potential adversary with regard to adjudication, the momentary composition of the court and the alignments of judges on it, the extent to which the countries from which they come have critical interests in the potential dispute or parallel interests in cognate disputes, the costs of losing and the extent to which the government of the loser can mobilize its population to accept the loss, and so on. Because adjudication has certain properties that, in different contexts, may discriminate in favor of or against one of the parties, responsible legal advisers must decide carefully which bilateral matters should be made subject to an adjudicative jurisdictional clause and which should be reserved for other dispute resolving modalities. That national policy is meaningful only if the presumption of confinement operates and is applied through good faith interpretations. The International Court has cast this essential condition for submission to jurisdiction into doubt. In the absence of this control mechanism, the general utility of the Court as a dispute resolver declines.

The demise of restrictive jurisdiction and, in particular, of the presumption of confinement will have major effects on the process of making international law as well. International agreements are a mode of communication and redaction of commitments, but their content and, in particular, their degree of obligation may vary widely. There are agreements which are intended by both parties to be kept meticulously and which are premised on the maxim *pacta sunt servanda*. There are, however, other agreements, redacted in exactly the same form and legal dialect, which are not accompanied by comparable expectations. A modus vivendi, for example, expresses the terms of an arrangement deemed to be mutually convenient but not necessarily deemed to be binding. One party, departing from the terms of a modus vivendi, may not be in breach in the same fashion in which a party "violating" the terms of a treaty would be. In the recent past, standard-setting agreements have become an important technique in the lawmaking process. They are agreements which establish standards to which states are urged to adapt their own actions but which scrupulously avoid imposing obligations for a violation and usually do not include dispute resolution mechanisms. Soft agreements like these are not defects of the international system. They are important phases in the lawmaking process, permitting states to establish target goals, to begin to adapt national behavior to them and to accommodate internal disruptions that may ensue, giving all parties respite before they decide whether to proceed toward a more binding form of agreement.

The undermining of notions of restrictive jurisdiction and premises of confinement will have negative consequences on this important form of lawmaking.

The Breakdown of Case Law as a Control

In all legal systems, stare decisis is a communication from courts to all those influenced by the law they process that judicial applications will not be capricious and unpredictable but will respect prior holdings and, in similar circumstances, give effect to them. This reassurance permits courts to reinforce the expectations which lawmakers have tried to establish, while it helps members of the community plan their enterprises in ways that take account of community policy. The morality of case law, like that of all law, rests on respect for expectations that have been established and authorized by appropriate community processes.

The doctrine of stare decisis performs a special, if latent control function in international adjudication. An international court cites its prior holdings, even when it is not institutionally required to do so, to affirm this commitment and to reinforce expectations of authority. For courts whose jurisdiction depends on the consent of the litigants, this reassurance imports a critical control factor and is an indispensable communication for those who consider voluntarily subjecting themselves to its jurisdiction. Authoritative communications from the past become relevant to future planning precisely because the courts in question have committed themselves to respect and give effect to those expectations. When an international court plays fast and loose with its own case law, it undermines the confidence of others in its reliability, deters litigants from resorting to it, and thereby reduces its own potential contribution to the resolution of disputes.

This is not to suggest that stare decisis imports immutability. Modern laws are not inscribed in stone with the vaunted finality of the decrees of the Medes and the Persians. In modern contexts, law is perforce conformity and conformation: conformity with the past and a conformation of the future.[77] The problem, then, is not revision of prior holdings as such, but sufficient respect for them for courts to revise particular prescriptions, when necessary, in a fashion open enough to reinforce the commitment with regard to the rest of the body of case law.

The expectation that international tribunals will follow the law, whether its origin is statutory, customary, or judicial, also serves as a type of latent control function. This is the larger systemic function of judicial reasoning. A deterioration in the expectation of a court's respect for its own jurisprudence will deter potential litigants, who have other places to go, from seeking applications of the law by institutions whose behavior has become increasingly unpredictable. This problem appears to be bedeviling both the International Court with regard to its case law and certain international commercial tribunals with regard to party-designated law, the latter through the device of the so-called *lex mercatoria*. I will take up this matter in chapter 4. Here, I would like briefly to examine certain breakdowns of stare decisis in the International Court and their control implications.

Military and Paramilitary Activities (Nicaragua)

In the nature of international adjudication, nonappearance by a defendant state is not an uncommon occurrence. Article 53 of the Statute of the International Court of Justice deals with it explicitly:

> 1. Whenever one of the parties does not appear before the Court, or fails to defend its case, the other party may call upon the Court to decide in favour of its claim.
> 2. The Court must, before doing so, satisfy itself, not only that it has jurisdiction in accordance with Articles 36 and 37, but also that the claim is well-founded in fact and law.[78]

In the Merits Phase of the Military and Paramilitary Activities case,[79] the International Court purported to restate and strictly apply its prior case law about its own obligations to test evidence required to establish an applicant's claim when the respondent state refuses to appear: "There is however no question of a judgment automatically in favour of the party appearing, since the Court is required, as mentioned above, to 'satisfy itself' that the party's claim is well founded in fact and law."[80] Judicial self-satisfaction of the law in a case of nonappearance is not a serious obstacle. The court recalled that in the Icelandic Fisheries case, it had observed that: "It being the duty of the

Court itself to ascertain and apply the relevant law in the given circumstances of the case, the burden of establishing or proving rules of international law cannot be imposed upon any of the parties, for the law lies within the judicial knowledge of the Court."[81] In Nicaragua the court reaffirmed this view: "For the purpose of deciding whether the claim is well founded in law, the principle *jura novit curia* signifies that the Court is not solely dependent on the argument of the parties before it with respect to the applicable law . . . so that the absence of one party has less impact."[82] Because the court knows the law and is not, in any case, restricted to the parties' legal arguments (in contrast to an adjudication on an agreed basis, where, in the absence of a *jus cogens*, it presumably would be restricted to what the parties had jointly prescribed for it),[83] a defendant's nonappearance would not seriously disable the court in determining whether a claim is well-founded in law.

The situation is more complex with regard to the court's self-satisfaction on the facts, for the facts may be largely within the province of the parties. But in Nicaragua the court stated: "[T]he Court cannot by its own enquiries entirely make up for the absence of one of the Parties; that absence, in a case of this kind involving extensive questions of fact, must necessarily limit the extent to which the Court is informed of the facts."[84] In the second clause here, the court has edged away from the injunction of Article 53(2), laying the basis for a qualification and reduction of the peremptory and unqualified requirement of the statute that "the Court must . . . satisfy itself . . . that the claim is well-founded in fact and law." The court continued

> It would furthermore be an over-simplification to conclude that the only detrimental consequence of the absence of a party is the lack of opportunity to submit argument and evidence in support of its own case. Proceedings before the Court call for vigilance by all. The absent party also forfeits the opportunity to counter the factual allegations of its opponent. It is of course for the party appearing to prove the allegations it makes, yet as the Court has held: "While Article 53 thus obliges the Court to consider the submissions of the Party which appears, it does not compel the Court to examine their accuracy in all their details; for this might in certain unopposed cases prove impossible in practice."[85]

Thus, the court significantly reduced the burden which Article 53 imposes on it. If the court is not obliged to examine the accuracy "in *all* their details" (emphasis added) of the applicant's claims, certain claims may be either accepted without being tested, to the point of judicial satisfaction that they are well-founded, or accepted without being tested at all, in other words, by default.

The court developed this amendative interpretation first by reaffirming the language of Article 53(2) and then ascribing the qualification to a previous court whose holding is quoted. In invoking the Corfu Channel Judgment as authority for a partial default judgment, the court implied that it was doing no more than restating a doctrine of its own case law to which it had adhered for some forty years. In fact, the court cited only one-half of the relevant sentence in the Corfu Channel case and, in so doing, created the impression that Corfu was holding something it was not. The pertinent section of Corfu Channel states:

> The position adopted by the Albanian Government brings into operation Article 53 of the Statute, which applies to procedure in default of appearance. This Article entitles the United Kingdom Government to call upon the Court to decide in favour of its claim, and, on the other hand, obliges the Court to satisfy itself that the claim is well founded in fact and law. While Article 53 thus obliges the Court to consider the submissions of the Party which appears, it does not compel the Court to examine their accuracy in all their details; for this might in certain unopposed cases prove impossible in practice. *It is sufficient for the Court to convince itself by such methods as it considers suitable that the submissions are well-founded.*[86] [Emphasis added.]

This section of Corfu was concerned with the methods to be used for fulfilling the requirement of Article 53(2). The point it makes is obvious and innocuous: in satisfying itself that the applicant's claim is well-founded, the court may have to resort to methods different from those which the absent defendant might have used. The selective quotation in the Nicaragua case, which suppresses the final sentence in the paragraph in Corfu, leaves the impression that it is long-standing jurisprudence that the court is entitled to reach judgment in Article 53 cases without satisfying itself that the factual claims made by the applicant state are well-founded. It is not.

The PLO Mission Opinion

In 1947 the United States and the United Nations, newly established in New York City, concluded what has come to be known as the Headquarters Agreement.[87] The agreement sets out the basic rights and obligations of each of the parties and constitutes an indispensable part of the environment necessary for an organization which, although international, must maintain and operate its headquarters within the territory of a single state. The agreement was quite comprehensive and included a dispute settlement procedure.[88] By a joint resolution of August 4, 1947, Congress authorized the President to bring the agreement into effect.[89] Congress anticipated that the agreement would be interpreted in the course of its implementation and that this might involve some changes. Hence its authorization included an empowerment to conclude "such changes therein not contrary to the general tenor thereof and not imposing any additional obligations on the United States as the President may deem necessary and appropriate."[90]

Section 11 of the Headquarters Agreement obliged the various levels of authority within the United States not to impose impediments to transit from or to the Headquarters District upon representatives of members, officials of the United Nations, experts performing missions, representatives of the press, representatives of nongovernmental organizations recognized by the UN, and "other persons invited to the Headquarters District by the United Nations."[91]

Early in its history, the General Assembly began to invite observers to its meetings—some for brief terms, some for longer terms.[92] These observers have become important and sometimes indispensable participants in the work of the United Nations.[93] In a relatively short period of time, the status of "Permanent Observer" was established and recognized. The U.S. government has routinely provided the benefits of the Headquarters Agreement to these Permanent Observers, on the common understanding that they fell within Section 11's category of "other persons invited to the Headquarters District."

In 1974 the Palestine Liberation Organization (PLO) was invited by the General Assembly to "participate in the sessions and the work of the General Assembly in the capacity of observer."[94] The PLO established an Observer Mission, and since that time has maintained a permanent office in New York City. The PLO is listed in UN publications as a member of a category of "organizations which have received a standing invitation from the General Assembly to participate in the sessions and the work of the General Assembly as observers."[95]

Shortly after the invitation was extended, the B'nai B'rith Anti-Defamation League, a private organization in the United States,[96] sought to enjoin the U.S. government from granting visas to members of the PLO. A district court rejected the request on the ground that the United States was obliged to issue visas on the basis of its obligations in the Headquarters Agreement.[97]

There the matter rested until public opinion in the United States was aroused by the Achille Lauro incident in 1987, in which Palestinian "irregulars" seized an Italian cruise ship with the intention of using it for an operation against Israel. The mission went awry; in the course of its conclusion, the Palestinians murdered a passenger, an elderly American confined to a wheelchair.[98] In December 1987, in the face of resistance from the Reagan administration, Congress passed the Anti-Terrorism Act of 1987.[99] Section 1003 of the act provided:

> It shall be unlawful, if the purpose be to further the interests of the Palestine Liberation Organization or any of its constituent groups, any successor to any of those, or any agents thereof, on or after the effective date . . . (3) notwithstanding any provision of law to the contrary, to establish or maintain an office, headquarters, premises, or other facilities or establishments within the jurisdiction of the United States at the behest or direction of, or with funds provided by the Palestine Liberation Organization or any of its constituent groups, any successor thereto, or any agents thereof.[100]

The original targets of this legislation were the PLO Observer Mission in New York and the PLO information office in Washington, D.C. This was clear from the final text of the bill as well as from statements made on the floor of each house when revisions of the bill were introduced in late April and May 1987.[101] In September 1987 the executive branch ordered the PLO to close its information office in Washington, D.C., in the hope of placating Congress and arresting the progress of the Anti-Terrorism Act.[102] Congress was not dissuaded, however, and when the act was incorporated into a larger omnibus appropriations bill in October 1987,[103] now exclusively targeting the PLO Mission, the president signed it, despite continuing misgivings about the act's legality.[104]

The UN Secretariat believed that the implementation of the Anti-Terrorism Act would violate the Headquarters Agreement, but it was unable to secure from the United States a commitment to refrain from implementing the act.[105] Nor could the United Nations persuade the United States to cooperate in initiating arbitration in accordance with the agreement's dispute resolution mechanism.[106] When negotiations deadlocked, the General Assembly entered the picture. At the conclusion of a special session convened to deal with the impending application of the U.S. statute, the General Assembly resolved that the Anti-Terrorism Act was inconsistent with the United States' obligations to the United Nations under the Headquarters Agreement.[107] The General Assembly asked the International Court of Justice to issue an Advisory Opinion on whether the United States was obliged to participate in arbitration as requested by the United Nations pursuant to the Headquarters Agreement's dispute resolution clause.[108]

On March 11, 1988, ten days before the act's effective date and while the ICJ opinion was pending, the Department of Justice informed the PLO Observer Mission that it would have to close.[109] The PLO refused to comply and indicated that it would resist the demand for closure. The Justice Department then initiated an action to secure the closure of the Observer Mission, as the statute prescribed, in the Federal District Court for the Southern District of

New York. While that case was pending, the International Court issued a unanimous opinion, confirming the General Assembly's conclusion that the act violated the Headquarters Agreement and that the United States was obliged to commence arbitration.[110]

Shortly afterward, the Federal District Court in which the Department of Justice had filed suit ruled, *per* Judge Edmund L. Palmieri, that congressionally mandated closure of the PLO Observer Mission would indeed constitute a violation of the Headquarters Agreement and that, as Congress had not explicitly indicated an intention to violate the agreement, courts were to assume that it had not intended to do so. Thus, the court found against the Department of Justice.[111]

On August 29, 1988, the Reagan administration decided not to appeal the decision,[112] effectively terminating the United States' effort to close the PLO Observer Mission.

In the international judicial phase of this case, which the ICJ heard under the rubric Applicability of the Obligation to Arbitrate under Section 21 of the United Nations Headquarters Agreement of 26 June 1947,[113] the United States and the United Nations agreed that the proper interpretation of the Headquarters Agreement[114] precluded the United States from requiring the PLO Observer Mission at UN Headquarters to close. It was also clear that there was a dispute about the closing of the PLO Observer Mission in New York. If there were no dispute, it is difficult to see what the parties were negotiating about. The question posed to the court by the General Assembly was whether, in the circumstances, the United States was obliged to go to arbitration under Section 21(a) of the Headquarters Agreement. Section 21(a) provides that: "Any dispute between the United Nations and the United States concerning the interpretation or application of this agreement or of any supplemental agreement, which is not settled by negotiation or other agreed mode of settlement, shall be referred for final decision to a tribunal of three arbitrators."[115] The United Nations claimed that, given an arbitration clause in the agreement, once a dispute erupted and one party called for arbitration, the other party was obliged to arbitrate. The United States did not really contest that point, but claimed that the existence of a dispute notwithstanding, the critical question was whether, in the circumstances of the case, arbitration was appropriate at that particular moment. The United States contended in its written statement to the court: "The United States will take no action to close the Mission pending a decision in that litigation. Since the matter is still pending in our courts, we do not believe arbitration would be *appropriate or timely*"[116] (emphasis added). Thus, the central legal question of the case was whether arbitration had to be compelled at that moment or whether an international tribunal had some prudential discretion to determine whether it was appropriate or timely to compel arbitration immediately or to postpone it or defer decision while the parties resorted to some other mode of dispute resolution. Only if the court confirmed the legal proposition that it was endowed with prudential discretion in the matter, would it then reach the factual question of whether the circumstances of the case warranted its exercise.

The court rejected the United States' legal contention: "The Court could not allow considerations as to what might be 'appropriate' to prevail over the obligations which derive from Section 21 of the Headquarters Agreement, as 'the Court, being a Court of Justice, cannot disregard rights recognized by it, and base its decision on considerations of pure expediency.' "[117] The impression created by the quotation from the Free Zones case is that a jurisprudence of more than fifty years standing holds that, in determining the appropriate moment for compelling arbitration, the court is precluded, by its nature as a court, from considering and taking account of prudential factors such as the appropriateness and timeliness of arbitration in the particular case.

Once again, the court, by selective quotation, created exactly the opposite impression of what the court in the precedent being invoked had actually said. Consider the exact words of the Permanent Court in Free Zones: "*And although* the Court being a Court of Justice, cannot disregard rights recognized by it, and base its decision on considerations of pure expediency, *nevertheless there is nothing to prevent it, having regard to the advantages which a solution of this kind might present, to offer the parties, who alone can bring it about, a further opportunity for achieving this end*."[118] In the Mission opinion, the court quoted only a dependent clause and suppressed the most important part of the prior court's holding. Deleting the conjunction "although," which introduced the dependent clause, obscured the fact that the fragment the court was quoting was only a dependent clause, a syntactical construction which is invariably qualified, if not contradicted, by the independent clause it accompanies.

The ELSI Case

On February 6, 1987, while the United States was denouncing the Truman Declaration, it filed, by prior agreement with Italy, an application against Italy for alleged expropriations of United States property. The case was heard by a chamber. The United States claimed that Italy had violated international legal obligations under the Treaty of Friendship, Commerce, and Navigation the two governments had concluded on February 2, 1948, and a supplementary agreement of 1951.

The American company involved, Raytheon, had a wholly owned subsidiary in Palermo, Sicily, Elettronica Sicula S.p.a. or ELSI, which had encountered serious business difficulties and which the parent corporation had determined to close down in an orderly fashion. On April 1, 1968, the mayor of Palermo requisitioned the plant. A prefect rendered a decision characterizing the seizure by the mayor as unlawful and politically motivated: "under the influence of the pressure created by, and of the remarks made by the local press, therefore we have to hold that the Mayor, also in order to get out of the above and to show the intent of the Public Administration to intervene in one way or another, issued the order of requisition as a measure mainly directed to emphasize his intent to face the problem in some way."[119] But higher instances in Italy did not provide a meaningful remedy and the matter was brought, under diplomatic protection, by the United States to the chamber. The standard under which it was brought was provided by the U.S.-Italian FCN Treaty which made actionable "arbitrary" and "discriminatory" measures taken by one party against the nationals of the other. The chamber based its holding on the treaty.

> [T]he fact that an act of a public authority may have been unlawful in municipal law does not necessarily mean that the act was lawful in international law, as a breach of treaty or otherwise. A finding of the local courts that an act was unlawful may well be relevant to an argument that it was also arbitrary; but by itself, and without more, unlawfulness cannot be said to amount to arbitrariness.[120] . . . Arbitrariness is not so much something opposed to a rule of law, as something opposed to the rule of law. This ideal was expressed by the court in the Asylum case, when it spoke of "arbitrary action" being "substituted for the rule of law." . . . It is a wilful disregard of due process of law, an act which shocks, or at least surprises a sense of juridical propriety. Nothing in the decision of the Prefect, or in the judgment of the Court of Appeal of Palermo, conveys any indication that the requisition order of the Mayor was to be regarded in that light.[121]

Ultimately, the chamber rejected the United States claim.

The requisitioning of a factory owned by foreign investors, not by citizens, by the mayor of the town in which it was located and the endorsement of that action by the highest instances in Italy was not deemed to be a denial of justice, even though lower courts indicated and the chamber in effect acknowledged that the action was taken for political reasons. The chamber found that an act taken in violation of Italian law, which was arguably unreasonable and improperly motivated, and which the prefect found to be "destitute of any juridical cause which may justify it or make it enforceable," was not "arbitrary" in terms of international law or the FCN Treaty.[122] Indeed, the chamber noted "That the fact that an act of public authority may have been unlawful in municipal law does not necessarily mean that that act was unlawful in international law, as a breach of treaty or otherwise."[123] The test, according to the chamber, is that the alleged arbitrary action must be a "wilful disregard of due process of law, or an act which shocks, or at least surprises, a sense of juridical propriety."[124]

Now, I would submit that the doctrine the chamber in the ELSI case enunciates is an innovation in international law and purports to change the law with regard to the protection of foreign investment. My concern, in the context of this discussion, is not that change, as such, but the way the chamber achieved it. The chamber stated, in paragraph 128 quoted above, that its idea of arbitrary action was not innovative but was being derived from the Asylum case of 1950: "This idea [the chamber's notion of arbitrariness] was expressed by the Court in the Asylum case, when it spoke of 'arbitrary action' being 'substituted for the rule of law.'" The Asylum case raised questions about the circumstances which justified granting diplomatic asylum. The section of the judgment from which the chamber excerpts the nine words it quotes reads as follows:

> In principle, therefore, asylum cannot be opposed to the operation of justice. An exception to this rule can occur only if, in the guise of justice, arbitrary action is substituted for the rule of law. Such would be the case if the administration of justice were corrupted by measures clearly prompted by political aims. Asylum protects the political offender against any measures of a manifestly extra-legal character which a government might take or attempt to take against its political opponents.[125]

The critical words in the court's judgment with special relevance to the ELSI case equated arbitrary action with circumstances in which "the administration of justice were corrupted by measures clearly prompted by political aims." But the chamber ignored the reference to political motives for acts, which were manifestly present in the ELSI requisition and, instead, pretended that the Asylum case had spoken only of procedural violations, a willful disregard of due process of law. This is not what the Asylum judgment, which supposedly provided authority for the statement, was saying.

Substantively, the chamber may have had ample reason to change international law in this regard. But the method, involving a misrepresentation of its own case law, was not the way to do it.

The point is not that revisions in case law (or, *mutatis mutandis*, statutory law) are externally prohibited, but that the communication of respect for law serves as an informal control mechanism. When it is flouted, the implication is that this control is no longer available. In tribunals of consensual jurisdiction, the natural reaction is withdrawal.

Conclusion

The International Court of Justice, like the Permanent Court before it, does not provide us with an explicit system of control. Control was built into the system in a latent fashion through a number of practices and doctrines. Restrictive jurisdiction, presumptions of confinement, and respect for stare decisis all functioned as informal control mechanisms. Each of these mechanisms has undergone significant changes. None now functions as a control.

The International Court of Justice, though a decision institution that is distinct and unique in the United Nations system, is also profoundly influenced by the context in which it operates. Three features in that context have influenced the court's self-redefinition and revision of its control system.

(1) For more than four decades, the United Nations Charter provided an elaborate plan for the maintenance of international order but the cold war paralyzed the UN institutions that had been assigned the competence to effect it. It was no surprise that other entities within the UN system that found that they were able to operate should have sought to assume and discharge some of the functions that the Security Council was incapable of implementing. The General Assembly itself sought to expand its own powers in this regard, first through the formation of the "Little Assembly," that was to meet continuously, later by passage of the Uniting for Peace Resolution.[126] The court, too, felt some pressure to fill the vacuum created by the Security Council's paralysis. Most of the critical jurisdictional innovations were hard cases that were not being processed by the Security Council: the Nuclear Tests case with its potential impacts on arms control and the environment; the Nicaragua case with its potential effects on regional and superpower relations; and Burkina Faso v. Mali[127] with its potential for regional effects. In the last case, a chamber of the court actually functioned as a mini–Security Council, designing and imposing a cease-fire in the midst of the adjudication. A majority of the judges apparently concluded that the role of the court had changed or had to change or that controls that might have been a critical part of the court's effectiveness in the past were no longer relevant.

(2) This judicial activism was certainly influenced by the increasing dependence of the court on the General Assembly. The method of selection of its judges, the old "Root-Phillimore plan," had sought to balance the interests of large Permanent Members of the UN who, though a numerical minority, were key players in the effective power process of the world with those of smaller but more numerous states. The method for balancing was a system of simultaneous voting in the Security Council and the General Assembly; the successful candidate had to be elected by both bodies. It now appears that the General Assembly has become the dominant partner in this process and that

election and reelection to the court for all but candidates from the strongest states require active campaigning in the assembly. There is no evidence that a record of support for initiatives dear to a majority of the assembly has hurt a candidate's prospects.

(3) Related to the second factor was the introduction of judges from legal cultures that do not necessarily accept the notion of judicial independence. High U.S. officials voiced this complaint at the jurisdictional phase of the Nicaragua case. It was then considered the height of bad taste to talk in this fashion but tastes change and newly liberated peoples in Eastern Europe are the first to decry the lack of judicial independence in communist and totalitarian states.

In the unique constitutional structure of the United States with its tripartite division of powers among the branches, each of which is designed to check and balance the other, an activist judiciary has been permitted to assume and perform certain implicit legislative functions in ways compatible with the interests of more powerful groups in the political system. As long as this latent lawmaking function has been consistent with the real configuration of power in the national political process, the court has been able to continue in this role. But when the court gets out of step with that power process, the court is pressed in a variety of ways until it changes its policy vector or until its personnel are replaced by those who share views more congruent with the contemporary effective power process.

The International Court has tried to activate itself, first and necessarily through a redefinition of its jurisdiction which permits it to seize more disputes than it could have were it applying its classic doctrine of restrictive jurisdiction, and second, through a rather aggressive lawmaking rather than law-applying role. But unlike an activist national court, whose jurisdiction is compulsory and ultimately relies on the support of effective power in the community, the jurisdiction of the International Court remains voluntary and the effective power process, symbolized by the Security Council but actually consisting of a much more complex system of relationships, does not appear to support its initiatives. Yet because the dominant organ in selection of judges continues to be the General Assembly, there is no corrective dynamic, comparable to the one in the United States which periodically acts to reestablish a rough congruence between authority and effective control.

It is clear that the more powerful states have preferred a less active International Court, performing a precise but limited role, policed by control mechanisms such as restrictive jurisdiction and a functional stare decisis. It is clear that they are unlikely to resort to the court if those control mechanisms are not operative or credible. It is also clear that a number of smaller and often newer states do find an International Court which has shrugged off those control mechanisms useful for some purposes. The question is what effect these changes will have on the future work of the court and its contribution to the maintenance of world order.

For many international lawyers, the International Court is a type of secular religion. There is a tendency to exaggerate what are seen as millenial trends. Proponents of the court and its new self-defined role point to a burst of increased activity. Many invoke the Diplomatic Hostages case as an example in which the United States used the court as, they believe, it should have been used. What people overlook is that the case was sent to the court by a government that was completely stymied, had no other ideas, felt it had nothing to lose, was already planning a covert operation to achieve its aim, counted on submission to the court being perceived as a significant action but surely (one hopes) knew that the court's decision would have no effect on the outcome. The Diplomatic Hostages case was a dramatic failure for the court. Nor did the United States submission of the ELSI case mean that the United States had rediscovered the virtues of the court. It was submitted on the day the United States denounced the Truman Declaration under which it had accepted the optional jurisdiction of the court. As everyone who follows these matters knows, ELSI, which had been prepared for ad hoc arbitration, was submitted to the court instead in order to head off an anticipated public outcry in the United States and abroad over the U.S. withdrawal. (The outcry, in fact, never materialized.)[128]

The only successes the court has enjoyed have been in cases in which *both* parties consented to jurisdiction and wanted the court to resolve their dispute. The court's rejection of its controls and its aggressive reaching for jurisdiction has made prudent legal advisers with big and difficult cases that might be submitted in this fashion stay away.

To an extent the court has already been curbed because of these control violations. In the chamber procedure, as it has been revised, the litigant states select only those judges they wish or trust, as the case may be, to sit in a minicourt. The judgment rendered is deemed to be a judgment of the court. The increased use of chambers of the court is, in my view, a clear indication of lack of confidence in the court. And it is sad, for a court of chambers is not the same as a world court.

I would like to see the court play a useful role in world politics. But the use of chambers and the numbers and the types of cases now on the plenary court's docket do not augur, for me, a continuing important role for the court in the world order that seems to be evolving. These numbers could flatten further and the cases could oscillate increasingly between the marginal, the trivial, and the bizarre. Over time the institution processing such cases could, for all its ritual and pomp, take on some of their character and be even less likely to be viewed as an attractive option for major dispute resolution. It is significant that in every major crisis since the Nicaragua case, voices have urged that the matter at the heart of the crisis be sent to the court. None has been. I would guess that without a revival of the control mechanisms that operated in the past, none will be.

Ironically, all this occurs as we are entering a period in which there is greater need for institutional third-party decision-making. Institutions are proliferating. ECSC fora are regularly exploring new possible arrangements. The court, as a highly subsidized and extremely economic mode, could be an attractive option. There are many proposals to use the court, but no one seems to have enough confidence in the institution to really press them to fruition.

This is a good time for the court to repair its damaged control mechanisms. We are in a period in which the Security Council is operating approximately as the charter regime envisaged it. Hence the court need not imagine that it must shoulder the burden of world security that a paralyzed Security Council had dropped. The court could perform the functions for which it had been designed and thereby make a real and substantial if not glamorous contribution to world order. But the court will not realize its promise if it is perceived as operating without controls.

The court is the sum of its judges. They or the leaders among them can make a change. If they do not, others will have to. Until all the political organs of the United Nations decide that there is no point in maintaining a budget item for an institution of marginal contribution and themselves insist, by selection of judges and communication of dissatisfaction, on the operation of controls, the court, I fear, will be a shadow of what it might have been.

But the chances for repair are limited, for the breakdown of the informal and internalized control system of the ICJ exemplifies many of the ambiguities of changes in control configurations. In the wake of these changes, the United States, an important consumer of international third-party decision, withdrew from the optional jurisdictional clause of the court, and a number of other states may have reconsidered the extent to which they can use the institution. Meanwhile other states and many scholars have applauded the development. Some view the court's shrugging off of its erstwhile controls as a liberation, an emancipation, international law unbound. Thus, the breakdown does not necessarily signal the end of the operation of the court. It does suggest, however, that the major states will find it increasingly risky to use it. Hence, its clientele may henceforth be a different group of states. That, in turn, could further affect its jurisprudence and may have additional implications for control.

Whoever henceforth uses the court, one structural consequence of the breakdown of informal and internalized control mechanisms is their externalization, at greater cost to the system. In the absence of reliable internal controls, states resorting to the court will increasingly fall back upon the classic control device of the unilateral claim of *excès de pouvoir*. This may not help the operation of the court or amplify its contribution to world order.

3 The ICSID Experiment: The Breakdown of International Institutional Control Mechanisms

One of the major objectives of international commercial arbitration has been to keep dispute resolution out of the courts of one or the other of the parties and to protect litigants from the costs of plodding through the long corridors of national judicial bureaucracies, with mandatory calls at each successive cubicle to rehear all or part of the case. At least, national courts would provide a measure of control. Of course, the optimum control institution for international commercial arbitration would be self-contained at the international level, completely avoiding national courts, but would perform all necessary control requirements. This sort of control institution has proved elusive. It is now relatively easy to establish workable international arbitral institutions, as their proliferation demonstrates. It has proved much more difficult to create comparably workable explicit control institutions, whether through some form of review or appeal.

There is one dramatic exception. World Bank arbitration, thanks to the opportunities presented by its structure and the imagination of its conceivers, provides us with an example of an entirely internal and international control mechanism.

The Background of ICSID

In 1963 the International Bank convened a conference to create a system of international arbitration associated with the bank.[1] The nexus between a public international development bank and international arbitration may not be immediately apparent, but, in fact, it is very close. The purpose of the planned arbitration center was closely related to the major purpose of the International Bank: to encourage and accelerate economic development in the poorer countries. Since it had become apparent that available public funds were quite insufficient for the task, the bank sought to recruit private capital by encouraging direct foreign investment in developing countries. But potential investors had become skittish about investing in poorer countries, at a time when a synergy of recent independence and radical ideology was provoking expansive claims of sovereignty and national rights to expropriate foreign property.

The new arbitral center sought to create an impartial and reliable system of arbitration, under the aegis of the World Bank, for disputes between direct foreign investors and host governments. The assurance of such a system, it was thought, would assuage the anxieties of foreign investors and encourage them to invest, while, at the same time, cooling the enthusiasm of host governments for expropriatory initiatives. The fundamental idea underlying the ICSID experiment was brilliantly simple: developing countries anxious to induce private foreign investment in their countries would agree to submit disputes about those investments to a tribunal while the governments of foreign investors would agree to refrain from what is often euphemistically called "diplomatic protection," a term which includes national actions on behalf of investors abroad ranging from the gentlest of persuasion to very high coercion.

As in all international commercial arbitration, the designers of the World Bank scheme knew that they had to provide a neutral forum, which would avoid both the courts of the host state, which foreign investors usually felt could be prejudicial to their interests, and the courts of the foreign investor which the host government would usually assume to be less than sympathetic to its aspirations. Moreover, for many states, the prospect of submitting to the jurisdiction of a foreign court was taken as an affront to its sovereignty and national dignity.

The International Centre for the Settlement of Investment Disputes or "ICSID," as the World Bank system came to be acronymically known, addressed both of these problems. Sensitive to the political elements in the cases it would be processing, the ICSID system also sought to reduce the role of national courts in enforcement even more than in other available systems of private international arbitration by providing for direct enforcement with no possibility of challenging an award in those national courts where enforcement of awards would otherwise have been sought. The developing countries which were anxious to attract foreign investment would have been loath to submit to the jurisdiction of a foreign court in an enforcement action. From the perspective of the foreign investor, such enforcement, as of 1963, hardly looked worth the effort. If the developing country even had assets in an industrialized state, those assets were probably protected by the then still broad doctrine of sovereign immunity.

The ICSID Control Scheme

But how then police the many normative requirements and standards of the proposed system? To have used national courts, as the control system of noninstitutional private international arbitration does, would have defeated one of the cardinal purposes of ICSID, which was to avoid national courts. The drafters of ICSID took an entirely different tack, drawing on an idea that had gestated since 1928.

In the past most international tribunals were formed for a particular dispute or class of disputes and then, *functus officio*, dissolved after they had rendered their awards. Their members would return, often by comparatively primitive means of transportation, to their distant countries. Not only were there no existing control institutions; it was often virtually impossible to reconvene the tribunal which had rendered the award for even the limited purpose of clarification or rectification. Unless special provision had been made, the tribunal no longer existed legally and factually. If one sought an organized control mechanism, one had to create a new tribunal.

The creation of the Permanent Court of International Justice in 1920 opened new opportunities which were quickly appreciated. The idea of employing the court as a review or appeal authority was forwarded first by Szymon Rundstein, the Polish member of a Committee of Jurists which the League of Nations had established to study the possible revision of the Statute of the Permanent Court. In 1928 Rundstein proposed that states interested in averting the problems caused by claims of arbitral nullity could make a declaration, under Article 36(2) of the Statute of the Permanent Court, which would commit them in advance to submit to the Permanent Court claims of excessive jurisdiction and violations of rules of international law by arbitral tribunals. The Permanent Court was to act as a *cour de cassation*; after its decision, the original tribunal would modify its award in the light of the court's ruling.

Point 5 of Rundstein's draft provided: "Eventual revision of an award belongs to the competence of the international arbitral or judicial tribunal which has been established by the signatory parties, except where they confer on the Permanent Court of International Justice jurisdiction as a tribunal for revision."[2] Note the assumption that the original tribunal was still in operation and had not become *functus officio*. Rundstein assumed that the original tribunal would still be operating but would suspend itself until the contested issue was resolved by the court. Apparently, Rundstein was thinking of institutions like the Mixed Arbitral Tribunals of the Peace Treaties of the First World War.[3] His assumption made his proposal relevant only to a limited number of what proved to be ephemeral international arbitral phenomena.

In 1929 Finland proposed that the question of enfranchising the Permanent Court with an arbitral review competence be placed on the agenda of the League of Nations.[4] Shortly thereafter, the General Assembly asked the Security Council to consider: "What would be the most appropriate procedure to be followed by States desiring to enable the Permanent Court . . . to assume, in a general manner, as between them, the functions of a tribunal of appeal from international arbitral tribunals in all cases where it is contended that the arbitral tribunal was without jurisdiction or exceeded its jurisdiction."[5] Meanwhile, the idea was also being explored in nongovernmental fora. At its 1929 meeting, the Institut de Droit International recommended: "States, in their conventions on arbitration, as well as in the *clauses compromissoires* signed by them, agree to submit to the Permanent Court of International Justice for decision all disputes between them relating to either the competence of the arbitral tribunal, or to an *excès de pouvoir* by the latter alleged by one of the Parties."[6]

In 1930 the Committee of Jurists, which had been appointed by the League Council, submitted a report and proposed three alternative draft protocols, each of which incorporated and developed the earlier proposals.[7] Under Article 3 in each of the alternatives, a party alleging the nullity of an award for specified grounds had to submit its allegation to the Permanent Court. Common Article 4 provided: "The Permanent Court of International Justice shall declare the award which is impeached to be null, in whole or in part, if it recognizes the application to be well founded. By such annulment, the parties to the dispute shall be replaced in the legal position in which they stood before the commencement of the proceedings which gave rise to the award which has been impeached."[8]

The idea languished during the rest of the League period but was revived, after the formation of the United Nations, by the late Professor Georges Scelle, when he was rapporteur for the International Law Commission's project on international arbitration,[9] an ill-fated enterprise we considered in the first chapter. Scelle was instructed by the commission to prepare a comprehensive code of international arbitration which would establish unified standards for every phase of the process. In dealing with the subject-matter of control systems, claims about improper actions on the part of the tribunal and challenges or refusals to comply with awards because of those actions, he decided to revive the abortive League plan. In Scelle's conception, the International Court of Justice would be enfranchised to act as the final review tribunal for challenges to arbitral awards.[10]

The Scelle plan, like its predecessor, was stoutly resisted. The ILC draft, with its innovative control system, was rejected by the United Nations General Assembly. Thereafter, the ILC concluded the project by transforming it into a set of "Model Rules."[11] The question of exactly who they were to be a model for was not specified. But the idea was not dead.

In designing their control system, the drafters of the ICSID Convention drew upon the experience of both the League and the United Nations International Law Commission. But they modified it in one critical way. Rather than incorporating the International Court of Justice, as had the abortive proposals of Rundstein and then Scelle, the new convention created its own internal, international review instance.

ICSID Convention Article 52(1) broke no new ground in setting out the grounds for annulment of an ICSID award. It stated:

> Either party may request annulment of the award by an application in writing addressed to the Secretary-General on one or more of the following grounds:
>
> (a) that the Tribunal was not properly constituted;
>
> (b) that the Tribunal has manifestly exceeded its powers;
>
> (c) that there was corruption on the part of a member of the Tribunal;
>
> (d) that there has been a serious departure from a fundamental rule of procedure; or
>
> (e) that the award has failed to state the reasons on which it is based.[12]

Article 52 thus authorizes either party to request by application to the secretary-general of the Arbitration Centre annulment of an award rendered by an ICSID tribunal for a limited number of specified reasons, comprised of the familiar terms of art of arbitral nullity (as quoted above). The application for annulment had to be made within 120 days of the date on which the award was rendered.

The innovation in ICSID was the control entity to which claims for nullification were to be submitted. Once the request has been lodged, the chairman of the ICSID Administrative Council (ex officio the president of the World Bank) appoints an ad hoc committee of three persons from a panel of names proposed by states' members and kept by the secretary-general, none of whom may have the nationality of the state-party or the foreign investor.[13] Name notwithstanding, the committee is, in effect, another tribunal, following the same procedures prescribed in the convention for the original tribunal,[14] though its mandate is more circumscribed than the tribunal whose award it is reviewing. In the course of its proceedings, the committee may stay enforcement of the award.[15] If it finds that there has been a violation of one or more of the standards, the ad hoc committee is authorized to annul the award in whole or in part. If the award is nullified by the committee, either party may submit the dispute to a new tribunal, constituted in accordance with the convention.[16]

Klöckner: Arbitral Review Amok

ICSID began operation in 1966. By 1983 it had entertained fourteen arbitrations, five of which had proceeded to award. Throughout this period, there was no recourse to the review option provided by Article 52. The ICSID control scheme existed on paper as a theoretical possibility, but without the rich background material, doctrinal illumination, or analogues in other operating arbitral systems that might have given users of the convention an idea of how it would actually operate.

The situation changed dramatically with the case of Klöckner v. Government of Cameroon.[17] The essential relationships between the parties in this case were concisely described by the tribunal in the first phase of the case:

> This was a joint venture between Kloeckner, a multinational European Corporation, and a developing country. The plant to be built was an example of imported modern technology and engineering. Cameroon had no experience in manufacturing fertilizer products. The factory was to be acquired with the Government's guarantee of payment; its output being of major importance for the country's agriculture, and agriculture being in turn the very foundation of Cameroon's economic ambitions. Cameroon counted on Kloeckner to supply all that was necessary to ensure the success of the project. Kloeckner had carried out the initial feasibility study. It had designed the plant and carried out the technical studies. Kloeckner had undertaken to organize the long-term financing, over ten years, of the project. It built or bought from others all the machinery and all the material. It coordinated the work of suppliers and sub-contractors. It was to execute, operate, and manage the project, procure necessary raw materials, and organize the marketing of output. By accepting—and indeed seeking out—these responsibilities, Kloeckner had taken on a serious obligation. Kloeckner claimed to be capable of supplying all the know-how, all the material, and all the management skills necessary to ensure the project's success, the Government's only role being to supply a site and to guarantee payment of the contract price.[18]

These relationships were concretized in a network of agreements. In 1971 Klöckner, the West German multinational, and the West African government of Cameroon, had concluded a so-called "Basic Agreement," which created a type of joint venture in the form of a Cameroonian company, SOCAME, which was to construct and manage a fertilizer plant. Klöckner, owning 51 percent of SOCAME, would control it; the government was to hold the remaining 49 percent. The Basic Agreement assigned to Klöckner the responsibility "for the technical and commercial management of the Company (SOCAME) under a management contract for at least five years, beginning with the start-up of operations." The agreement also contained an arbitration clause, referring disputes to ICSID.

Three months later, Klöckner and Cameroon concluded another agreement, this one a turnkey contract for the factory to be built or supplied by Klöckner; in the subsequent disputes, this was referred to as the "Supply Contract." SOCAME would pay Klöckner for the factory, but the government of Cameroon guaranteed SOCAME's payments. This turnkey or supply contract also contained an ICSID arbitration clause.

In 1973 the Cameroon government and SOCAME, now in operation and controlled by Klöckner, concluded another agreement, the so-called "Convention," defining additional rights and obligations of the parties and referring to all the previous agreements. The convention also contained an ICSID clause. In 1977 Klöckner and SOCAME, which Klöckner still controlled, concluded a management contract. This new contract referred to the previous contracts in which the fundamentals of the management agreement had been set out and further elaborated those management responsibilities.

While each of the other contractual documents chose ICSID arbitration, the management contract contained an arbitration clause referring disputes to the International Chamber of Commerce. Now this was rather unusual, but one can imagine complex transactions in which there might be cogent reasons for using several different dispute resolving institutions. In agreeing to build and manage a port for a government, the prime contractor might wish an ICSID clause in agreements with the government, except for jurisdiction over maritime collision disputes that could be assigned to a tribunal specialized over maritime matters. Contracts with foreign subcontractors might include an ICC clause. Contracts with local subcontractors might refer to the local arbitration system. But the rich variety of contractual partners in this hypothetical was hardly matched in the Klöckner-Cameroon relationship. In fact, this curious and belated reassignment of part of the dispute-resolving competence of this particular integrated operation to a different arbitration system may not have been an act of caprice or an accident, as we will see in a moment. Certainly, by the time the management contract was concluded, arbitration was no longer a remote contingent possibility. Klöckner had known for some time that there were serious difficulties with the project, that some facts on which original projections of profitability had been based had changed drastically and that, in fact, the factory could not be profitable. (In the arbitration, Cameroon presented evidence, which apparently persuaded the tribunal, that throughout its life, the factory barely attained 30 percent of its promised capacity.) Klöckner did not share this new information with the Cameroonian government.

After the factory started up, output fell far below original projections. In 1978 the Cameroonian government sought the views of an outside consultant, who recommended that the factory be redesigned in order to modify its processes. Money, of course, would be required. Cameroon invited Klöckner to participate, but Klöckner refused to make any additional capital contributions to SOCAME and instead yielded its majority shareholding.

Even after the supplementary investment and redesign, the factory proved unworkable and SOCAME refused to pay Klöckner for it. Klöckner then initiated ICSID arbitration against the government of Cameroon for payments it had guaranteed. Because the various arbitration clauses now referred different parts of the transaction to two different arbitral systems—ICSID and ICC—Klöckner confined its claim to a demand for the guaranteed payment for the turnkey delivery of a factory (the supply contract), a matter subject to ICSID jurisdiction, while contending that any counterclaims based on allegations about violation of its management obligations that Cameroon might want to raise had been assigned by the parties to another arbitral system (ICC) and, hence, could not be heard in ICSID. With regard to the factory's performance, Klöckner insisted that it had no obligations with regard to its workability. Cameroon counterclaimed for violations of obligations under the various agreements. It insisted that it was entitled to a factory that worked and not just a factory. Its counterclaims also raised matters concerning management of the enterprise. Klöckner insisted that these matters had been assigned to the International Chamber of Commerce in Paris and not to ICSID in Washington.

Klöckner's demurrer to these counterclaims was one of the most interesting aspects of the case. The final management contract, which spelled out the details of the management relationship that had been expressed more generally in some of the previous instruments, incorporated, as mentioned earlier, an ICC rather than ICSID arbitration clause. Klöckner, as the then majority owner and effective manager of SOCAME, was, in one sense, concluding an agreement with itself. Why did it elect ICC arbitration? Conceivably, it may have thought that ICSID was inappropriate, for SOCAME was not the host state. But, then, other agreements with SOCAME had incorporated ICSID clauses. It is also possible that this was the result of carelessness or error. But if the factual account in the first award is accepted, Klöckner may have realized, as early as 1973, that the original projections of profitability which it had prepared for the Cameroonian government, and were apparently the basis for the decision about the transaction, were obsolete. Even with additional funds, it was not at all certain that the planned enterprise could turn a profit. Klöckner, at this time in control of SOCAME, did not share this information with the government. In a sense, the success or failure of the factory may not have been of central urgency to Klöckner, for its payments were guaranteed by the government of Cameroon and backed up, as it were, by an ICSID clause.

It is possible—this is pure speculation—that Klöckner, in 1977, still in charge of SOCAME, inserted the ICC clause in the management contract as a worst-case contingency. It may have hoped that if Cameroon concluded that it had been treated unfairly and refused to pay its guarantee and Klöckner initiated arbitration under the ICSID clause, the only issue over which ICSID would have jurisdiction, if the strategy worked, was the question of whether or not a factory was built and delivered. All of the questions about Klöckner's management behavior and, in particular, whether it concealed vital information which might have permitted Cameroon to reduce its exposure or even to cut its losses terminally by aborting the project earlier, would not be subject to ICSID jurisdiction, if, according to this gambit, they had been assigned to the ICC. A favorable jurisdictional decision that the issue properly before an ICSID tribunal was the factory and not the quality of its management would have been virtually outcome-determinative.

If this was Klöckner's strategy, it was confounded by the ICSID tribunal, which concluded, over the strong dissent of Klöckner's party-appointed arbitrator, that the tribunal had jurisdiction over management issues by virtue of the Basic Agreement.[19] Klöckner's second line of defense to Cameroon's complaints about the quality of the factory was that its only obligation was to supply a factory. It had no obligation to supply a factory that worked.

In turning to this latter question, the tribunal held that Cameroonian law applied. Because Cameroon had been divided, during the colonial period, between Britain and France and had inherited systems of British common law and French civil law which continued to operate in its two component regions, the tribunal applied Cameroonian conflicts of law and concluded that French civil law, as incorporated in Cameroonian law, applied.[20]

This law, the tribunal held, included the obligation of a party to disclose to the other party material information of interest to it.

> We take for granted that the principle according to which a person who engages in close contractual relations, based on confidence, must deal with its partner in a frank, loyal and candid manner, is a basic principle of French civil law, as is indeed the case under the other national codes which we know of. This is the criterion that applies to relations between

> partners in simple forms of association anywhere. The rule is particularly appropriate in more complex international ventures, such as the present one.[21]

Within that normative framework, the tribunal concluded:

> In the present case, as we have suggested, we do not feel that Kloeckner had dealt frankly with Cameroon. At critical stages of the project, Kloeckner hid from its partner, information of vital importance. On several occasions, it failed to disclose facts which, if they had been known to the government, could have caused it to put an end to the venture and cancel the contract before the expenditure of the funds whose payment Kloeckner now seeks to obtain by means of an award. When a partner in a financially complex international venture learns of certain facts which could influence the attitudes and the actions of the other partner with respect to the project; when the first partner fails to disclose this information to the other; and the second thereupon continues with the project and incurs additional costs, the first partner has not acted frankly and loyally vis-a-vis his partner, and he cannot rightly present a claim to funds whose expenditure would perhaps never have been necessary if he had been frank and candid in his dealings. In a very significant sense, the fault is his. The fact that the funds were spent becomes his responsibility and not that of his partner. In this respect, we decide that Kloeckner violated its fundamental contractual obligations and may not insist upon payment of the entire price of the Turnkey Contract.[22]

Cameroon argued that Klöckner's failure to perform had relieved Cameroon of its own obligation to pay Klöckner. It invoked the French contracts law principle of *exceptio non adimpleti contractus*, which permits one party to a contract to refrain unilaterally and lawfully from performing its obligations under the contract when faced with material nonperformance by the other party.[23] Klöckner, according to the majority of the tribunal, had failed to perform in a way which justified the application by Cameroon of the *exceptio*.

The issue of adequacy of performance turned on whether the obligation was to supply a factory that worked or simply to supply a factory, without regard to whether it was operable. Klöckner argued that it fulfilled its requirements under the contract by supplying a factory. The tribunal held:

> In order to perform the relevant contracts correctly, it was not sufficient to supply a fertilizer factory; the factory had to have the required capacity and had to be managed in the manner necessary to obtain the

> proposed goals. . . . Kloeckner had undertaken to ensure continuous functioning and maintenance of the factory (technical management) as well as to perform its commercial management. . . . The most conclusive proof of Kloeckner's failure to perform its duty of technical and commercial management results simply from the shutdown of the factory in December 1977, by decision of Kloeckner personnel sent to Cameroon, after 18 months of underproduction and operating losses.[24]

Accordingly, the tribunal decided by majority to reject Klöckner's claim as well as Cameroon's counterclaim. In effect, the award was a victory for Cameroon.

Klöckner's party-appointed arbitrator, Professor Dominique Schmidt, appended an unusual fifty-three-page dissenting opinion. Ordinarily, dissenting opinions express a different legal view, leading to a different outcome but acknowledge the authority of the award. Professor Schmidt did not dissent in this sense. He stated that the award was null, because of, in the words of its author, "important mistakes, the numerous contradictions and failures to state the grounds, and the misrepresentation of contractual clauses."[25]

Klöckner promptly applied to the secretary-general of ICSID for nullification of the award under Article 52 of the ICSID Convention, essentially on the grounds spelled out in Professor Schmidt's dissent. The chairman of ICSID's Administrative Council (who is, by virtue of Article 5 of the convention, the president of the World Bank) appointed a three-person ad hoc committee composed of distinguished professors and eminent arbitrators from Switzerland, Austria, and Egypt.

The ad hoc committee's decision[26] was extremely long (176 typed pages) elaborate, and careful. In places it is stunning and brilliant, but it is also marked by a tendency toward hairsplitting, or "legal purity," as the committee put it, without, it would appear, any intended irony. It justified its purist approach on theoretical grounds.[27] There are good arguments to be made for strict application of a review procedure. But, as is often the case, any legal approach which resolutely tries to avoid reality runs the danger of colliding head-on with it.

As the first ad hoc committee operating under the convention, its members were manifestly sensitive to the fact that their decision would profoundly shape expectations about control systems of arbitration, in general, and ICSID review, in particular. On its own motion, the committee purported to issue an authoritative interpretation of the control procedure of ICSID. It took up this burden, it said, in view of the fact that this was "the first Application for Annulment ever lodged against an ICSID award" and in view of the "interest to the parties and to the new Tribunal that may be constituted under Article 52(6)."[28]

The committee's appreciation of its longer-term mission was not modest. Even after nullifying the award, it appended a long obiter dictum, comprising almost two-thirds of its decision. The purpose of the excursus was explained in a grandiloquent style, by now familiar to readers of this unusual document. "While it is superfluous here to return to each criticism of the Award, it is incumbent upon the Committee, in the interest of the Tribunal itself and in the higher interest of the arbitration system set up by the Washington Convention, not to leave any of the claimant's essential complaints unanswered."[29] The fact that a matter had nothing to do with its mandate under the convention was apparently no reason to refrain from commenting on it. Even matters such as "particularities of structure and presentation of the Award"[30] were favored with gratuitous evaluations. Nor was it only the award that was graded by the committee. The states-parties to the ICSID Convention themselves were graciously advised about how they might go about revising the rules.[31]

Constitutive Rulings

At the most basic level, the committee made what amount to four constitutive rulings about ICSID review. These rulings, which would have a decisive effect on the disposition of the Klöckner case, were also designed to shape all future procedures under Article 52. Let us consider them briefly.

A presumption in favor of the validity of the award under review. The committee posited a presumption in favor of the validity of the award under question. In cases in which doubts were raised, "analysis should be resolved *in favorem validitatis sententiae.*" This particular holding, to which the committee returned on a number of occasions in its decision, appears to be mandated by the structure of ICSID review. The alternative, that the award does not enjoy such a presumption, would, in effect, transform the procedure under Article 52 into a de novo arbitration. If the award did not enjoy a presumption of validity and the burden of proof was not on the challenging party, the procedure would be rearbitration.

Hair trigger: the automatic technical discrepancy standard. The second constitutive holding was that review was to be technical and mechanical; the ad hoc committee was to have no prudential competence. In keeping with that conception, the committee posited an automatic requirement of nullification if a defect were established. The gravity or significance of a particular defect was not to be taken into account.[32] In effect, this requirement made

Article 52 into a hair trigger, a mechanism of extraordinary sensitivity that would set off nullification at the slightest provocation, without regard to the magnitude of the defect established.

In terms of legal theory, the committee had elected, in effect, to adopt a "rule" rather than a "standard" approach. Where a large number of similar cases come to a decision-maker and the value of any case is substantially less than the transaction costs involved in deciding it, considerations of economy may dictate that each case be decided by a "binary" rule in which many variables are fixed a priori and only two choice options, on the order of "a" or "not-a," are allowed the decision-maker. A rule approach is effected by evidentiary limitations on everything except what is needed to establish the relevance of the binary rule to the case at hand. All other evidence is simply inadmissible. A rule approach may also be dictated by intense policy demands. Some defects, for example corruption of a chairman, may be deemed per se to require nullification even if the consequences are minimal.

The "rule" approach may be contrasted with a "standard" approach, in which each case is examined in terms of its special facts and related to and decided in accord with the full array of community policies. A much wider array of evidence is perforce admissible in a standard approach. In many contexts the preferability of a "rule" over a "standard" approach is arguable. But the principle of economy, the proliferation of similar cases, and the need for economy on which the rule approach is based can hardly apply to the limited number of cases with widely varying and complex fact-patterns that come to ICSID tribunals.

Choosing whether to use a rule or standard approach is a constitutive decision. Like all such decisions, one would expect a canvassing of the aggregate consequences of the alternatives in terms of the fundamental goals and objectives of arbitral review in the ICSID system. But the Klöckner committee's constitutive decision was not based on this sort of exercise nor was it inferred from jurisprudence nor tested by reference to past practice. It was derived essentially from textual interpretation which the committee derived from the convention. Article 52(3) of the ICSID Convention states that "the Committee shall have the authority to annul the award." From this the committee concluded that if it found a defect, it was obliged to nullify the award.[33]

This is a doubtful interpretation. It would appear from the language of that provision, in the context of the convention as a whole, that its purpose was not to install a rule of compulsory nullification but simply to confirm *who* nullifies. Article 52(3) establishes that the committee *does not* report back to the secretary-general with a recommendation or opinion, for the provision does not assume that the actual competence to annul is located in the permanent administrative apparatus of ICSID. Rather, it is the committee which makes the decision on annulment.

Such an interpretation would have allowed a committee some discretion as to whether or to what extent to nullify. The Klöckner committee construed the provision as an injunction to it to annul an award even if there were no injury to the other party or no substantial cause for grievance.[34]

The expansion of grounds for annulment. In a third constitutive ruling, the committee rejected the notion that its role and competence were limited to testing the award only in terms of the grounds listed in Article 52.[35] Article 52, it will be recalled, does not simply say that *any* departure from any of the prescriptions of the convention warrants annulment. Instead, it lists specific grounds, some of which differ in language and scope, from coordinate sections of the convention. For example, a party may request annulment under Article 52(1)(e) on the ground that "the award has failed to state the reasons on which it is based." Article 48, which is comprised of a series of instructions to the tribunal seised of the case, states in subparagraph 3 that "[t]he award shall deal with every question submitted to the Tribunal, and shall state the reasons upon which it is based." Article 52(1)(e) is plainly narrower than Article 48(3). *Stricto sensu*, nullification would be inappropriate under Article 52(1)(e) if the reasons for the award reached were stated, but the award did not deal with every question submitted to the tribunal nor did it set out the reasons for the particular disposition of each question.

The committee decided to ignore the clear differences between the language of Article 52(1) and other sections of the convention and, instead, chose to coordinate sections of the convention with Article 52(1) by reading that provision as a type of *renvoi* to the rest of the convention. In effect, the committee interpreted the convention as authorizing and requiring it to examine a challenged award's compliance with *all* the standards set out in the rest of the convention.[36]

We will consider the soundness of the committee's interpretation later. Here, we are concerned with the implications of the holding for Klöckner and subsequent cases. A strict reading would have limited the ambit of the control function to the enumeration in Article 52(1). The committee's interpretation greatly enlarged its own work as well as expanded future possibilities for challenging awards. Implicitly, it also affected the latent compromising function of arbitration, a matter which will be considered below.

A formal rather than substantive test of reasons. In a fourth constitutive ruling, the committee adopted a formal rather than substantive requirement for adequacy of reasons. In the committee's view, as long as the tribunal's "answers seem tenable and not arbitrary, *they do not constitute a manifest excess of powers*."[37] In case of doubt, as noted earlier, "analysis should be resolved *in favorem validitatis sententiae*."[38]

This formalistic approach, which seemed to have been designed to help sustain challenged awards, actually reduces the effect of the presumption in favor of validity, for it produces a curious passivity and unwillingness to try to penetrate the thinking of the tribunal whose award is under attack. Thus, in elaborating its conception of its mandate, the committee said:

> [I]t is not for the Committee to imagine what might or should have been the arbitrators' reasons any more than it should substitute "correct" reasons for possibly "incorrect" reasons, or deal "*ex post facto*" with questions submitted to the Tribunal which the Award left unanswered. The only role of the Committee here is to state whether there is one of the grounds for annulment set out in Article 52 of the Convention, and to draw the consequences under the same Article. In this sense, the Committee defends the Convention's legal purity.[39]

What emerges, then, is a formalistic approach which eschews a real effort at reconstruction of the objectives or deeper ratiocination of the award under review. Under such an approach, a committee would theoretically nullify an award for faults in logic somewhere between first premise and conclusion, even though it might be arguable, even clear, that the conclusion was correct.

This particular construction of the convention is textually plausible and consistent with the core idea animating arbitral review. The alternative, a substantive test, runs the danger of sliding into appeal. But the committee's construction is not informed by any sense of the control function in arbitration and, as a result, poses certain risks for the future of ICSID arbitration. Due to varying levels of personal ability and the diversity of legal cultures, different arbitrators perceive and analyze legal questions differently, reason differently and at extraordinarily different lengths, and write judgments with greatly varying degrees of skill and elegance, often in a language to which they are not native. If a subsequent ad hoc committee, composed in part of people from still different legal cultures, decides that it is not obliged to try to "get into the skin" of the tribunal and reconstruct the reasoning of the award it is reviewing, and does not approach its task with full recognition of the difficulties of construing any human communication, a fortiori, transnational legal communications, the probability of nullifying on grounds of inadequate reasons increases. And if the committee is unwilling to try to determine whether, reasons notwithstanding, a plausible and defensible (if not wise) answer was reached, nullifications with formal but no material justification will occur.

Appeal rather than review consequences. The committee postulated constitutive rulings that restricted substantive inquiry and was at pains to emphasize that it was involved in a review of particular grounds established in Article 52 of the ICSID Convention and not an appeal on the wisdom or "correctness" of the award. This is a proper concern of everyone engaged in arbitral review. Notwithstanding, the committee tended to slip into appeal. In addition to finding that there were defects in the award which warranted nullification, the committee made certain key decisions on some legal issues of the merits, some of which it even suggested might be used by a subsequent tribunal.[40] This is a radical and interesting redefinition at the constitutive level of the review function. We will consider its implications below.

Although the ad hoc committee reaffirmed a commitment *in favorem validitatis sententiae*, the net consequence of its constitutive holdings was, as we will see, a weakening of that presumption and a marked tilting in review in favor of the challenging party.

Substantive Holdings

Klöckner, it will be recalled, had challenged the validity of the entire award on jurisdictional grounds, contending that the tribunal had, among other things, exceeded its jurisdiction by basing its award on alleged violations of management responsibilities. Klöckner averred that allegations about those matters were subject to the ICC jurisdictional clause in the management contract. Because the tribunal had purported to decide them, it had exceeded its jurisdiction and its award was null.

The committee purported to examine every possible construction of the two jurisdictional clauses. It did not conceal its serious doubts about the tribunal's jurisdictional conclusions. Nevertheless, the committee did not substitute its own judgment for that of the tribunal and did not find a ground for nullification here. "Such an interpretation of the agreements and especially of the two arbitration clauses, whether correct or not, is tenable and does not in any event constitute a manifest excess of power. To this extent, the complaint, while admissible, is unfounded."[41] Although the committee did not find the tribunal's reasons persuasive, they were, it found, not implausible. Hence they benefited from the presumption in favor of validity.

> [T]he Tribunal refused to accept, in the absence of completely precise and unequivocal contractual provisions, that the parties to the Management Contract wanted to "derogate" from the Protocol's ICSID clause. The Tribunal may have implicitly accepted that the ICSID clause constituted for both parties an "essential jurisdictional guarantee," the

relinquishment of which could neither be presumed nor accepted in the absence of clear evidence.[42]

This was a liberal and extremely tolerant holding. In light of the analytic method of the rest of the committee's decision, it is puzzling. The tribunal's jurisdictional decision was probably the most questionable part of its award. After all, the parties had decided to structure their transaction in four agreements and to assign arbitral jurisdiction over different parts of the agreements to different arbitral institutions. Yet the tribunal, rather than accept the legal characterization the parties had jointly selected, had looked at the integrated transaction as a factual matter and then used that perspective to override contractual options plainly adopted by the parties. In doing this, the committee only asked itself whether this arrangement was "tenable," without determining whether governing legal systems might make other judgments. "Tenability," absent reference to an encompassing system of law, can become quite subjective.

The committee's conclusion in this part of the decision is all the more puzzling in that a contrary finding on the tribunal's jurisdictional decision would have produced an annulment for *excès de pouvoir*, in a more economical fashion than the methods actually selected by the committee. It also would have done less injury to the review function of ICSID. One may note in passing that arbitrators at the present time rarely find themselves without jurisdiction. As we saw earlier, that development may have long-term implications for both willingness to submit to arbitration and, at the international level, the lawmaking process.

The minimum standard of plausibility and the presumption in favor of validity did not avail the award on other matters. Klöckner had attacked the award on the ground that the tribunal had not applied the proper law. The tribunal, as will be recalled, had explicitly designated that part of Cameroonian law based on French law as the applicable law. Klöckner had been particularly offended by the tribunal's use of the "obligation to disclose everything to a partner." The tribunal had said: "We assume that the principle according to which a person who engages in close contractual relations, based on confidence, must deal with his partner in a frank, loyal and candid manner is a basic principle of French civil law, as is indeed the case under other national codes which we know of."[43] Klöckner's gravamen, it appeared, was not the selection of the proper law as such, but whether the tribunal had made a mistake in applying that proper law.

In an arbitral review format, this was a difficult, even tricky argument for Klöckner to make. The usual practice of review instances has been well summarized by a U.S. federal court. "To vacate an arbitration award for manifest disregard of law there must be 'something beyond and different from a mere error in the law or failure on the part of the arbitrators to understand or apply.' . . . Plaintiff has not demonstrated, as it must, that the majority arbitrators deliberately disregarded what they knew to be the law in order to reach the result they did."[44] The Klöckner tribunal had certainly *identified* the proper law (or laws). The claim that it might have mistakenly applied that law, a legitimate ground for appeal, would not have been admissible in review, for it would have required the committee to redecide the merits.

In light of the committee's tolerant treatment of the tribunal's jurisdictional holding, one might have thought that the tribunal's holding would satisfy the requirements of the ICSID Convention, especially if it were buttressed by the presumption in favor of validity. But the committee found it wanting. "It may immediately be noticed that here the Tribunal does not claim to ascertain the existence (of a rule or a principle) but asserts or postulates the existence of such a 'principle' which (after having postulated its existence) the Tribunal *assumes* or takes for granted that it 'is a basic principle of French civil law.' "[45] The committee was particularly troubled by the award's observation that "this is the criterion that applies to relations between partners in simple forms of association anywhere,"[46] that "the rule [sic] is particularly appropriate in more complex international ventures, such as the present one,"[47] and that the arbitrators declared that they were "convinced that it is particularly important that *universal requirements* of frankness and loyalty in dealings between partners be applied in cases such as this one."[48]

The committee felt that it was insufficient to refer to a "basic principle" without more specific references.[49] It was also troubled by the failure to distinguish between "rule" and "principle."[50] In keeping with its own constitutive holdings, the committee did not attempt to discover, for itself, whether the tribunal's reference to a "basic principle" could in fact be related to rules in the governing law which would have established that the tribunal was correct but careless in its method of citation. (The tribunal's sweeping proposition, one may note, is problematic in arms-length commercial transactions.) The defect, in the view of the committee, was fatal.

> [I]n the absence of any information, evidence or citation in the Award, it would seem difficult to accept, and impossible to *presume*, that there is a general duty, under French civil law, or for that matter other systems of civil law, for a contracting party to make a "*full* disclosure" to its partner. If we were to "presume" anything, it would instead be that such a duty (the basic idea of which may, of course, be accepted as it follows

> from the principle of good faith; cf. Article 1134, para. 3 of the French Civil Code) must, to be given effect in positive law, have conditions for its application and limits![51]

As a result, the committee concluded that a ground for annulment had occurred.

> [I]n its reasoning, limited to postulating and not demonstrating the existence of a principle or exploring the rules by which it can only take concrete form, the Tribunal has not applied "the law of the Contracting State." Strictly speaking, it could not be said that it made this decision without providing reasons, within the meaning of Articles 48(3) and 52(1)(e). It did, however, act outside the framework provided by Article 42(1), applying concepts or principles it probably considered equitable.[52]

The committee concluded that the award was a single unit and that this ground necessitated a total annulment.[53]

Citation method is certainly an important part of our science, but international commercial law draws perforce on lawyers trained in many different legal systems, each of which has a different style or dialect of citation, ratiocination, and redaction. Some systems redact judgments in what Karl Llewellyn called "the grand style";[54] this is the style of the International Court, for example, of which the chairman of the Klöckner tribunal had been the president. Other systems, for example, the United States in its current practice, use idiosyncratic and highly particularistic citation methods. Citations are sprinkled to support even the most self-evident of propositions with the abandon of a Northwest Coast indian throwing an epic potlatch.

Strictly speaking, the tribunal had fulfilled the requirements of both Article 52 and Article 42. It provided reasons for its judgment which sounded in the applicable law. The tribunal's reference to other systems of law was neither optional nor incorrect.[55] By referring to international and "general principles," the tribunal would have demonstrated that Cameroonian law was not inconsistent with international law and hence continued to apply. If there had been a conflict, Cameroonian law, under one theory of interpretation of the ICSID Convention, might have had to yield to international law.[56]

This part of the decision of the committee is cast in terms of inadequate reasons and thus avoids the appearance of an appeal of a mistaken application of law. Though the committee was at pains to distinguish this claim from a claim of an erroneous application (*error in judicando*), it is difficult to escape the impression that the real thrust of the committee's concern was that the tribunal's legal conclusion of an obligation imposed on Klöckner *de tout reveler* constituted a mistake in law. Of course, the committee could not frame its objections in those terms, for that would have manifestly transformed the review into an appeal. Perhaps that accounts for the tortured and ultimately unpersuasive formulation of inadequacy of reasons.

Had it been as sensitive to the formative effect of its work on the ICSID control system as it said it was, the committee might have reflected that the route it was taking might well be tantamount to the worst of possible worlds. It served as precedent for review of the wisdom and correctness of an award *as well as* for a very detailed technical examination of awards. If its conception of the proper role of the ad hoc committee in the ICSID system were to become authoritative, the probability of future nullifications would increase without a corresponding increase in desirable control.

An inadequate conception of control function is also apparent in the ad hoc committee's treatment of procedure. Klöckner had petitioned for nullification on grounds of procedural violations. The committee implied that some of the procedures undertaken by the tribunal may have compromised Klöckner's procedural rights, but felt that Klöckner's claim was barred since Klöckner had not promptly raised objections. Such a holding could act to increase procedural factiousness in future ICSID arbitrations, since it seems to require a litigant to argue each procedural matter it feels is or may be improper the moment it arises. If it does not, *pace* the committee, it may be barred from raising it at the review phase. Happily, this implication appears to have been decisively reversed by the secretariat of ICSID, which reportedly rejected a request for an ad hoc committee to review an interim award in a subsequent case and indicated that the proper moment for review of all issues was at the end of the procedure.[57]

Because the ad hoc committee nullified the entire award, a second arbitration initiated by Klöckner was, in principle, obliged to relitigate everything again. There was no res judicata, however fragmentary, remaining from the first award. A second tribunal was empaneled. It was chaired by Carl Salans and included Juan Antonio Cremades and Jorge Casteñeda. It rendered an award in January 1988 which has not been published. It has been reported to have been in favor of Klöckner though giving it only a fraction of the amount it claimed. That award has been challenged in another Article 52 procedure. The ad hoc committee in this case, chaired by Ambassador Sompong Sucharitkul and composed of Judge Mbaye of the International Court and Professor Girardina of Italy, rendered a decision which has not been published but has been reported to have nullified partially the award.

AMCO and the Effort to Repair the ICSID Control Function

Some students of international commercial arbitration feared that Klöckner, as a precedent authorizing a detailed scrutiny of awards in the review phase, could encourage losers in subsequent ICSID arbitrations to challenge their awards. Whatever the reason, the very next award decided by an ICSID tribunal, AMCO v. Republic of Indonesia,[58] was promptly brought by the loser, Indonesia, to the secretary-general with a petition for annulment under Article 52.

The AMCO case was in many ways the paradigmatic dispute about contemporary direct foreign investment. Indonesia was in the hapless but classic position of a developing country: resource rich and capital poor and thus desperately seeking foreign capital to jump-start productive economic activity. Indonesia had developed a broad program to attract foreign investment by awarding licenses with concessions and incentives for approved foreign investors. Each foreign investment was negotiated separately, but they were all similar in general terms. In return for a commitment to invest a prescribed amount of foreign capital in Indonesia for an approved project, the government would grant a package of concessions, tax holidays, and other inducements.

AMCO, a U.S. company, negotiated this type of model agreement with Indonesia. AMCO committed itself to build and manage a hotel in Jakarta, in collaboration with an Indonesian joint venturer, a private company largely organized by military officers. AMCO promised to invest $3 million of foreign currency in Indonesia as part of its program. The agreement contained an ICSID arbitration clause.

After the hotel was built, the Indonesian joint venturer lodged many complaints. At the same time, the Indonesian government alleged, in various forms, nonpayment of the capital sums which AMCO had agreed to introduce into Indonesia. AMCO did not respond. On the night of March 30, 1980, police and military personnel seized the hotel and expelled the management. Shortly afterward, the competent Indonesian government agency concluded that AMCO had not fulfilled its foreign capital obligations and terminated its license. After unsuccessful efforts to have the decision reversed in Indonesian courts, AMCO exercised its right to ICSID arbitration, claiming not less than $9 million plus interest.

The ICSID tribunal's award considered two basic claims: expropriation and breach of contract. The tribunal concluded as a matter of fact that:

> [O]n or about the critical period there was a taking of Claimants' rights to the control and management of the land and all the Kartika Plaza Building. . . . [A] number of army and police personnel were present at

> the hotel premises on the Ist [*sic*] April, 1980 and by their very presence assisted in the successful seizure from P.T. AMCO of the exercise of its lease and management rights.[59] . . . As a taking per se is not necessarily an unlawful act attributable to a state, the tribunal proceeded to examine whether this taking "amounts to an expropriation which according to Indonesian Law and to International Law can give rise to a claim for compensation."[60] The first question was whether Indonesia itself was the agent of the taking. The tribunal held that the Indonesian government had not expropriated: . . . The taking was instigated by P.T. Wisma and was carried out for the benefit of the same.[61] . . . The Tribunal was not provided with any evidence that the takeover of the hotel and thereby the taking of the Claimants' exercise of their rights to control and management was due to a governmental decision.[62]

This may have been a courtesy to sovereign sensibilities, for the award still concluded that Indonesia had failed to protect an alien from suffering these acts,[63] that the takeover was unlawful,[64] and that the Indonesian Court ruling did not purport to legitimize the act.[65]

With regard to AMCO's claim for breach of contract, the tribunal found that the relationship between AMCO and Indonesia was more in the nature of a license, though "not alien to the general concept of contract."

> Being an agreement aimed at producing legal effects in the economic field, creating obligations for the applicant and obligations for the State, even if in the latter case they are conditional, the legal combination formed by the application and by the approval thereof is not alien to the general concept of contract according to Indonesian law. Nor is it alien to general principles of law.
>
> However, it is not *identical* to a private law contract, due to the fact that the State is entitled to withdraw the approval it granted *for reasons which could not be invoked by a private contracting entity, and/or to decide and implement the withdrawal by utilizing procedures which are different from those which can and have to be utilized by a private entity*. (Italics in original)[66]

Indonesia was entitled, according to the tribunal, to terminate such a relationship for, among other things, nonfulfillment of its terms.[67] But in order to be lawful, the termination had to meet procedural requirements and be substantively justified.[68] AMCO had not met its full requirement of foreign capital, which was a violation, but the tribunal found that it was immaterial. Even if the violation had justified termination, Indonesia had to terminate in accord with international due process and, under its own law, had to give certain prescribed warnings. If Indonesia had violated due process, it was liable, even if the termination had been substantively justified.[69] And Indonesia had violated due process, the tribunal held, for though written warnings had been given,[70] they had not emanated from the right agency nor used the proper language.[71]

The tribunal decided not to inquire into the cogency of other grounds for revocation that had been considered by the appropriate Indonesian authority,[72] for the act was, in its view, already unlawful.[73]

But the tribunal awarded the claimant only $3,200,000 plus 6 percent interest, a sum considerably less than it had claimed. Indonesia had counterclaimed for all the monies, which, except for the tax holiday granted by the license, the claimants should have paid as taxes and import duties. The tribunal rejected the counterclaim: "[S]ince the Tribunal finds that the revocation of the license was unlawful, as a consequence, the revocation of the tax facilities was unlawful as well."[74]

The award was unanimous and, given the fraction of the claim actually awarded, bore the signs of an internal tribunal compromise. Compromise is a curiously unstable phenomenon in arbitration. There are structural pressures both for and against it and structural costs when a compromise is struck for all or part of a decision. The option in three-party arbitration of selection of party-appointed arbitrators introduces and implicitly endorses certain intracameral dynamics for compromise, while the requirement of a thoroughly motivated judgment restrains it. If reasons are viewed as, in key part, a ritual rather than as a real record of the actual ratiocination of the tribunal, the compromise dynamic can operate. But if the reasons requirement is transformed into a ritual, then the control function which operates through the requirement of manifest reasons is lost.

If the AMCO award was a compromise, it would help to explain the award's curious reasoning which was laconic in some parts and opaque and puzzling in others. To cite one dramatic example, the tribunal found that AMCO indeed had not invested the $3 million of foreign currency it had committed itself to bring into the project as part of the terms of the license it had secured. The shortfall, according to the tribunal's calculation, was some 16 percent. Under its own theory, this would have justified the termination. The tribunal summarily concluded that this was not "material," without explaining why or under what legal system materiality was being tested.[75]

If compromise is to work, its crafters must correctly identify and accommodate the essential concerns of each of the parties to it. When more than money is involved, a viable compromise will be more than a matter of numbers. It is precisely in this sense that the AMCO compromise proved problematic. The award was unanimous, was for substantially less than

AMCO had claimed, and might have been viewed from Indonesia's perspective as amounting to less than the general transaction and nuisance cost of continuing the dispute. Indonesia apparently felt that it had to challenge the award, for if a country establishes a program to induce foreign investment and grants licenses on the basis of that program but discrepancies of as much as 16 percent of the foreign commitment to invest are internationally determined to be irrelevant such that the government may not terminate the license, the host country will find itself in the position of being unable to enforce its own law.

On Indonesia's application, the chairman of ICSID's Administrative Council established an ad hoc committee. Its chairman, Professor Seidl-Hohenveldern of Austria, had been a member of the Klöckner ad hoc committee. A prominent Philippine lawyer, now a justice on the Philippine Supreme Court, and an Italian professor were the other members of the committee.[76] In 1986 the committee annulled the original award in part.[77] It found that the shortfall of 16 percent had been understated. Of the $3 million which AMCO had been expected to invest, the committee believed that less than $1 million had actually been invested.[78] But the committee did not nullify the entire award. It confirmed many of the factual and legal holdings of the tribunal.

Constitutive Rulings

The fact that the case immediately after Klöckner was also being challenged was plainly not lost on the AMCO committee. The Klöckner committee had been sensitive to and, indeed, had explicitly addressed the constitutive dimension of its operation. Yet it developed a theory that facilitated challenges to awards, thanks to its constitutive holdings and, in particular, the large number of detailed grounds it made available. Without acknowledging Klöckner's authority or openly entering the lists against it and without enunciating its own explicit constitutive principles, the AMCO committee also addressed the constitutive dimension in its decision, making constitutive rulings, some explicit, some implicit, that revised Klöckner.

By implication, the AMCO committee confirmed the presumption *in favorem validitatis sententiae*. It appears to have ignored the Klöckner committee's expansion of the grounds for nullification and moved quite far from Klöckner's technical and formal approaches. It will be recalled that the Klöckner committee had rejected a prudential competence: after posing the question of whether it could refrain from annulling if it found that the first tribunal's departure was of no consequence, it concluded that the convention gave it no discretion in the matter and established instead a hair trigger.[79] The AMCO ad hoc committee did not accept this theoretical position. In a number of places, as we will see, the AMCO committee found certain things in the award to be technical discrepancies in terms of one of the grounds specified in Article 52 but refused to nullify because it found that the matter was obiter dictum.[80] In other places, the committee noted the existence of a ground of nullity but refused to nullify because the discrepancy was *de minimis*.

Thus the ad hoc committee refused to nullify on the ground that an alleged international principle of due process was violated. The committee found that the tribunal had made the wrong choice of law and had based this part of the award on a norm from the wrong legal system, but the committee found that the *content* of the international principle the tribunal had applied was materially the same as the applicable law, Indonesian law. This time the relevance of the tribunal's holding was not minimized by calling it obiter dictum. The tribunal's failure to apply the law prescribed by the ICSID Convention was confirmed. It was technically a violation of Article 52. But since the committee concluded, from the testimony of the parties, that the proper law, had it been applied, would have yielded exactly the same result, it refrained from nullifying on that ground.[81]

In a sense, Klöckner and AMCO join issues here, presenting, *grosso modo*, two different interpretations of the competence and functions of an ICSID ad hoc committee. One approach may be referred to as the "technical discrepancy" approach. It is highly technical and rests on the conviction that a committee must declare nullification if it finds a technical discrepancy from the convention without regard to whether the technical discrepancy caused injury to the party alleging it or distorted the award. The other approach may be referred to as the "material violation" approach. It would ignore a technical discrepancy if, in the context of the case, it did not constitute a material violation of the standards of the convention. This approach, akin to the American appellate practice of harmless error, is consequentialist and consistent with the doctrine *de minimis non curat praetor*.

Each of these approaches has a different modus operandi. In the technical discrepancy approach, the committee does no more than determine if something done by the tribunal that rendered the award sounds in one of the grounds itemized in Article 52(1). Any confirmed technical violations of the convention require nullification per se. There is no need to explore whether the "mistake" causes an injury to the party alleging nullity nor, in such an inquiry, to assess whether the correct discharge of the arbitral function would have yielded the same result. There is also no reason for an ad hoc committee to assess what the correct answer would have been in order to determine whether the violation of Article 52(1) is significant. By definition there can be no violation of the convention that is not significant. Nor is there need or authorization to think in terms of control function.

In terms of the theory of arbitral review, there is something to be said for the technical discrepancy approach. It keeps the review agency from getting too deeply into the merits of the award and exercising (or reexercising) judgments about them. And it restrains the reviewer from making comparative judgments about which parts of a tribunal's statute or of arbitral procedure are more important than others. (Some of these apparent advantages may be illusory, for the use of the *ratio decidendi-obiter dictum* distinction seems to permit a reviewer applying the technical discrepancy approach to ignore some technical discrepancies and to refrain from nullifying because of them.) But appraised in terms of the control function, the technical discrepancy approach may, as we will see, prove deficient.

In contrast, the material violation approach explores what the correct component of the award, in terms of its premises, would have been in order to determine whether or not a ground of nullity of sufficient consequence and injury to the party initiating the review warrants a total or partial nullification of the award or may be ignored. This approach necessitates not merely interpretation of the explicit award, but requires efforts at reconstruction of the ratiocination of the tribunal whose award is under review. While classical arbitral review prohibits examination of the merits of the dispute, the material violation approach does involve an inquiry into the "right" answer. But the examination is purely instrumental and is undertaken only if a preliminary finding of a technical violation has been made. Klöckner, it will be recalled, would nullify at that moment, without regard to whether or not the technical discrepancy led to a material discrepancy. AMCO, in contrast, would examine whether the technical discrepancy constituted a material violation. The purpose of this investigation is not to substitute a committee's view for that of the tribunal. It is only to stop the committee from nullifying an award on technical grounds when the award itself is materially correct. Yet because of the doctrine of res judicata, these instrumental findings may have consequences in possible subsequent phases of the dispute.

The method of inquiry of the material violation approach is marked by both negative and affirmative formulations and perforce statements of correct answers that would be revisory in consequence were the committee endowed with the competence to substitute its view as a new award binding on the parties.

Substantive Holdings

A central part of the dispute was whether Indonesia could lawfully revoke AMCO's license. A core question here was the substantive lawfulness of the revocation. That lawfulness depended, according to the original tribunal and to both of the parties, on compliance by AMCO with its commitments to Indonesia.

The award found compliance; discrepancies between obligations of investment in Indonesia and actual performance were deemed not to be material.[82]

The ad hoc committee nullified this part of the award for failing to apply fundamental provisions of Indonesian law and failing to state reasons.[83] The award had established a number of common points as between the parties:

> [I]f the failure to fulfill their obligations, as alleged by Respondent, could be established, the revocation of the license could be justified.[84] . . . [A] contract can be terminated by one of the parties where the other party does not fulfill its obligations.[85] . . . [T]he revocation of the investment application's approval by the host State can be justified only by *material* failures on the part of the investor. . . . [T]he sub-lease agreements between P.T. AMCO ASIA and P.T. AEROPACIFIC were not, in any event at the date of the revocation, a material failure justifying the same.[86] . . . [T]he applicant undertook to invest the sum of US $3,000,000.[87] . . . [T]he full capital of P.T. AMCO INDONESIA (that is to say the investment to be made) was to be paid within ten years.[88]

The critical question with regard to the lawfulness of Indonesia's revocation was whether these requirements, which both parties accepted, had been complied with.

The parties agreed that there had not been compliance. Issue was joined over the magnitude of the discrepancy between the investment required and the funds actually committed, and this discrepancy's legal significance. Of the two versions presented, the tribunal, it will be recalled, had accepted the smaller shortfall and found that it was legally immaterial.[89] The ad hoc committee nullified this portion of the award:

> [I]t was firmly established, in the view of the ad hoc Committee, firstly that according to relevant provisions of Indonesian law, only investments recognized and definitely registered as such by the competent Indonesian authority (Bank Indonesia) are investments within the meaning of the Foreign Investment Law.[90] . . . It was also clearly established . . . that P.T. Amco failed to obtain definitive registration with Bank Indonesia of all the amounts claimed to have been invested by it in the Hotel project.[91] . . . The evidence before the Tribunal showed that as late as 1977, Amco's investment of foreign capital duly and definitely registered with Bank Indonesia in accordance with the Foreign Investment Law, amounted to only US $983,992. . . . The Tribunal in determining that the investment of Amco had reached the sum of US

> $2,472,490 clearly failed to apply the relevant provisions of Indonesian law. The ad hoc Committee holds that the Tribunal manifestly exceeded its powers in this regard and is compelled to annul this finding.[92] . . . If it be assumed that BKPM's finding that P.T. Amco's share capitalization figure of US $1,399,000 had in fact included US $1,000,000 of loan funds, was correct, then the Tribunal had effectively failed to apply Article 2 of the Foreign Investment Law which limits qualified foreign investment to investment of equity capital. The Tribunal, in any case, failed to state reasons for counting the entire US $1,399,000 as equity capital and not merely US $399,000. . . . If, upon the other hand, it be assumed that the BKPM finding was *not* correct and the entire US $1,399,000 had somehow become "equity capital", then the Tribunal had still failed to apply Article 2 of the Foreign Investment Law and to state reasons.[93] . . . [T]he ad hoc Committee feels obliged to consider that the Tribunal manifestly exceeded its powers in failing to apply fundamental provisions of Indonesian law and failed to state reasons for its calculation of P.T. Amco's investment.[94]

The method used here is a good example of the material violation approach. It necessarily generates affirmative conclusions, for it tests claims of nullity not on the purely technical grounds of Article 52(1) but on grounds of whether the alleged nullification really makes any difference in the context of the case. The nullity of the award is established by reference to the substantively accurate position. Hence the AMCO committee concluded not simply that the award was null on the formal ground of absence of express reasons. Insofar as the committee could have reconstructed the tribunal's ratiocination, it might have found that the tribunal's conclusions had been at least substantively plausible, if not substantively correct. But the ad hoc committee found that the tribunal's ruling was wrong on material grounds, for the investor actually brought an amount far less than required (indeed far less than the award found). Hence the license had been properly revoked.

A number of consequences flowed directly from nullification of this part of the award. The first, obviously, was the nullification by necessary implication of the award's finding of nonmateriality of the discrepancy between AMCO's obligation and AMCO's performance.[95] The tribunal's conclusion that BKPM (the Indonesian financial control agency) was unjustified in revoking AMCO's license also had to be annulled.[96] This, too, was the result of a materiality test. For the ad hoc committee, Indonesia's failure to protect adequately against a taking by unauthorized personnel, though procedurally defective, was substantively justified.

Consider the contrasting consequences of the different methods with regard to the procedural defects in the license termination. If the Klöckner committee's theory had been applied, this probably would have been decided otherwise for, in a technical sense, it was a violation. Under the AMCO committee's theory, though, it was not. The committee also found that a material approach in this part of its inquiry was mandated by Indonesian law: "The fundamental character of Indonesian administrative law seems, to the ad hoc Committee, to be such that a conclusion on the legality of an act of an Indonesian public authority, and on its implications for responsibility for damages, can be reached only after an over-all evaluation of the act, including consideration of its substantive bases."[97] Because the revocation was substantively lawful, the ad hoc committee found that the tribunal's award of compensation for procedural violations also had to be nullified.[98]

The previous nullifications appeared to entail nullifications with regard to the temporal extent of AMCO's claim to manage the hotel.[99] This too nullified a key part of the award and established, by implication, the temporal limits of any subsequent claim.[100]

Indonesia had contended that the award should be nullified because the tribunal should have accepted Indonesia's warnings to AMCO as sufficient within the meaning of Indonesian law. The ad hoc committee rejected this contention.[101] But the "warning" and "hearing" issues were then deprived of legal consequence, for they constituted a technical rather than material violation.[102]

As a consequence of the method the committee developed, part of the AMCO award was nullified.[103] The only issue remaining to be relitigated by a new tribunal, were it established, would have seemed to have been the question of damages (if any) for the nonfeasance from the time of the taking until the time of the justified and lawful revocation of the license. But, as is often the case, things proved to be more complex.

AMCO II

Shortly after the ad hoc committee in AMCO partially annulled the award, AMCO, as it was entitled under the ICSID Convention, applied for a new arbitration. It will be convenient to refer to this new phase of the case as AMCO II. A new tribunal was established, chaired by Professor Rosalyn Higgins of London. One of the first issues the AMCO II tribunal had to deal with was just how much of the dispute before the first tribunal would be heard again. This was a matter of interpreting what issues had been nullified by the ad hoc committee and what issues had not and were hence res judicata and not available for relitigation. The framework within which this interpretation was to take place was the scope to be attributed to the concept of res judicata in international arbitration. The question was, it soon became clear, to be treated in large part as one of policy.[104]

These questions were hardly theoretical or academic. Their resolution would have major impacts on the parties in the case no less than on parties in future arbitrations. How the matter was to be resolved had the potential for shifting the ICSID structure from one of symmetrical party equality in the context of the speed and economy of arbitration to one inclining in favor of successive losers. Though there were a few analogies in older cases, this was, in many ways, a case of first impression.

The first question posed to the second AMCO tribunal was the extent of the res judicata effect to be accorded the premises and reasoning of the ad hoc committee. If the mode of nullification adopted by the AMCO committee were endorsed and effect were given to its explicit as well as implicit confirmations of parts of the original tribunal's award, the scope of the new arbitration would be quite narrow. AMCO would be allowed, in this second phase of the case, to argue for little more than compensation for the period from March 31–April 1 when the unlawful taking occurred, until the time when the license was terminated, some three months later, by the competent Indonesian court. Damages would, accordingly, be quite small. At the same time, Indonesia would be entitled to bring counterclaims for reimbursement of many of the concessions it had made to AMCO under the license, which the first tribunal had concluded AMCO had violated. Indonesia also had substantial tax claims.

Thus, a broad conception of res judicata would limit what the plaintiff could get, but posed so many dangers in the form of counterclaims to the plaintiff that it might have deterred it from reinitiating the arbitration entirely. The broad conception of res judicata would also have had consequences for future cases, for the margin for relitigation in successive tribunals would always be narrower.

If, in contrast, res judicata were to be interpreted narrowly to exclude reasoning and its premises as well as implied confirmations, the margin for relitigation would, in many cases, be much broader. This could provide a greater incentive to the losing party to seek recourse under Article 52. The implications for the ICSID control system are plain.

The AMCO II tribunal grappled with this problem in the first phase of the case.[105] It showed great sensitivity to the issue of the scope of its own future jurisdiction, but appeared to be oblivious to the control dimension of the decision it was making. It adopted a narrow approach to the findings of the ad hoc committee.

> If the present Tribunal were bound by "integral reasoning" of the *ad hoc* Committee, then the present Tribunal would have bestowed upon the *ad hoc* Committee the role of an appeal court. The underlying reasoning of an *ad hoc* Committee could be so extensive that the tasks of a subsequent Tribunal could be rendered mechanical, and not consistent with its authority—as indicated in Article 52(6), which speaks of "the dispute" being submitted to a new Tribunal.[106]

The reasoning in this statement is not without problems. It rests on two grounds to support its conclusion. The first ground concerns a fear of transformation of review into appeal. Arbitral review can slide into an appeal on the merits and, given the structure of international arbitration, this may not be desirable. But is that the issue at stake here? It is not an ad hoc committee's reasoning in support of its conclusions (which is explicitly required by the convention) that transforms a review into an appeal. Nor is there a transformation of review into appeal because effect is given by subsequent tribunals to the integrated reasoning of the ad hoc committee. We encounter an appeal, rather than a review, when an ad hoc committee moves beyond an examination of the probity of procedures to an examination of the "correctness" of legal application and nullifies for that reason, substituting its own view for that of the original tribunal. That may be improper or, at the least, undesirable, but it is not related to the question of giving effect to reasons.

The second reason invoked by the AMCO II tribunal is that assigning res judicata effect to the ad hoc committee's reasoning could drastically reduce the scope of relitigation for a subsequent tribunal. There is a logical pathology here. A consequence of a choice cannot be a reason for a choice until one has established by reference to law or policy that the consequence is a desirable or undesirable legal or policy consequence.

AMCO II does not address the policy issue but reasons that giving effect to the reasoning of the committee by means of a broad conception of res judicata would be inconsistent with the convention which allows either party to resubmit the "dispute." As part (and possibly a large part) of the dispute would not be resubmittable, convention-granted rights, this line of reasoning goes, would be violated.

Consider the difficulties in this line of reasoning. If it is valid, there can be no place for res judicata in the ICSID control scheme, for any res judicata effect, whether broad or narrow, must reduce the arbitrability of what constituted the "dispute," whatever its parameters may have been, in the first phase. But there must be a place here for res judicata by virtue of a committee's convention-granted power to annul only partially. Otherwise, we must ignore the explicit power of a committee to annul only part of an award and conclude that even when a committee annuls partially, a subsequent tribunal must treat it as a total nullification and hear the dispute de novo, lest the convention-granted right to bring the "dispute" to a new tribunal be infringed. AMCO II's reasoning here leads it into a cul-de-sac in which it seriously undermines the convention power of partial nullification.

The reasoning of the AMCO II tribunal is not only defective on its own terms, but also begs the real issue, which is one of policy. AMCO II rejects a broad conception of res judicata including integral reasoning because it fears that this could limit its own jurisdiction and, more generally, the ambit of functioning of subsequent tribunals, impaneled after a nullification. This is, of course, true. The question is whether it is desirable on policy grounds. I submit that it is, for it would focus the control system and prevent its abuse by attenuating, at each successive phase, the matter in dispute, obviating the rehearing of matters that were not defective, not nullified, and hence not entitled to rehearing, thereby limiting the scope of rehearing and reducing the incentive of abusive review. In the absence of such a restrictive approach, each successive tribunal would have to decide *pro hac vice* how much res judicata effect to accord to the previous decision. As litigants will not know in advance, one party will have good reason to try its luck.

Given the fact that ICSID Article 52 procedures are more likely to proliferate, the efficacy of ICSID and its survival as a meaningful dispute-resolving mechanism will depend upon preserving this balance. In my view the balance will be seriously disturbed if an award deemed by an ad hoc committee to be defective in severable part necessarily and automatically entails the nullification of a greater part of the labor of the parties and the first tribunal. The net result will be to require the parties to invest major resources in a relitigation of matters which, in the view of the first tribunal and in the view of an ad hoc committee that scrutinized its work, are untainted, directly or indirectly, by a ground of nullity and hence had been decided within the terms of arbitral jurisdiction.

One must bear in mind that even an institutionalized system of review, if wrongly designed or wrongly interpreted, is susceptible to abuse. The losing party to a second arbitration may request the installation of an ad hoc committee in the hope that even a minor, technical defect will, *pace* the Klöckner committee, entail the nullification of the entire award and provide a potentially infinite series of opportunities to win or, at least, to stave off losing and paying. The utility of the convention's system of partial nullifications and its implied corollary of a broad res judicata is that each subsequent arbitration will be permitted to hear only the annulled portions of the preceding award, thereby reducing, at each successive stage, the incentive and rewards for abuse.

Nor should the financial consequences of mandatory total relitigation be minimized. Arbitral costs may total millions of dollars, sums which developing countries can ill afford. If the prospective costs are so great as to require the country to settle in ways adverse to its rights, then Article 52 becomes a weapon for extortion and undermines ICSID's mission. Investors, as well, may be prejudiced, for heavy litigation costs may make private investors decide that ICSID and, possibly, a particular private investment in a foreign country are no longer attractive.

To contend, as a matter of policy, that the doctrine of res judicata should insulate those matters decided by a first tribunal which were not nullified as well as the broader reasoning of the ad hoc committee addresses, of course, only part of the problem. The question of how a subsequent tribunal discharges its obligations under the convention and under international law and how, in particular, it interprets those parts of the prior award which are deemed to have survived the partial nullification decision of an ad hoc committee no less than how the committee decision itself is to be interpreted is another matter.

Although the merits of these decisions are of far less interest to us in this discussion than are the evolving control dimensions, it may be of interest to note that the tribunal in AMCO II rendered its decision on the merits on May 31, 1990, awarding AMCO $2,567,966.20 plus 6 percent interest.[107] Because AMCO I and the ad hoc committee had confirmed that AMCO had violated the terms of the license and, *pace* AMCO I, such a violation warranted Indonesia's termination of the license, compensation for procedural violations by the Indonesian administration could not sustain an award of $2.5 million. Instead, the tribunal developed a rather innovative theory of the "tainted background," according to which, certain undefined tainting factors in the background (or foreground, as it developed) of the impugned national decision could render it a violation of law, even if it were substantively correct. If a tainting factor were found, full compensation could be ordered as if the substantive claim were well-founded.[108]

The theory apparently dispenses with traditional tests of the required actionability of the alleged taint and thus functions as something of an *ex aequo et bono* formula. With its flexible notion of background, it dispenses with traditional tests of relevance and causality. It could prove to be difficult for defendants to argue against it.

At the time of this writing, both AMCO and the Republic of Indonesia have applied for the annulment of the AMCO II award. An ad hoc committee has been impaneled.

MINE v. Guinea

After the Currie Lecture was delivered and published in the *Duke Law Review*, the ad hoc committee in the MINE case rendered a decision which appears to be the beginning of a process of ICSID institutional self-correction.[109] It is particularly important to the thesis I have developed, for it amounts, in its substance, to a sweeping repudiation of many of the theoretical assumptions of the Klöckner committee.

In 1963 the government of Guinea and the Harvey Aluminum Company established a joint venture called Compagnie des Bauxites de Guinée or CBG. Its purpose was to mine bauxite. Harvey's interest was subsequently transferred to Halco, a company owned by six major aluminum producers who contracted to purchase bauxite from CBG. Article 9 of the Harvey Agreement authorized Guinea to transport up to 50 percent of the exported material, but at rates not exceeding market rates.

On the basis of its Article 9 rights, Guinea contracted, in 1971, with the Maritime International Nominees Establishment or MINE, a Liechtenstein company, to create another joint venture, whose purpose was "l'armement et la gestion de navires au long-cours sous forme d'achat, de location-vente our d'affrétement dans des conditions conformes aux interêts des parties."[110] Governance of the joint venture was by an administrative council of ten members, five appointed by each of the venturers, with the president to be appointed by the Guinean government, the vice president by MINE. The council could be convened by the president and had to be if three members of the council requested it. Article 5 of the joint venture agreement provided that all formal decisions, all policy and implementation decisions, and all administrative decisions having a value of more than one million Guinean francs were to be taken by "double signature" of the president and vice president. Article 12 obliged MINE to make available to the joint venture, at its request, "le personnel technique nécessaire à son bon fonctionnement, personnel ne pouvant être fourni par le GOUVERNEMENT." A joint venture company called SOTRAMAR was formed. Thus MINE undertook to provide the necessary technical personnel and to charter and make available to the joint venture the necessary ships as well as to guarantee them financially. The 1973 agreement contained a dispute resolution clause calling for ICSID arbitration.

By 1973 no charter parties had been concluded and Guinea notified the bauxite takers in CBG that they would have to make their own transport arrangements for that year. There was considerable disagreement between Guinea and MINE as to the responsibility for this state of affairs. MINE asked for a meeting of the administrative council, which the president did not call.

Guinea, for its part and without notifying MINE, concluded that MINE was unwilling to carry out its obligations and, in 1974, contracted with another company, AFROBULK, for the execution of its Article 9 rights for a period of two years and, thereafter, for the creation of a joint venture.

MINE thereupon invoked the arbitration procedure, alleging breach of contract, with two general grievances: first, failure to perform internal obligations, specifically Guinea's alleged failures to take the measures necessary to make SOTRAMAR viable; and, second, external violations, specifically, Guinea's unilateral notification to the bauxite takers that they should make their own arrangements for transportation in 1973 and its unilateral agreement with AFROBULK to execute the Article 9 rights. Guinea defended that it was MINE that had breached the agreement by failing to conclude freight contracts and to charter vessels and that, therefore, the contract with AFROBULK was a lawful measure mitigating damages.

The request for arbitration was submitted on May 7, 1984, but the arbitration tribunal was only constituted in June 1985. Curiously, all of its members were American nationals. The tribunal rejected Guinea's defense that MINE had breached the contract. It found that Guinea's contract with AFROBULK "was contrary to the spirit, and express provisions of the Convention"[111] and that "Guinea's conduct in secretly negotiating the AFROBULK arrangement, and in denying its existence to MINE thereafter, exhibits bad faith on its part, violating the principle of good faith set forth in the French Civil Code."[112] A unanimous award was rendered on January 6, 1988, ordering Guinea to pay MINE $12,249,483, a total that was arrived at after setting off a $210,000 counterclaim that was awarded to Guinea.

On March 28, 1988, within the statutory 120-day period for filing annulment requests, Guinea applied for a partial annulment on the basis of Article 52(1), paragraphs e, b, and d. Specifically, with regard to Article 52(1)(e), Guinea alleged that the tribunal had failed to state any reasons for its decision on damages and that it had failed to address certain allegedly pivotal questions. With regard to Article 52(1)(b), Guinea alleged that the tribunal failed to apply "any law, much less the correct law" as to both liability and damages. With regard to Article 52(1)(d), Guinea alleged that the tribunal had departed from a fundamental rule of procedure by adopting a measure of damages that had not been advanced or discussed by the parties.

On December 14, 1989, an ad hoc committee was formed composed of Judge Keba M'baye of the International Court of Justice, Aron Broches, the former general counsel of the World Bank and the first secretary-general of ICSID, and Professor Sompong Sucharitkul, who served as president.

Constitutive Rulings

The implications for the ICSID system of the lengthening series of nullifications was explicitly put into issue in the proceedings. MINE, as part of its defense and surely with no small measure of self-interest, urged a restrictive approach because "a series of annulments of ICSID awards might impair the effectiveness and integrity of ICSID as an international institution for settlement of disputes."[113] While the committee dismissed, without further explanation, such a "pure statistical approach . . . as a wholly inappropriate measure of ICSID's effectiveness,"[114] the committee's decision shows a deep concern with the role of the annulment procedure within the ICSID system. Almost a fifth of the operative parts of the award represents a considered examination of this issue.

Reduced range of annulments. The emphasis is decidedly on closing the aperture and introducing restrictions. The first restriction has to do with the Klöckner ad hoc committee's conception of the range of grounds for annulment. Thus, in paragraph 4.06, the MINE committee states

> Article 52(1)(b) does not provide a sanction for every excess of its power by a tribunal but requires that the excess be *manifest* which necessarily limits an *ad hoc* Committee's freedom of appreciation as to whether the tribunal has exceeded its powers. Again, the text of Article 52(1)(d) makes clear that not every departure from a rule of procedure justifies annulment; it requires that the departure be a *serious* one and that the rule of procedure be *fundamental* in order to constitute a ground for annulment. (Italics in original)[115]

Rejection of mandatory annulment. The committee also rejected Klöckner's conception of mandatory annulment on the finding of a ground of nullity. Basing itself on textual interpretation, the MINE committee stated that an ad hoc committee is *not* obliged to nullify an award simply because one of the grounds of annulment is established.

> Article 52(3) provides that an *ad hoc* Committee "shall have the authority to annul the award or any part thereof on any of the grounds set forth in paragraph (1)." The Convention does not require automatic exercise of that authority to annul an award whenever a timely application for its annulment has been made and the applicant has established one of the grounds for annulment. Nor does the Committee consider that the language of Article 52(3) implies such automatic exercise.[116]

The choice available to an ad hoc committee, according to the MINE committee, derives from an inherent discretion.

> An *ad hoc* Committee retains a measure of discretion in ruling on applications for annulment. To be sure, its discretion is not unlimited and should not be exercised to the point of defeating the object and purpose of the remedy of annulment. It may, however, refuse to exercise its authority to annul an award where annulment is clearly not required to remedy procedural injustice and annulment would unjustifiably erode the binding force and finality of ICSID awards.[117]

Confirmation of res judicata. The committee was also at pains to emphasize the res judicata effect of any portion of a previous award which was not annulled.[118]

Ex aequo et bono decisions must be manifest. Having assigned itself a discretionary power, the committee's general analysis on particular grounds of nullity, did not (indeed, did not have to) depart markedly from the earlier case law. The committee confirmed that "a tribunal's disregard of the agreed rules of law would constitute a derogation from the terms of reference within which the tribunal has been authorized to function. Examples of such a derogation include the application of rules of law other than the ones agreed by the parties, or a decision not based on any law unless the parties had agreed on a decision *ex aequo et bono*."[119] But, the committee immediately added, the derogation must be "manifest,"[120] an adjective which is puzzling in this context. If the original tribunal goes out of its way to conceal an *ex aequo et bono* decision in what appears to be a legal formula, it will not be manifest. Such concealment is usually the case. One rarely finds in the annals of international arbitration, statements on the order of the New Testament: "this is the law, but *I* say unto you." I would assume that the committee's intention here is that, however concealed the decision *ex aequo et bono* is, when it is exposed in an ad hoc committee procedure, it is its nonlegal quality that must be manifest. Consistent with prior holdings, the committee emphasized that this pathology was to be distinguished from erroneous application of the law[121] in order to prevent ICSID review from becoming a form of appeal.

A higher threshold for procedural pathologies. The committee also tried to restrict the ambit for nullifications for procedural pathologies by postulating that Article 52(1)(d) required "quantitative and qualitative criteria."[122] "The departure must be substantial and be such as to deprive a party of the benefit or protection which the rule was intended to provide." But "even a serious departure from a rule of procedure will not give rise to annulment, unless that rule is 'fundamental'" and, most significantly, "[t]he term 'fundamental rule of procedure' is not to be understood as necessarily including all of the Arbitration Rules adopted by the Centre."[123]

Reduced reasons requirement. The MINE committee also introduced some drastic restrictions on the reasons requirement. It summarily discharged a tribunal from having to produce an award dealing with "every question" submitted to it. Only a failure to state reasons for those grounds on which the award is actually based will, in its view, constitute a ground for annulment.[124] And, as far as the requisite substance of the reasons themselves are concerned, the committee held that

> the requirement that an award has to be motivated implied that it must enable the reader to follow the reasoning of the Tribunal on points of fact and law. It implies that, and only that. The adequacy of the reasoning is not an appropriate standard of review.[125] . . . [T]he requirement to state reasons is satisfied as long as the award enables one to follow how the tribunal proceeded from Point A to Point B and eventually to its conclusion.[126]

On the other hand, "the minimum requirement is in particular not satisfied by either contradictory or frivolous reasons."[127] One would assume that this means that if a tribunal cites, as its reason for a proposition, a case which is plainly not in point, that will not be deemed to meet the reasons test. Any other interpretation would reduce the role of reasons to empty formality and could hardly fulfill the objects and purposes of this requirement of the convention. And while every question need not be answered, "a tribunal's failure to address a question submitted to it may render its award unintelligible and thus subject to annulment for failure to state reasons."[128]

Substantive Holdings

Failure to cite correct law. The constitutive rulings were reflected in the specific treatment of the applicant's claims. Guinea contended that the tribunal "failed to apply any law, let alone the correct law" and that there was an "almost total lack of citation to legal authorities."[129] The committee stated, as its baseline for appraisal, its independent view of the applicable law: "When the Agreement is silent or incomplete, recourse must be had to Guinean law in its entirety, subject to the qualification that the only rules of Guinean law (public or private) that are applicable are those that were in existence at the date of the Agreement."[130] On this basis the committee dismissed the tribunal's error in citing to Article 1134 of the French Civil Code instead of to the identical Article 1134 of the Code Civil de l'Union Francaise. Because the provisions are identical, the discrepancy was technical and there was no material violation. "[T]he Committee does not consider that this error warrants annulment."[131] In fact, the citation density of the

MINE award under review was very low, but the committee appears to have validated the material components of the award by reference to its own view of the proper law.

Failure to state reasons. If one were to take as a normative standard the style of citation in an American student law journal, in which the requirement for footnotes seems to follow the linear inch rather than some notional criterion, the pages of arbitral awards would consist largely of footnotes. In practical application, the MINE committee reduced the requirement to provide reasons for every statement with its own "rule of reason" which was given a number of applications.

Guinea had cited as an example of the tribunal's alleged failure to give reasons its statement that changed commercial circumstances brought about during the 1973 Middle East war did not make it "legally impossible for either side to perform" the agreement."[132] This was, Guinea alleged, unsupported and inconsistent with the tribunal's finding "that neither short-term nor long-term contracts of affreightment were available, through no fault of the parties."[133]

The statement is quite conclusory and does jump over some necessary reasoning, especially if it is accompanied by a statement that there was a state of commercial impossibility. But the committee rejected Guinea's argument on the factual ground that neither party had argued legal impossibility or implied a legal impediment. This holding is puzzling, for it seems to suggest that when a tribunal adduces its own legal view, which it is entitled to do, rather than adopt a view of one of the parties over which issue has been joined, the reason requirement is either suspended or is lower. In fact, the committee appears to be using its own test of material accuracy and internal relevance, for it says that "there was no necessity for the Tribunal to give reasons for stating an obvious truth from which it drew no conclusions."[134]

Guinea also argued that key arguments it had lodged had not been addressed by the tribunal. The committee contended, rather weakly, that the tribunal had been "aware" of the arguments, but it could only point to those sections of the award in which "Guinea's Assertions" had been recapitulated.[135] But ultimately, the committee acknowledged that "[t]he Tribunal did not explicitly address and decide either of Guinea's arguments."[136] But again the committee avoided a technical discrepancy by applying a material violation approach: "The Tribunal did not have to address these specific conflicting contentions of the parties because it did address and resolved [*sic*] Guinea's principal argument to the effect that after the July 1973 agreement ('arbitration') with the bauxite receivers, MINE, in the Tribunal's paraphrase, 'demonstrated its lack of will and competence to put SOTRAMAR in operation, thereby breaching its obligations under the Convention.'[137] By rejecting

Guinea's factual assertions and stating, albeit rather summarily, that many conditions of the package still had to be negotiated, the committee was able to conclude that "the award," in the words of the committee, "is supported by reasons which can be followed without great difficulty." This conclusion also obviated the need to address other Guinean arguments, for, by the disposition of this issue, they had become "irrelevant."[138] The same analysis discharged the tribunal from any obligation to deal with Guinean arguments about the limits of good faith and rights of mitigation, for it had already decided that MINE had not been in breach.

Damages. The tribunal's statement of law regarding damages was terse and devoid of, in the language of the committee, "statutory or case law references."[139] According to the tribunal: "The Tribunal accepts the general principle that MINE is entitled to be compensated for the profits it would have earned if Guinea had not breached the Convention. The lost profits need not be proven with complete certainty, nor should recovery be denied simply because the amount is difficult to ascertain."[140] In applying this conception, the tribunal rejected summarily, at best, the three alternative theories of damages proferred by MINE. Two of the theories were not deemed "usable."[141] The third was not considered. Instead, the tribunal used the figures in the two-year AFROBULK contract which Guinea received, since it had already determined that this rightly belonged to SOTRAMAR, and extended them over a period of ten years. The reasons for this abbreviated period were explained by the tribunal in the following terms: "While the Convention was to last 30 years, the Bauxite Receivers under the Harvey Agreement were bound to CBG for only 20 years, and 10 years appears to be a reasonable period considering that the Convention contained provisions for early termination."[142] The tribunal awarded simple interest on each year's estimated lost profits at the average U.S. prime rate.

The committee annulled the portions of the award relating to damages for failure to state the reasons on which they were based and the failure to address issues. Article 16 of the agreement between Guinea and MINE had limited damages in case of breach to one year. The tribunal either failed to consider this argument or considered it but thought it should be rejected. But "[t]hat did not free the Tribunal from its duty to give reasons for its ejection as an indispensable component of the statement of reasons on which its conclusion was based."[143] The committee also found that to the extent that the tribunal did purport to state reasons, they were inconsistent and in contradiction with its own analyses of the adduced alternative damage theories.

Costs. The tribunal had awarded $275,000 to MINE as costs, but without reasons, for which Guinea challenged it. The committee held that the awarding of costs is discretionary and is subject to no obligation to state reasons. Since Guinea did not allege abuse of discretion, that challenge failed. But because the basis for costs, that Guinea was the losing party, no longer remained, a domino-effect required that part of the award as well be nullified.

ICSID Control Out of Control: Some Recommendations

Since Klöckner, a significant number of ICSID awards have not been accepted as final. AMCO, as we have seen, reinstituted its claim. With the preliminary question of how much of the original award remains res judicata and how much must be decided anew resolved, the second phase was recently decided, only to stimulate an additional action, by each party, under Article 52. In the meanwhile, the *second* award in Klöckner v. Cameroon has been rendered, and the loser and the winner have asked for its review under Article 52. Another ad hoc committee was impaneled. None of these decisions has been published as of the completion of this study.

In a superficial sense, one may say that the ICSID control system is "working." In fact, it is not, for the function of a control system is not to undermine the operation of the dispute mechanism by extending disputes ad infinitum nor to deter potential litigants from incorporating this mode of dispute resolution in their agreements.

The international arbitration bar has digested the extraordinary opportunities presented by Article 52 procedures as construed by Klöckner and has transformed ICSID arbitration into a sequence of two-phased proceedings. The first phase of the first sequence is classically arbitral. Each party may select an arbitrator and participate in the selection of the chairman of the tribunal. In the second phase, the results of the first phase may be challenged before another tribunal. It uses ICSID procedures, but is called a committee. In this phase the secretary-general selects *all* the decision-makers. Only if the committee upholds the award in its entirety does the arbitration end. If there is a rearbitration, more, rather than less, is still in dispute.

If this becomes a routine feature of ICSID arbitration, it will signal a far-reaching qualitative change in ICSID procedure.

Henceforth, the first tribunal will, in effect, become something of a trial court of first instance, while the second tribunal, the ad hoc committee, will evolve into an androgynous creature, something between a court of cassation and a court of appeals. Which of these two characteristics will be dominant is as yet unclear. The parties will play an explicit role in the composition of the first and less important phase. The critical parts of a dispute will now be decided by three neutral arbitrators, none of whom has been appointed by either party. Precisely because the institution of the party-appointed arbitrator tends to reassure states and corporations nervously contemplating the downsides of big-ticket arbitrations, ICSID arbitration may come to look less attractive than other options.

The emerging jurisprudence encourages some of these developments. If the technical discrepancy approach of the first Klöckner committee is widely used, there will always be a better than even chance that at least part of the award will be nullified. If there is a partial nullification and the successive tribunal adopts the approach of AMCO II, the res judicata effect of the unnullified parts of the previous decision will be construed narrowly, to the advantage of the party attacking the award.

In light of these developments in the control systems of Article 52, the future of arbitration at the World Bank seems uncertain. Until now, ICSID has enjoyed a rather rapid, wide subscription, but it is doubtful if prudent counsel will continue to recommend to their clients a system of dispute resolution that no longer economically resolves disputes. There is little reason to believe that future losers in ICSID arbitrations will not exercise their option under Article 52. The very availability of the procedure, as it has developed, virtually requires the professionally ethical counsel to recommend its vigorous exploitation.

Repairing the Breach in the ICSID Control System

A viable and useful dispute resolving instrument is now in peril because its control system has spun out of control. Several types of remedies are available. Adjustments by arbitrators and ad hoc committee members could repair the problem most economically, insofar as they can be accomplished in ways that do not themselves violate the convention. In addition, a variety of institutional changes, some more costly in terms of time and political capital, may be undertaken.

The ICSID Convention is a constitution and, as such, it could do little more than establish institutions that could elaborate the scheme through time. The designers of the system could not think through all of the implications and ramifications of the control system and provide, whether in the convention or in its legislative history, detailed instructions about the mission assigned to the committees. Whatever the mode of repair, a thorough reconsideration of the basic policies of the ICSID control system is most urgent. The core purpose of control in international arbitration is functional and not textual. It is to ensure that arbitral awards and the processes that precede them are fair and consistent with the expectations of the parties and the pertinent prescriptions of the community, such that confidence in arbitration as a method of dispute resolution is sustained. Without that expectation, the flow of private funds to developing countries is likely to be restrained. It serves well to remember that this was the intended contribution of ICSID arbitration to the larger mission of the World Bank.

In this context, control is not a question of protecting the "purity" of a convention, in the sense in which the Klöckner committee conceived its mission. It is rather a question of maintaining the vitality and integrity of a process of dispute resolution by providing a degree of supervision sufficient to correct violations of parties' expectations in a way that sustains confidence in the efficiency and fairness of ICSID arbitration. A control system which tests an award against every jot and tittle of the convention and creates a series of arbitrations, nullifications, and yet more arbitrations that extend ad infinitum is an absurdity because it undoes the very raison d'être of international arbitration—rapid, economical, and fair dispute resolution which does justice to the parties and encourages productive economic processes.

With these policies in mind, a number of initiatives may be taken by arbitrators, committee members, the ICSID administration, and the states-parties to the convention.

Modifications in Approach by Committee Members

The committees that have precipitated part of the problem are, given the structure of ICSID arbitration, the most appropriate avenues for remedying it. Probably the most urgent matter on the ICSID agenda is for future ad hoc committees to rethink their function and the principles they should apply in ICSID arbitration. The task is not unlike that facing Justice Marshall in Marbury v. Madison.[144] One would imagine that this searching inquiry is already underway. To contribute to it, I would propose a number of changes which future committees might consider undertaking.

Restrict nullification grounds to those explicitly set out in Article 52(1). There are, as we saw, discrepancies between the general procedural instructions in the ICSID Convention (only some of which are mandatory) and the specific grounds for nullification set out in Article 52. One possible interpretative response to this discrepancy is a conclusion of "exclusivity," that is, that the drafters intended Article 52 procedures to be limited to what was stated in Article 52: *expressio unius est exclusio alterius*. Another possible interpretation is "inclusivity," that is, that the drafters intended Article 52 to be read with and to incorporate other pertinent parts of the convention. Both interpretations are plausible. Each would have different consequences for the

ICSID control system. The exclusive interpretation restricts the grounds for nullification; the inclusive interpretation expands them. In cases in which textual construction produces a type of interpretative equipoise between two textually plausible readings, interpreters usually inquire as to the objects and purposes of the legislative exercise.

This is exactly what the Klöckner committee did not do. The Klöckner committee, it will be recalled, opted for the inclusive interpretation, deciding that the grounds of nullification set out in Article 52(1) could be illuminated by reference to coordinate provisions in other parts of the convention.

> Obviously, and in accordance with principles of interpretation that are recognized generally—for example, by Article 31 of the Vienna Convention on the Law of Treaties—Article 52 on the annulment of Awards, must be interpreted in the context of the Convention and in particular of Articles 42 and 48, and vice versa. It is furthermore impossible to imagine that when they drafted Article 52, the Convention's authors would have forgotten the existence of Articles 42 or 48(3); just as it is impossible to assume that the authors of provisions like Articles 42(1) or 48(3) would have neglected to consider the sanction for non-compliance.[145]

As an exercise in textual interpretation, this statement of interpretative method is problematic, for it overlooks the plain meaning of the provision and ignores the possibility (usually presumed, as a matter of minimum courtesy, in deference to the intelligence and purposiveness of the drafter) that the difference in language was intentional and not accidental and/or frivolous.

Even setting aside the possibility that manifest differences in language were intentional, the committee's construction is inconsistent with the convention. According to Article 44 of the convention, only Articles 41 to 47 may not be suspended by agreement of the parties.[146] The other procedural norms are dispositive and may be set aside by the parties. The tribunal seised of the case is the arbiter of its own procedures. With the exception of Articles 41 to 47, there is nothing in the convention to support the proposition that Article 52(1) should be read to incorporate the other parts of the convention. Quite the contrary. Nor is it even certain, under the canons of international interpretation, that Articles 41 to 47 themselves should be read into Article 52(1).

Most disturbing, the Klöckner committee's interpretation did not even consider the objects and purposes of the control system. Article 52(1), like all law, is a human artifact designed to achieve some objective. One would expect, at least, curiosity about the objective and the context in which it is to be achieved.

The Klöckner committee's interpretation invited and entertained claims for nullification of the award that sounded in other parts of the convention. Precedentially, it makes departures from any pertinent part of the convention a potential basis for a ground of nullity. This problem was further aggravated by the technical discrepancy and hair-trigger approach taken in Klöckner, which will be appraised below. I am not persuaded that this interpretation serves the purposes of the ICSID control system and would urge that it be replaced by an exclusive interpretation of Article 52(1).

The implications and consequences of this suggestion may be demonstrated by reference, once again, to the issue of reasons. Consider the linguistic differences between Article 52(1)(e) and Article 48(3).

Article 48 deals with the components of the award. Paragraph 3 of that provision states: "[T]he award shall deal with every question submitted to the Tribunal, and shall state the reasons upon which it is based." Note should be taken of the fact that no consequences follow on departures from Article 48. The nullification provision, Article 52, does not replicate the language of Article 48 but simply says that a party may request annulment inter alia on the ground "that the award has failed to state the reasons on which it is based." The difference between the two provisions is not trivial and the fact that the drafters adopted, within the same instrument, such materially different formulations regarding the requirement for reasons cannot be ignored. It is, of course, Article 52 and not Article 48 that governs in this matter.

The desiderata in the reduction of an award prescribed by Article 48 are considerably reduced in Article 52. That reduction is consistent with scholarly views. Carlston, the major authority in this area, states:

> [A]rbitration is a judicial process. The requirement that a decision be reached by a formally stated process of reasoning would, therefore, seem to be essential. It need not be in meticulous detail; a statement indicating in a general way the legal reasons upon which the award is based will be valid and binding. The circumstance, however, that upon certain aspects of the opinion reasons were lacking cannot reasonably be considered to result in the nullity of the entire decision.[147]

In an earlier study, I wrote: "A detailed justification of every premise, every step in a process of inference, and every subsidiary conclusion, is unfeasible. Excluding *per curiam* decisions, which are a rare international phenomenon, few, if any, international judgments and awards have been 'fully reasoned.' "[148] Jurisprudence, while less explicit, would appear to be consistent with these views. In the Case Concerning the Arbitral Award Made by the King of Spain on 23 December 1906 (Honduras v. Nicaragua),[149] which was decided by the International Court of Justice in 1960, Nicaragua sought to impugn an award rendered by the king of Spain on a number of grounds, including the alleged inadequacy of its reasons.[150] The award was short by current standards, seven and one-half pages long, of which some five pages involved reasoning. The court dealt summarily with the claim: "[A]n examination of the Award shows that it deals in logical order and in some detail with all relevant considerations and that it contains ample reasoning and explanations in support of the conclusions arrived at by the arbitrator. In the opinion of the Court, this ground is without foundation."[151] The court did not require the award to deal with all considerations, but only all "relevant" considerations. Nor did it require that every *question* raised be dealt with in a reasoned fashion but only that "the conclusions arrived at by the arbitrator" be supported by reasons. As for the quantum of reasons, the standard was not full but "ample."

The policy reasons accounting for this requirement in the context of a claim for nullification are hardly recondite. International arbitration perforce takes place in an international and transcultural environment in which, as noted above, lawyers from many different legal systems and cultures interact. Many of these cultures have different conceptions of what constitutes adequate reasoning in general and, in particular, what constitutes appropriate judicial reasoning. These variations in legal culture are multiplied by the extraordinary range of variation in the styles and detail of ratiocination that can be attributed to individual subjective factors. In this varied context, an insistence on a very detailed standard and/or a culturally unique ratiocinative style for the reasoning requirement would open up many awards to challenges to nullification and undermine the entire process of international arbitration. Hence there would appear to be very compelling reasons for the substantially reduced requirement found in international arbitral practice and adopted in the text of Article 52 of the ICSID Convention.

The strict construction of Article 52 which I am proposing is consistent with the canons of treaty interpretation, has authority in past practice, and, most important, would contribute to better performance of the control function within ICSID arbitration.

Use a material violation rather than technical discrepancy approach. Enough has been said to indicate the reasons why a technical discrepancy approach undermines the control function of ICSID and should be replaced by a material violation approach. The late Professor Kenneth Carlston has stated the matter better than anyone: "Not all departures from the terms of the *compromis* will lead to nullity. It is a matter of the substantial character of the departure, the prejudice involved, the importance of the departure from the standpoint of the practice of tribunals, and whether the injured party has by failure to object and subsequent participation in the conduct of the arbitration waived its right to contest validity."[152] The point is apparent in the formulation of the convention. Thus, for example, Article 52(1)(d) which deals with procedural violations, prescribes nullification when "there has been a *serious* departure from a *fundamental* rule of procedure" (my italics). Note that the provision does not say that nullification follows when *any* procedural provision of *the convention* has been violated. The procedural rule violated, whether found in the convention or not, must be fundamental. The mere fact that there has been a violation is not determinative. The violation must be serious.

The recommendation being forwarded here is a complete rejection of this constitutive decision of the Klöckner committee.

A material violation approach also has a substantive dimension, for, when applied in review, it obliges the ad hoc committee to confirm an award if the reasons, no less than the procedure, are wrong but the award is right. Theoretically, this is a radical proposition. In fact, it is practiced explicitly, even in some of the more conservative jurisdictions. Bucher writes, in the Swiss context: "Il n'y a pas lieu d'annuler la sentence lors qu'il est possible de justifier celle-ci sur la base d'une autre motivation que celle des arbitres."[153] Poudret writes that "l'autorité de recours peut toujours substituer ses propres motifs à ceux de la décision attaquée pour justifier celle-ci."[154] Blessing states "the Federal Supreme Court may supplant reasons expressed in the award by others that in its view justify the holding."[155]

Now, it is clear that when a tribunal finds its own reasons for an award after concluding that the reasons of the award under review fail, that it has made its own substantive inquiry. I propose that the same approach be adopted by ICSID ad hoc committees.

Where appropriate, use "confirmatory" formulations. Because an Article-52-type procedure responds to claims of nullity, there is an assumption that the formulations of an ad hoc committee should only be negative in consequence, that is, that a ground of nullification has been found and that all or part of an award must be nullified. As a practical matter, it is almost impossible to escape using what I will call, with apologies for the lack of grace of the term, "confirmative" formulations.

Some affirmative language is sometimes purely a matter of style, verbally affirmative but negative in consequence. In the dynamic context of an annulment process, affirmative language may be used for rhetorical variation. In the context of an inquiry as to whether there is water in a glass, it would be scholastic to search for the intended difference between statements like "The glass is empty" and "The glass has no water in it." Sometimes, diplomatic considerations dictate the mode of formulation. It is to be expected, especially in international arbitration where there is a potential national sensitivity which could complicate procedures, that an ad hoc committee will vary its language and will sometimes say that a claim of nullification has not been sustained by using the language of "confirmation" of the original award.

In a more substantive sense, it is generally impossible to avoid confirmative formulations. A rejection of a particular claim for nullification confirms the validity, if not the correctness, of that part of the challenged award. A nullification by implication may arise in a number of ways. In the Pious Fund case, a tribunal of the Permanent Court of Arbitration noted the interdependence of the reasons and the operative parts of an award.[156] The interrelated character of some awards means that nullification of one part may automatically entail the nullification of other parts. In awards such as these, there can be a type of "domino" effect. Where, for example, parts of an award are related to each other in terms of premise and conclusion and the premise or the procedures by which it was reached is deemed null, the conclusion is nullified by implication. A comparable result may be achieved when part of an award which has been challenged is not considered by the ad hoc committee because it becomes moot, due to the structure of the committee's decision. While this is not a nullification, it is also not a confirmation.

Explicit confirmations speak for themselves. An award or part of an award for which a party seeks annulment may be expressly not annulled. Implied confirmations may be inferred from the context and the reasoning of the ad hoc committee. Where, for example, part of an award is not challenged before the ad hoc committee, is not addressed by the committee, and is not nullified by implication, it may be deemed to have been confirmed by implication.

In some cases, an authority reviewing an arbitral award may not be able to avoid an affirmative finding. Consider the issue of jurisdiction. If a first instance finding of jurisdiction is annulled because it was inadequately motivated or the decision was reached by a procedure which seriously departed from a fundamental standard, the reviewing authority makes no affirmative decision on the issue of jurisdiction in its nullification. Theoretically, either party may reinvoke the jurisdictional clause. But if a losing party claims *simpliciter* that there is no jurisdiction, the response of the reviewing authority is confirmative. If it holds that there is no jurisdiction, the possibility of successive arbitrations based on it ends. Can that inquiry be undertaken without an independent consideration of the merits and a confirmative decision?

There appears to be a general doubt about an ad hoc committee's confirmation authority, which is confused, as we saw in our analysis of the AMCO II award, with the ever-present fear in arbitration that review might be transformed into appeal. The concern is misplaced. The ICSID Convention nowhere requires an ad hoc committee to use only negative formulations. The only instructions as to the modus operandi of the committee are the concluding sentence of Article 52(3) which states, "[t]he Committee shall have the authority to annul the award or any part thereof on any of the grounds set forth in paragraph (1)," and Article 52(4) which states that "the provisions of Articles 41–45, 48, 49, 53 and 54, and of Chapters VI and VII shall apply *mutatis mutandis* to proceedings before the Committee." None of these provisions indicate that negative formulations alone are permitted and that affirmative formulations, confirming parts of the award under review, are prohibited.

It appears that the ICSID drafters did not exclude a confirmatory competence for ad hoc committees. Article VI, Section 13 of the Preliminary Draft of October 15, 1963, said that the procedure contemplated "calls for an affirmative or negative ruling based upon one or the other of the three grounds."[157]

I submit that ad hoc committees may and, where appropriate, should engage in affirmations of parts of a contested award. In a later section, I will suggest, as a corollary to this proposal, that subsequent tribunals, in their determination of the extent of the res judicata effect of the previous award and the ad hoc decision nullifying it, in whole or in part, may give effect to both confirmative and negative formulations. In the control conception of the ICSID Convention, ad hoc committees are part of a process of dispute resolution. They are not discrete from that process, and they are its terminus only if they reject all claims of nullity, thereby confirming the challenged award. In case of partial or total nullification, the ad hoc committee knows that either party may reinstitute the arbitration before a second tribunal.[158] In case of a total nullification, the anticipation of a new phase of arbitration is not a major concern, for the second tribunal must essentially start from scratch. But insofar as the ad hoc committee is only partially nullifying, the committee is cognizant of the fact that one of the parties has the option of resubmitting the surviving parts of the dispute to a new tribunal.

Both the Klöckner and AMCO committees were aware of this dimension of their role. The Klöckner committee, it will be recalled, referred specifically to this possibility and even assigned to itself the performance of certain functions for the potential new tribunal.[159] This was startling, as Klöckner involved a total nullification. A fortiori, an ad hoc committee which issues a partial nullification may believe it is authorized and possibly obliged to clarify which parts of the award survive. Such a method is required if the ad hoc committee is also using the material violation approach. It is difficult to see why this would be inconsistent with the major purposes of Article 52. To insist that ad hoc committees shroud the reasons for their decisions in Delphic obscurity would certainly be absurd and hardly consistent with the obligation to express the reasons on which decisions are based.

This approach will not transform Article 52 procedures into appeals. Recourse under Article 52 becomes an appeal only when a committee confirms that a tribunal stated and intended a certain result, and the procedures used and result reached do not fit any of the specific fact situations in Article 52(1), but the committee disagrees with the tribunal's result and wishes to nullify it for that reason.

Where possible, reconstruct a tribunal's reasoning. Klöckner, as we saw, developed what it called a *praesumptio in favorem validitatis sententiae* under which an award was to prevail if it expressed formal reasons.[160] But the committee in that case did not seek to reconstruct the reasons which may have motivated the tribunal whose award was under review. I would suggest, as a corollary to the material violation approach proposed above, that subsequent ad hoc committees actively seek to get inside the skin of the tribunal whose award is under review and to track its explicit and implicit ratiocination before concluding that its reasoning is insufficient.

When there are indications that the award is a compromise, adopt a flexible approach to the ground of absence of reasons. Under classic arbitration doctrine, a tribunal may not render a decision which departs from the law governing the transactions without an express authorization by the parties to decide *ex aequo et bono*. It is unfair to the parties and dangerous for the future of arbitration if arbitrators can arrogate to themselves a change of the rules once parties have selected a set of them to govern their transactions. For this reason, any decision by a tribunal which purports to decide by equity without authorization from the parties is a classic *excès de pouvoir* and may be nullified.

In practice, however, arbitrations sometimes seek to arrange compromises between the parties. The dynamic of compromise is almost forced upon a chairman of a tribunal when his two colleagues are party-appointed. The party-appointed arbitrator, under several codes of arbitral ethics, may espouse the views of the party appointing him. He may not, however, communicate with that party. Thus, there are circumstances in which compromises may be affected within the tribunal and presented in the form of an award, without any direct communications with the parties. Larger changes in conceptions of the function of dispute resolution in the past decade have, if anything, accelerated this tendency. To an extent, conciliation and compromise have been woven into many of the processes of more explicit decision.

Securing a compromise is necessarily a delicate matter in itself, but it also puts special stress on the formal reasons which are still required to appear in the final award. Framing a compromise decision in terms of law becomes a ritual and art which is significantly different from the usual presentation of reasons as a way of explaining the ratiocinations of a tribunal and providing guidance for future parties who may look to the tribunal as a source of law. A compromise does not present itself explicitly as a compromise. When it is a cameral rather than party product, it must still be decked out in the usual language of the law. As a result, such compromise awards are inevitably not as tightly reasoned, no matter how great the craft skills of the arbitrators drafting the award, as would be one achieved by strict application of the law. If a control system such as that found in ICSID's Article 52 tests what is essentially a compromise award in a strict fashion, there is a high probability that the review committee will demonstrate some inadequacy in the reasoning purporting to sustain the award. Anticipation of this result could chill the operation of the latent compromise function of this mode of arbitration.

I would propose that ad hoc committees acknowledge the latent compromising competence of a tribunal and apply a different standard with regard to adequacy of reasons when there are indications that a compromise has been struck. One of the most dramatic of such indicators is a unanimous award.

The danger of decisions which have been made *ex aequo et bono* but without party authorization is that they are effectively unreviewable. That danger need not arise for latent compromises, if the *content* of the compromise is subjected to an *appropriate* test by the ad hoc committee. The compromise may be tested by reference to the law and policies of the community which govern the transaction. While a unanimous award is often a signal of a compromise, it does not necessarily signal that the compromise struck is one which adequately meets the minimum requirements of both parties. It would appear that in AMCO I, the unanimous tribunal in scaling down the claimant's demand from $12 million plus interest to some $3 million, thought that it was fashioning an adequate compromise. But, as we saw, the longer-term implications of the award would have undermined any competence in Indonesia (and, by analogy, in all other developing countries) to enforce their own law with regard to development projects. That, one may presume, was an intolerable situation for a country which had issued hundreds of such licenses and may have impelled Indonesia to seek nullification.

Ad hoc committees faced with an award that bears all the hallmarks of a compromise should test them in terms of the viability and fairness of the compromise and not in terms of strict textual reasoning. This proposal is, to be sure, quite radical in terms of arbitral theory, though not necessarily in terms of actual practice.

The Role of Arbitrators in Subsequent Tribunals

The reaction of arbitrators in subsequent tribunals to the previous phases of the case is an important link in the ICSID control system. Recommendations about how ad hoc committees should behave with regard to the control problem will have little effect if their decisions are ignored or minimized by subsequent tribunals. The arbitrators in these subsequent tribunals should shape their conduct in ways that take account of control needs.

Theoretically, a second tribunal might deem itself authorized to review, in terms of Article 52(1), the ad hoc committee's procedures and findings and accept only those which, as it were, are not "null." That sort of demarche would be unauthorized. A subsequent tribunal is not empowered, under the ICSID Convention or general international law, to nullify, as it were, findings of the ad hoc committee. To identify particular parts of an ad hoc committee decision as themselves an *excès de pouvoir* because, for example, they used confirmative rather than negative language or because they clarified what was nullified and what was confirmed in the award or because they took the material violation rather than the technical discrepancy approach, would elevate form over substance and, more serious, risk throwing the ICSID control system into even greater turmoil.

In my view the proper role of a second tribunal is to accept the decision of the ad hoc committee as binding and as a valid exercise of the committee's duty to interpret the convention, international law, and the award as it sees fit. The longer-term consequences of the alternative, an arrogated competence by the second tribunal to "review the reviewer," would lead to an infinite regression of nullification action. It would plainly be in violation of the purposes of the convention and frustrate its control function.

This is not to say that a second tribunal is able to avoid or is discharged from interpreting the ad hoc decision. But a sharp line must be maintained between interpretation, and review and nullification. Interpretation of any legal communication is to be performed in good faith in terms of the ordinary meaning of its words and in light of its objects, purposes, and context. A second tribunal should be engaging in interpretation but not second guessing.

What, then, are the hermeneutics which a subsequent tribunal should deploy in cases of partial nullifications? I would suggest a number of interpretative principles:

Use a broad yet supple conception of nullification. A subsequent tribunal, obliged to determine which parts of the first award survived and are hence res judicata and which are not, must necessarily engage in a broader analysis of the ad hoc committee's decision in light of the previous award. In doing this, a committee's use of devices such as the language of explicit confirmation should be viewed as an unequivocal rejection of a claim of nullification and, for purposes of subsequent arbitrations on the same dispute, clear indication that the matter concerned is res judicata between the parties. Ordinary principles of construction and inference should lead a new tribunal to conclude that an ad hoc committee may have confirmed certain points by implication. This particular recommendation will be difficult to apply in cases in which the award under review bears indications of a compromise. As we saw earlier, partial nullification of parts of a compromise may substantially deform subsequent arbitrations. Hence some adjustments may be required.

Use a broad and inclusive concept of res judicata. A qualified nullification of an arbitral award, by definition, only nullifies those parts of it that are tainted, in some way, by the ground of nullity and those parts, if there are such, that depend for their validity on the tainted parts. The point was probably made with greatest clarity and authority by Professor Heinrich Lammasch, the umpire in the review phase of the Orinoco Steamship case.[161] His decision there is considered a locus classicus, both because of the cogency of its reasoning and the fact that Lammasch was one of the great authorities on the nullification of international arbitral awards. He held: "[F]ollowing the principles of equity in accordance with law, when an arbitral award embraces several independent claims, and consequently several decisions, the nullity of one is without influence on any of the others, more especially when, as in the present case, the integrity and the good faith of the arbitrator are not questioned; this being ground for pronouncing separately on each of the points at issue."[162] This view is reinforced by the common interest in minimization of the expenditure of resources in dispute resolution.

Res judicata has been described by the Franco-Venezuelan Mixed Claims Commission in the Compagnie Orinoco Steamship case:

> Every matter and point distinctly in issue in said cause and which was directly passed upon and determined in said decree, and which was its ground and basis, is concluded by said judgment, and the claimants themselves and the claimant government in their behalf are forever estopped from asserting any right or claim based in any part upon any fact actually and directly involved in said decree. . . . The general principle, announced in numerous cases is that a right, question, or fact *distinctly put in issue and directly determined*, by a court of competent jurisdiction as a ground of recovery, can not be disputed.[163]

The application of the principle of res judicata depends upon the identity of (1) the parties, (2) the subject matter of the dispute, and (3) the *causa petendi.*

ICSID Article 52 contemplates this identity with regard to all three components of the dispute, for Article 52(6) allows for the resubmission of the "dispute" to a new tribunal. The word "dispute" in Section 2 of the same chapter of the convention refers to the complex of issues between the parties. Insofar as all or part of the resubmission under Article 52(6) is not a new case, res judicata would appear to apply to the unannulled portions of the first award. But which parts of an international judgment or award are res judicata, and which are not?

Obviously, the "housekeeping" parts of a judgment or award, which are sometimes lengthy in an ad hoc arbitration, are not res judicata. They deal with the infrastructure, as it were, of the tribunal and its process and, in the absence of a violation of some procedural norm which might constitute a ground of nullification, their importance ceases with the rendering of the award. Less obviously, res judicata does not extend to obiter dicta. Even judgment analyses in legal systems that ascribe precedential value to prior holdings ignore those matters which are not part of the *ratio decidendi* but represent digressions by the tribunal. While the theoretical demarcation between *ratio* and *obiter* is clear, specifying what is *ratio* and what is *obiter* in particular cases is often difficult.

Where arbitrators are not obliged or are not permitted to give reasons for their award, it is plain that the *ratio* is only the *dispositif*. Where, however, the constitutive statute of the decision institution *requires* that reasons be supplied, and where the statute authorizes nullification for failure to state reasons, it is plain that the basis of the operative part of the decision, as well as the ratiocination which supports it, are inseparable parts of the decision. It will be recalled that ICSID Article 48(3) requires a statement of the reasons for decisions about every question submitted to the tribunal. This provision applies to the proceedings of tribunals as well as ad hoc committees. According to Article 52(1)(e), the failure of an award to state the reasons on which it is based is a ground for nullification. In institutional arrangements such as these, the reasoning for the operative part of the award is integral and must be considered part of it.

This encompassing conception of res judicata is consistent with a basic trend in international law. In the Pious Fund case, before the Permanent Court of Arbitration, the tribunal said:

> [A]ll the parts of the judgment or the decree concerning the points debated in the litigation enlighten and mutually supplement each other and . . . they all serve to render precise the meaning and the bearing of the *dispositif* and to determine the points upon which there is *res judicata* and which thereafter cannot be put in question. . . . [T]his rule

> applies not only to the judgments of tribunals created by the State, but equally to arbitral sentences rendered within the limits of the jurisdiction fixed by the *compromis*. . . . [T]he same principle should for a still stronger reason be applied to international arbitration.[164]

Judge Anzilotti is frequently cited as contrary authority for his well-known dissenting opinion in Chorzow Factory. In fact, Judge Anzilotti's position was quite indistinguishable from the classic formulation in the Pious Fund. Anzilotti, it will be recalled, wrote: "When I say that only the terms of a judgment are binding, I do not mean that only what is actually written in the operative part constitutes the Court's decision. On the contrary, it is certain that it is almost always necessary to refer to the statement of reasons to understand clearly the operative part and above all to ascertain the *causa petendi*. But, at all events, it is the operative part which contains the Court's binding decisions."[165] If one examines international judicial discussions of the extent of res judicata, one will find that even statements that appear to limit the extent of res judicata usually are responding to some exceptional circumstance in the case at bar. When the Permanent Court said, in Polish Postal Service in Danzig, that "[i]t by no means follows that every reason given in a decision constitutes a decision,"[166] it was not implying that the operative parts of a decision are not res judicata.

The question posed after AMCO is not the general position of international law on the issue or the policy considerations that animate it, but whether the ICSID Convention, in its treatment of partial nullification, intended to depart from the approach taken by international law. The question is not an easy one to answer.

If an ad hoc committee explicitly and without qualification nullifies all of an award ("the award," "la sentence en tout," "anulación total"), as was the case, for example in the decision of the Klöckner committee, theoretically nothing remains and a claimant party can elect to resubmit the entire dispute to another tribunal if it wishes. In fact, unless the award is nullified for complete absence of jurisdiction (in which case, a successive arbitration is unlikely) or the award is nullified for arbitral misconduct, which could taint all parts of the award, there may be much, in terms of facts established and law applied to them, that is untainted in the nullified award. If an ad hoc committee issues a qualified nullification and annuls only part of an award ("any part thereof," "annuler la sentence . . . en partie," "anulación parcial"), it is not clear, on the face of the convention, whether the ad hoc committee's finding that part of an award is null results only in the nullification of the tainted part of the award or must result in the automatic nullification of the entire award. The lack of clarity is aggravated when the committee does not use the convention's language "in part" but instead, as in the case of AMCO, uses the phrase "with qualifications."

The lack of clarity is not dispelled in other paragraphs of Article 52 of the convention. Article 52(1) authorizes either party to request "annulment of the award," but the English, French, and Spanish versions speak only of a total nullification without mention of a partial nullification. It is arguable that the drafters, if they ever thought seriously about this matter, may have assumed that a party could only ask for total nullification, while the ad hoc committee could decide on a partial nullification. If this were the case, one might expect that references to the decisions of the ad hoc committee would have noted the possibilities of total or partial nullification. But Article 52(6) provides: "If the award is annulled, the dispute shall, at the request of either party, be submitted to a new Tribunal constituted in accordance with Section 2 of this Chapter." Paragraph 6 makes no reference to annulment of a part of an award, nor does it suggest that the word "dispute" is to be understood in a partial sense, that is, limited to those elements of the award which were not nullified, rather than in the original, unlimited sense in which it is used in Article 42. Unfortunately, the ICSID Convention does not have a definitions section. "Dispute" is not defined in Section 2 of the ICSID Convention in any of the authentic languages. The French version uses the word "différend." The Spanish version uses the term "differencia." In all three of the authentic languages, "dispute," "différend," and "differencia" are respectively the terms used to refer to the issues to be resolved by the tribunal.

Thus, the core text and context of the convention are not univocal with regard to the question we are addressing. While all three authentic texts, expressly and by implication, contemplate the ad hoc committee nullifying only part of an award, all the texts are unclear as to whether (1) a partial nullification necessarily entails the total demise of the old award and, as a consequence, the relitigation, at the option of the claimant, of all issues or (2) a partial nullification only permits a relitigation of those parts which were nullified.

The ICSID Rules of Procedure lay out the more detailed modes for the implementation of the broad language of the convention. These rules are a particularly important evidentiary source for understanding the convention, for they are not only an authorized and authoritative construction of the convention and part of the "context" within the meaning of Vienna Convention Article 31(2)(a),[167] but in addition they can be viewed, in certain ways, as a continuing elaboration of the text of the convention. As "subsequent" text, the rules acquire a special contingent force in interpretation, for insofar as there is a lack of clarity in the convention and it is dispelled by the rules, it would appear that the principle of *lex posterior* would hold in favor of the later expression of the parties' will.

The reason for this special status is to be found in the fact that the rules are drafted by an Administrative Council which, under Article 4, is composed of one representative of each contracting state. The Administrative Council is empowered, under Article 6, to "adopt the rules of procedure for conciliation and arbitration proceedings." Thus, in discharging this function, the Administrative Council is akin to a continuing conference in which all parties to the convention are fully and equally represented. With one qualification, the parties have accepted beforehand the results of this continuing conference.

Rule 55(3) provides:

> If the original award had only been annulled in part, the new Tribunal shall not reconsider any portion of the award not so annulled. It may, however, in accordance with the procedure set forth in Rule 54 [concerning stay of enforcement of an award] stay or continue to stay the enforcement of the unannulled portion of the award until the date its own award is rendered.[168]

Plainly the Administrative Council reads ICSID Article 52(6) in the light of ICSID Article 52(3) and concludes that a partial nullification precludes the subsequent tribunal from relitigating those parts of the dispute decided by the first tribunal which have not been nullified.

The secretariat, in its explanatory note to Rule 55, reads ICSID Article 52 in exactly the same way as does the council in its rules. Note D explains:

> Paragraph (3) [of Rule 55] provides that if the original award had only been annulled in part, then the new Tribunal shall not reconsider any portion of the award not so annulled. This is in accordance with the first sentence of Article 53(1) of the Convention, which indicates that awards shall not be subject to appeal except as provided in the Convention. If an *ad hoc* Committee empowered to annul all of an award has decided to annul only a part thereof, as it is entitled to do under Article 52(3) of the Convention, then the only possible remedy with respect to the unannulled portion is a request for revision made pursuant to Article 51 of the Convention.[169]

Thus there is ample authority in both international law and in the authoritative documents of ICSID to warrant a broad approach to res judicata. If it were adopted by subsequent ad hoc committees and subsequent second tribunals, it would substantially reduce the ambit of rearbitrations, thereby limiting the incentive to abuse the control procedure.

Institutional Alternatives for Closing the Breach

A number of essentially administrative steps have been taken to try to remedy the control problems created by Klöckner and AMCO. They have met with varying success.

Bond Requirements

After Klöckner, ICSID responded by insisting that the loser who was initiating the recourse post a performance bond for the face of the award. This would have rendered the decision of the ad hoc committee instantly self-executing in cases in which the first award was entirely sustained. The problems we have been considering do not derive from the possibility of a total confirmation of an award. Whatever the merits of this practice, it addresses a different problem and does not repair the control system of ICSID.

"Jawboning"

The secretary-general of ICSID has been trying to use verbal suasion to reduce the problem. At the twenty-second annual meeting of the Administrative Council of ICSID, held in Berlin from September 27 to 29, 1988, Dr. Shihata said:

> It may be expected that use of the annulment procedure would be a rare event because of the seriousness of the shortcomings against which it is meant to be a safeguard. This still seems to be the case, since the annulment procedure has only been invoked in three disputes before the Centre. However, if parties dissatisfied with awards regularly seek annulment such a practice may put in doubt the features which make ICSID arbitration an attractive means of settling investment disputes—namely its speed, comparatively low cost, and its effectiveness. It is also wrong to confuse the annulment proceeding with an appeals process which is not possible in respect of awards issued by ICSID's tribunals.[170]

Such jawboning, an oft-used administrative technique in other contexts, would appear to be very risky in these circumstances. One wonders whether it is wise for the ICSID secretary-general who appoints the members of ad hoc committees to be issuing such statements when three committees are in operation and one is the second successive committee in the Klöckner case.

Consistent Case Law Through Consistent Committees

It would appear that the secretary-general of ICSID has tried to secure more consistency in the decisions of ad hoc committees by creating a type of "super" ad hoc committee, which will be composed, insofar as possible, of the same members of each Article 52 action. This appears to be a sensible move.

Party Stipulation

In the future, parties anxious to avoid the Article 52 gauntlet might try to stipulate in their submission agreement that only fraud or corruption could be raised in an Article 52 proceeding following their arbitration. This would be parallel to certain national developments concerning limiting the review function by national courts of certain types of private international arbitral awards. In some, such as the United Kingdom,[171] a broad waiver for everything but arbitral misconduct is possible in international arbitration. In Switzerland all recourse may be waived for international arbitrations.[172] In Belgium, waiver or not, local courts may not play any postaward role in international arbitral cases whose venue was Belgium.[173]

Arguably, parties would be competent, under the terms of the ICSID Convention, to waive Article 52 procedures. Article 44 of the convention states that "[a]ny arbitration proceeding shall be conducted in accordance with the provisions of this Section and, except as the parties otherwise agree, in accordance with the Arbitration Rules in effect on the date on which the parties consented to arbitration." The section referred to is chapter 4, Section 1, while Article 52 is in Section 5. It is thus arguable that the text of the convention does not prevent the parties from opting out of the procedures of Section 5. But the wisdom of encouraging such waivers is doubtful, for the issue in control is often the aggregate system of arbitration and not simply the convenience of the parties.

Advisory Opinion by the International Court

The World Bank Arbitration Centre itself might seek an advisory opinion from the International Court, as it is entitled to do under the convention, either as to the competence of the parties to create a *lex specialis* by means of a waiver or to receive an authoritative interpretation of Article 52. Given the court's jurisprudence in the award of the King of Spain case,[174] an advisory opinion might well narrow the ambit of ICSID review.

Amendment

A more direct, though not necessarily more economical, method of rectification may be found in amendment. Articles 65 and 66 of the ICSID Convention provide a relatively economical procedure for amendments. Any member state may propose an amendment to the Administrative Council. The proposal must be considered at the next meeting. If a majority of two-thirds of the membership of the council agrees to accept the amendment, it is circulated to the contracting states and comes into effect thirty days after all of the contracting states have ratified their amendment. It would appear that prior to universal acceptance, the amendment would be effective as between contracting states that accepted it, but not as between an accepting state and a state which had not yet accepted it. Pending its universal acceptance, a new state adhering to the convention would have to indicate its acceptance of the amendment, if it too were to be bound.

Reconvening a special international conference to deal with these problems would be cumbersome and expensive. But since the Administrative Council procedure does not require the convening of another conference, a legislative restriction of Article 52 is possible. If it is undertaken, I would propose that Article 52 be amended such that only the five grounds of nullification listed in its first subparagraph would henceforth be actionable. Every other feature of the convention would be excluded. This could be accomplished by inserting the word "only" into Article 52(1). In addition, I would recommend that Article 52(3) be amended to instruct the ad hoc committee to nullify only in case of a material violation and not in case of a technical discrepancy. Although this would require the ad hoc committee to make certain conclusions of its own about the correct legal answer, a function it is likely to be performing in any case by indirection, it would also bar nullifications for purely technical reasons and for differences in ratiocinative and citative style. By requiring a technique of interpretation of awards of ad hoc decisions in terms of both explicit and implied nullification and explicit and implied confirmation, the ambit of review by subsequent ad hoc committees would be narrowed at each stage.

In addition, I would suggest that Article 52 be clarified to instruct subsequent tribunals convened after an ad hoc committee has nullified an award in part not to reconsider any finding of law or fact that, explicitly or implicitly, has not been nullified. With the exception of nullification on grounds of total absence of jurisdiction or because of fraud or corruption of a member of the tribunal, even a total nullification decision is likely to indicate that there are findings of law or fact by the original tribunal which have not been nullified, whether because the moving party did not challenge them, because they did not come within one of the grounds of Article 52, or because the ad hoc committee chose not to nullify. Principles of economy and fairness to the parties would suggest that subsequent tribunals dealing with the same dispute should not reconsider such matters.

Party Consultation

In the shorter term pending structural change, there are likely to be many more Article 52 procedures than were contemplated by the designers of ICSID. For these, the secretary-general might establish an informal procedure of consulting with the parties about the identities of two of the members of the ad hoc committee as well as the acceptability of certain chairmen. While such consultations could not be binding on the secretary-general, they might alleviate some concerns that ICSID had ceased to be a system of party-appointed arbitration.

Conclusion

Our review of the vicissitudes of the ICSID control system might carry the subtitle "Death and Rebirth." The designers of ICSID arbitration created a potentially effective control mechanism. It was seriously damaged by an initial misapplication, which, for all of its technical brilliance, showed no appreciation of the control dimension. For a period it seemed that ICSID's prospects as an important mode of dispute resolution were dim. But a patient and apparently effective process of reconstruction has been underway. Each subsequent ad hoc committee decision has grappled with the control dimension and has helped to recast it in the form in which it had been conceived. The process has not concluded, and a number of other steps might be taken. But the prognosis is good.

4 Non-Institutional International Commercial Arbitration: The Breakdown of the Control System of the New York Convention

The great bulk of international commercial arbitration, thousands of cases each year, is conducted under the auspices of a number of private international organizations. Prominent among them are the International Chamber of Commerce (ICC) in Paris,[1] the American Arbitration Association (AAA) in New York,[2] the London Court of Arbitration (LCA),[3] and the Stockholm Chamber of Commerce (SCC).[4] In addition the United Nations Conference on International Trade Law (UNCITRAL) has prepared a set of rules which are administered by a number of the existing organizations.[5] There is no UNCITRAL organization comparable to the ICC or AAA.

The Public International Infrastructure of Arbitration

Private international commercial arbitration depends, for its effectiveness, on substantial and predictable governmental and intergovernmental support. Plainly, an arbitration clause between businessmen in two separate jurisdictions will be effective only if, should one of the parties ignore the arbitration clause and try to select a convenient or favorable court, the courts in *all* relevant jurisdictions refuse to exercise judicial jurisdiction over the case other, perhaps, than to compel, on request, the reluctant party to go to arbitration. At the other end of the arbitral process, parties are unlikely to invest the time and money necessary to prosecute an arbitration if, upon award, the loser cannot be compelled to honor it. In the course of arbitrations, many types of orders which a tribunal may issue but not be able to implement will require the support of national courts either at the place of arbitration or elsewhere. There are many opportunities to frustrate an arbitration. National courts are the critical defense line against such efforts.

All of the possibilities for defeating arbitration commitments exploit differences in national legal arrangements in the various pertinent jurisdictions.

Dealing effectively with them is a prerequisite to a system of arbitration. But this requires securing uniform arrangements about arbitral commitments in different states.

Routine international commercial arbitrations are made possible by the interaction of two factors: (1) international agreements among all the pertinent jurisdictions to compel arbitrations to which parties have committed themselves in a contract and to enforce awards that ensue and (2) national legislation in the various jurisdictions likely to be concerned with arbitrations which are supportive of the activity.[6] The international agreement network is dominated by a single multilateral convention, but is supplemented in important, and for some cases, decisive ways by bilateral treaties. The national legislative dimension is, of course, shaped by the international agreements, but it, in turn, inevitably shapes and adapts them in each forum to various national values.

Control is as urgent in this form of arbitration as in any other. But the control systems which undergird this mode of nongovernmental dispute resolution are necessarily different from those we have examined. Given the enormous diversity of arbitral tribunals, legal cultures, and litigants, the sorts of implicit control arrangements we considered in the introductory lecture,[7] insofar as they are ever successful in transnational contexts, would plainly promise little success here. Control systems such as those devised by ICSID were animated in large part by a desire to bypass national courts in the postaward enforcement phase of the international awards issued by ICSID tribunals. Hence the creation of an entirely internalized control system within the World Banks arbitration center itself. But the possibilities of establishing an ICSID-style hierarchical form of internalized review in the broad area of international commercial arbitration are limited.[8] None of the world arbitral systems we are considering is embedded in institutions which could perform the function of the secretary-general of ICSID as part of the powerful World Bank. The ICC does have an internal "court," but its functions can hardly be compared to the procedures under Article 52 of the ICSID Convention. Even if an institution purported to review, as the self-styled ICC court does, matters of form, the awards would still require an additional national institution to effect enforcement. Ultimately, the ICC, like all other arbitral systems in this genre, depends perforce on national courts.[9]

Where an effective and distinct institutional framework does not exist and cannot be created, the designers of control systems have little choice but to seek to adapt and channel what is available: national judicial systems. The Convention on the Recognition and Enforcement of Foreign Arbitral Awards, signed in New York in 1958 and frequently referred to as the New

York Convention, is the most comprehensive and, until now, successful effort to do this.[10] It has been adopted by more than seventy-five states.[11] To all intents and purposes, that part of the planet which is actively engaged in international commercial arbitration operates under the convention's regime. Its title states that the convention is concerned with "recognition and enforcement." In fact, it also coordinates a complex coarchical international control system.

As in the other forms of control we have examined, here, too, change is the order of the day. The two key components of the control mechanism of this form of international commercial arbitration are evolving in ways which, in my view, could seriously undermine the effectiveness of this system of arbitration. The very notion of the responsible performance by national courts of important control roles assigned to them under the international agreement central to the entire regime is being challenged.

The Control Scheme of the New York Convention

The New York Convention applies to foreign awards, which include awards rendered abroad as well as awards rendered within the state in which enforcement is sought if the state chooses to characterize them as "non-domestic." Article 1(1) provides: "This Convention shall apply to the recognition and enforcement of arbitral awards made in the territory of a State other than the State where the recognition and enforcement of such awards are sought, and arising out of differences between persons, whether physical or legal. It shall also apply to arbitral awards, not considered as domestic awards in the State where their recognition and enforcement are sought." Article 1(2) extends the reach of the convention to both ad hoc arbitrations as well as awards emanating from "permanent arbitral bodies."

With regard to arbitration agreements meeting the requirements of Article 1, the convention obliges the courts of any contracting state to compel arbitration if a party to a written agreement to arbitrate, which satisfies the personal and material requirements of the convention, seeks instead to initiate court action in its territory and the would-be defendant, the other party to the arbitration agreement, insists upon its right to arbitration. Article 2(3) provides: "The Court of a Contracting State, when seized of an action in a matter in respect of which the parties have made an agreement within the meaning of this article, shall, at the request of one of the parties, refer the parties to arbitration, unless it finds that the said agreement is null and void, inoperative or incapable of being performed." Note that there is no obligation to compel arbitration if the arbitration agreement invoked is null and void, inoperative, or incapable of being performed. The national court which has been petitioned may also refuse recognition and enforcement, even when there is an agreement, if it finds that its own law does not permit arbitration of the subject-matter of the dispute.[12] These exceptions should not be interpreted as weakening the regime. By providing explicit and carefully bounded safety valves for precisely those arbitral matters which national legal systems would find difficult to compel or enforce, they greatly reinforce expectations of enforceability of all the other matters (and they are the vast majority) in this regime.

More important for our subject, the convention provides for the recognition and enforcement of awards that qualify under the convention. Article 3 provides:

> Each Contracting State shall recognize arbitral awards as binding and enforce them in accordance with the rules of procedure of the territory where the award is relied upon, under the conditions laid down in the following articles. There shall not be imposed substantially more onerous conditions or higher fees or charges on the recognition or enforcement of arbitral awards to which this Convention applies than are imposed on the recognition or enforcement of domestic arbitral awards.

The technical requirements referred to in Article 3 are set out in Article 4.[13] The other less technical conditions, which have the potential for intruding the national legal values of the enforcement arena into the decision of the arbitrator, do not exclude the application of national law, but insulate the foreign award from discrimination by requiring that whatever conditions the national court imposes be no more onerous than those set out in the convention.

Those conditions are set out in Article 5. As part of its enforcement system, the convention establishes grounds on which a national court in which recognition or enforcement is sought may deny the request. The grounds of nullity in the New York Convention comprise the traditional bases of arbitral review we have already encountered in the ICSID Convention. The first paragraph of Article 5 provides:

> Recognition and enforcement of the award may be refused, at the request of the party against whom it is invoked, only if that party furnishes to the competent authority where the recognition and enforcement is sought, proof that:
>
> (a) the parties to the agreement referred to in Article II were, under the law applicable to them, under some incapacity, or the said agreement is not valid under the law to which the parties have subjected it or, failing any indication thereon, under the law of the country where the award was made; or

> (b) The party against whom the award is invoked was not given proper notice of the appointment of the arbitrator or of the arbitration proceedings or was otherwise unable to present his case; or
>
> (c) The award deals with a difference not contemplated by or not falling within the terms of the submission to arbitration, or it contains decisions on matters beyond the scope of the submission to arbitration, provided that, if the decisions on matters submitted to arbitration can be separated from those not so submitted, that part of the award which contains decisions on matters submitted to arbitration may be recognized and enforced; or
>
> (d) The composition of the arbitral authority or the arbitral procedure was not in accordance with the agreement of the parties, or, failing such agreement, was not in accordance with the law of the country where the arbitration took place; or
>
> (e) The award has not yet become binding on the parties, or has been set aside or suspended by a competent authority of the country in which, or under the law of which, that award was made.

In addition to these grounds, all of which are consistent with the classical theory of arbitral control, Article 5(2) sets two additional justifications for refusing to enforce:

> Recognition and enforcement of an arbitral award may also be refused if the competent authority in the country where recognition and enforcement is sought finds that:
>
> (a) the subject matter of the difference is not capable of settlement by arbitration under the law of that country; or
>
> (b) the recognition or enforcement of the award would be contrary to the public policy of that country.

The two additional grounds, set out in Article 5(2), are, in effect, safety valves akin to those inserted into Article 2. A national court petitioned to enforce may refuse to do so, not because the award fails to meet some of the international standards of the convention, but because its enforcement would offend the court's fundamental domestic policies. These safety valves, by making explicit what national courts would probably be pressed to do anyway under pressure of endogamous political pressures, have made adherence to the convention easier and actually reinforced expectations of enforceability. They are of less interest to us and, indeed, have proved to be less important in the history of the convention than are the alternative grounds that constitute the international control system.

The regime in Article 5 is a policy statement about arbitral control. Incorporating, as it does, the courts of many different but coarchical national jurisdictions for particular disputes that are expected to involve more than one, it must express as well a so-called private international law system of allocation of competence. This allocative function of international law is necessitated when distinct and separately organized political communities are incorporated into larger interactive processes so that a significant number of persons, things, and events may be subject to simultaneous or sequential regulation by different communities. By allocating among the various states in such a larger process competences to making and applying law for these persons, things, and events, and recognizing and giving effect to the proper application of those competences, private international law stabilizes expectations about them and makes possible productive processes of interaction and exchange between different communities.

Because international arbitration is an event which, by definition, is subject to the simultaneous or sequential competences of two or more states, the careful allocation of those competences, as they relate to the regulation of arbitration, is also required. The convention establishes the conditions under which an arbitral event in one jurisdiction will be given full effect in another jurisdiction. But here, as well as in other areas, control of the system of allocation is important. That is the function of Article 5. Five of the grounds of Article 5, which are to be applied by the national courts of states-parties in reciprocal fashion, constitute the matrix of an international control system.

The first ground of Article 5(1) deals with defects in the arbitral agreement, whether because of the competence of the parties purporting to make the agreement, under whatever system of law is deemed relevant, or because of the invalidity of the agreement under the law governing it or, in the absence of an indication by the parties of that law, under the law of the place of the award. The arbitrators may have rejected a claim based on the standards in Article 5(1)(a), but the losing party may raise it again at the enforcement phase before a national court which may decide it anew. A ruling by the arbitrators rejecting allegations based on these grounds is not dispositive, nor does it function as res judicata for the reviewing court.

The second subparagraph concerns procedures which may have deprived a party of the opportunity to present its case. Notice relates both to constitution of the tribunal and its operation: the appointment of an arbitrator or the initiation of the proceedings. The final clause of this provision makes clear that the international policy is that both parties be given appropriate opportunities to present their cases.

Subparagraph C is an omnibus provision dealing with the general problem of excess of jurisdiction or *excès de pouvoir*. The provision allows the reviewing court to enforce that part of the award which did not exceed jurisdiction.

Subparagraph D is a more elaborate procedural test. Enforcement may be refused if the composition of the tribunal or the process of arbitration was not in accordance with the agreement of the parties or, in the absence of agreement, in accord with the law of the country where the arbitration took place. Note that both of these grounds give priority to the choice of law of the parties. Were the parties to select a set of arbitral rules which was duly followed but which proved to be inconsistent with local law, the latter inconsistency would not provide a ground for refusal to recognize and enforce under Article 5 of the convention. Many national systems require that a departure from the prescribed procedure be "serious." That qualification does not appear in the convention, but has generally been so interpreted by national courts applying it.[14]

How the Control System Works

Now, it is obvious that the intersecting interests in efficiency and minimization of national judicial interference in international arbitrations must strike an exceedingly fine balance between arbitral autonomy and a minimum competence for national judicial review. Too much autonomy for the arbitrators creates a situation of moral hazard. If abuses occur, and the theory of moral hazard holds that they are more likely to in the absence of controls, national courts will become increasingly reluctant to grant what amounts to a preferred, fast-track enforcement of awards. But too much national judicial review will transfer real decision power from the arbitration tribunal, selected by the parties in order to be non-national and neutral, to a national court whose party neutrality may be considerably less. Each of these possible developments would ultimately reduce the attractiveness of arbitration as a private means of dispute resolution.

To prevent such abuses, the convention establishes two tiers of review competence. It makes a sharp distinction between what we may call "primary" or "venue" jurisdictions and "secondary" or "enforcement" jurisdictions. Traditionally, the place of arbitration was called the forum or the *lex loci arbitri*. Since those terms are closely related to other functions performed by this venue, I propose that we use a different, though hardly arcane term to distinguish our specific concern with the operation of the control system. "Primary" jurisdictions will refer to those in which the arbitration was sited and the award was rendered or those whose law governed the award, or in other words the state where the arbitration took place, "the arbitration state," or the state whose law governed the arbitration, the "law state." "Secondary" or "enforcement" jurisdictions will include any other jurisdiction, subject to the convention, in which enforcement is sought.

The carefully prescribed and limited grounds for reviewing an award set out in the convention are the same for primary jurisdictions, which are selected jointly, whether directly or through delegation, by the parties, and for secondary jurisdictions, those jurisdictions which a hypothetical unscrupulous loser of a valid award could search out in an effort to undo the award's intended effect or an unscrupulous winner of a potentially defective award could seek in order to win enforcement. But the convention regime restricts the consequences of such an abuse in a secondary, unilaterally selected forum by varying the consequences of primary and secondary forum action. Indeed, the legal effects which the convention assigns to the national judicial acts of the primary and secondary jurisdictions vary significantly. The secondary jurisdiction may only decide whether or not to enforce the award. The "nullificatory" consequences of decisions in secondary jurisdictions, if they can even be called that, are limited to this question of enforcement and in that forum. But nullificatory consequences of decisions in primary jurisdictions have a universal effect. In terms of the dynamic of the convention, once an award has been set aside in a primary jurisdiction, it is not supposed to be enforceable anywhere else.

Once a venue or a governing law is selected, the convention gives to it a primacy with regard to the validity of an award. If an award is rendered, let us say, in Switzerland and is nullified under Swiss law, nothing should be enforceable in any other jurisdiction. However, if the award is rendered in Switzerland but enforcement is refused in France where the award debtor has property, the French judgment should have no effect outside of France, even if it explicitly bases itself on a ground of nullity which would have nullified the award *erga omnes* had it been rendered in a primary jurisdiction. The award creditor may still seek enforcement simultaneously or sequentially in any other jurisdiction which is party to the convention. The critical difference, then, is radius of effects. As opposed to the nullification of the hypothetical award in Switzerland, a nullification in France has no effect beyond France.

A similar but, in a systemic sense, less cogent primacy is given to the *law* under which the award was made. This means that if the award were rendered in Switzerland but under, let us say, Indian law, a mix of venue and law which is available to the parties, and the award were subsequently nullified by an Indian court, that nullification, like nullification in Switzerland, would terminate the validity of the award in all other jurisdictions. In terms of the logic and dynamics of a control system, the assignment of primacy coordinately to a legal system whose law the parties had chosen but which has no other connection with the arbitration is puzzling. Control under the New York Convention essentially involves policing procedure and not substance. In 1990 a federal district court in the Southern District of New York ruled, in interpreting the New York Convention, that "the competent authority of the country under the law of which, [the] award was made refers exclusively to procedural and not substantive law, and more precisely, to the regimen or scheme or arbitral procedural law under which the arbitration was conducted, and not the substantive law of contract which was applied in the case."[15] The court explained its view, in saying, "Any suggestion that a Court has jurisdiction to set aside a foreign award based upon the use of its domestic, substantive law in the foreign arbitration defies the logic both of the Convention debates and of the final text, and ignores the nature of the international arbitral system."[16] This particular judgment appears to be a clarification, if not a refinement, of the control system. It remains to be seen whether it will be accepted by courts in other jurisdictions.

For a control system like that established in the New York Convention to work, the primary and secondary assignments must be mandatory. Because of the language in the English text of the convention, the control system has appeared to some to be optional rather than imperative: "recognition and enforcement of the award *may* be refused" but may be refused "only" if there is proof of a defect, as detailed by the convention. The French text of the convention, which is equally authentic, suggests that the control system is mandatory.[17] The Spanish text is even more clearly mandatory.[18] This particular textual discrepancy between equally authentic languages is not uncommon in multilingual treaties, for the discretionary power intended and expressed in English by "may" is difficult to convey in French and Spanish, and the combination of "may . . . only," which is, at once, permissive and restrictive, is not easily rendered in many other languages.

The New York Convention is a treaty and as such should be interpreted according to international law, which has now been codified in the Vienna Convention on the Law of Treaties.[19] It provides for interpretation in good faith in accord with the plain meaning of the terms of the instrument, read in context, taking account of the major purposes of the drafters, legislative history, and subsequent practice.[20] While text is important, an interpretation which is only textual is not complete. And, of course, one should seek to accommodate the different but equally authentic language versions in international treaty interpretation.

The English text's allowance of discretion is not an invitation for caprice. Its presence in Article 5 may be plausibly understood as a policy decision by the drafters to adopt a material violation rather than technical discrepancy approach.[21] The national court seised of the case is allowed to reserve for itself some prudential discretion to refuse enforcement when the discrepancy that has been raised against enforcement is technical but the award lacks material defects.

But the allowance to courts of discretion or prudential space with regard to technical, nonmaterial defects is not the same as allowing a national option under which a signatory state may elect to remove local courts from any control role under Article 5. In my view a coherent control theory and a proper interpretation of the texts *require* the jurisdictions implicated in the arbitration to perform, as the case may be, a primary or secondary control function under Article 5. While that obligation is subject to local interpretation and, perforce, some healthy variation, the convention's control system would become meaningless if there were no such core obligation. Assurances of the performance of primary control functions permit responsible agencies in the secondary states to lend state power to the enforcement of actions that are otherwise privately effected and relatively unregulated, indeed substantially unchecked.

A number of scholars have urged an interpretation which makes the obligations imposed on the primary jurisdiction entirely discretionary.[22] Strictly as a textual matter one can make this argument, but international treaty interpretation may not, as I have said, look only to the text. Moreover, if the regime is optional, it is difficult to see why this part of the treaty was drafted. For reasons which I will develop below, I believe that this is a reading which is not supported by the essential control theory which underpins the convention and would lead to an absurd result.

The distinction between primary and secondary jurisdictions is, in my view, central to the control system of the New York Convention and has been an important reason for the attractiveness of the regime to its various consumers. Limiting the effects of decisions in secondary jurisdictions provides an important protection for the winner and vindicates one of the key reasons for going to international arbitration. The parties initially sought the nonnational, if not neutral, jurisdiction for their arbitration in order to avoid the potential bias of a particular national court or courts which might have a predilection for its national or affiliate. But arbitration is not an autonomous system. Because there is no international arbitral sheriff to enforce an award, those same national courts that could be skirted in the earlier phases must now be recruited for enforcement once an award is confirmed. And because the loser's national courts may be called on to enforce if the loser, as is likely, keeps substantial assets there and because one of the parties' common purposes was to stay out of each other's courts insofar as possible, it is necessary to design a system which confines the radial effects of the res judicata of these secondary enforcers to their own fora in order to avoid the possibility of frustrating the entire arbitration. Otherwise, the loser could retreat to its own national courts, try to secure the nullification of the award there and then use that judgment as a defense everywhere else.

Limiting to a maximum of two (and possibly only to one) the jurisdictions which can be primary in a particular case is also critical to the control scheme. Without the primary-secondary jurisdictional distinction, all states-parties to the New York Convention would be jurisdictionally equal. If any of the almost eighty fora of the convention enjoyed the power accorded to primary jurisdictions, the unscrupulous arbitration loser could quickly abandon the neutral forum upon which both parties had agreed and seek a favorably inclined jurisdiction. He could secure a full "nullification" there and then use it as a defense to enforcement in all other fora.

But this control system must also have a primary jurisdiction. If no forum enjoyed the nullificatory power with universal effect accorded to primary jurisdictions under the convention, the winner of a defective award could fail in enforcement in any forum and still continue to go to others in an effort at enforcement, harassing the other party and forcing it either to settle for a nuisance value factored by the number of jurisdictions in which it could be pursued or to expend great amounts of time and effort to block and block again enforcement efforts without ever securing a terminal annulment. Such undesirable effects are limited if only one primary jurisdiction has the capacity to nullify an award *erga omnes*.

There are good reasons to entrust a particular primary jurisdiction with this exclusive power. It has been selected by both of the parties or, in the absence of such a designation, by the arbitrators they appointed, whether directly or indirectly. Presumably neither party, acting rationally in its own interest, is likely to agree to a venue which it feels would discriminate against it in favor of its adversary. As a result, the dynamics of this sort of selection process work to ensure that the primary jurisdiction itself is impartial, in the sense that fewer of its interests are engaged in the case than those of other jurisdictions. On the other hand, the primary jurisdiction is also the beneficiary of the invisible trade benefits of the arbitration and, as such, may reasonably be asked to shoulder the possible costs of supervision. Of course, each primary forum's nationals will have the benefit of a minimum level of judicial supervision when they use other states as the venue for arbitration.

Limiting the supervisory or control function of the secondary jurisdictions in the New York Convention's control system is feasible only if a primary jurisdiction is available to scrutinize the process by which the award is reached so that the award is minimally acceptable. The leading scholar on the New York Convention, Dr. Van den Berg, writes:

> [A]n elimination of the ground for refusal that the award has been set aside in the country of origin would, in my opinion, be undesirable. A losing party must be afforded the right to have the validity of the award finally adjudicated in one jurisdiction. If that were not the case, in the event of a questionable award, a losing party could be pursued by a claimant with enforcement actions from country to country until a court is found, if any, which grants the enforcement. A claimant would obviously refrain from doing this if the award has been set aside in the country of origin and this is a ground for refusal of enforcement in other Contracting States.[23]

If the buck does not stop at the primary jurisdiction, it may not stop anywhere.

The possibility of the scrutiny of the award, in terms of the standards of the primary jurisdiction, whatever they are, is an indispensable part of this control scheme: it is one-half of the quid pro quo that is at the base of the implicit compact between primary and secondary jurisdictions. Without an assurance of the continuing possibility of such scrutiny at the behest of the loser, any secondary jurisdiction will be, quite reasonably, reluctant to buy a "pig in a poke" and to enforce an unsupervised private act (far less supervised than a foreign judgment) whose effectiveness requires the application of its own official power and whose consequence will be the removal abroad of the treasure of someone subject to local jurisdiction.

The relation between the primary and secondary jurisdiction in this regard may be compared to that of the various jurisdictions involved in the enforcement of foreign judgments.[24] The Uniform Foreign Money Judgment Recognition Act[25] provides for local enforcement of foreign money judgments subject to their meeting a limited number of tests set out in Section 4 of the act. The very first ground provides:

> A foreign judgment is not conclusive if
>
> (1) the judgment was rendered under a system which does not provide impartial tribunals or procedures compatible with the requirements of due process of law.

Under the modern theory, the presumption is that a foreign judgment will be enforced and local property will be transferred in accordance with its terms. That presumption operates because it is assumed that the foreign jurisdiction from which the judgment emanated was responsible and that minimum standards of due process were the norm there. When there are indications that that assumption is well-founded, governments, through their courts, are prepared to deploy national power to effect transfers of wealth within their jurisdiction based upon a foreign judgment, whose content is not reexamined locally. That foreign judgment is respected, not because it is assumed that it has been decided in precisely the same way the enforcement forum's court would have decided it, but because the foreign court enjoyed jurisdiction, met minimum international procedural standards, and could be counted upon to apply both fairly.

Suppose, however, that the jurisdiction from which the foreign judgment emanated has created, in the interest of speed and economy, a special regime or a *lex specialis*, according to which judicial processes involving foreigners may dispense with all internal controls that legally apply to "domestic" cases and issue a "special" judgment—an "export model," without the safety features provided by expensive judicial supervision and procedural requirements required for the local market. Would a special judgment of this sort be likely to receive the deference of foreign or secondary jurisdictions, or would it be subjected to a much larger degree of de novo examination?

A foreign arbitral award emanating from a primary jurisdiction is in a similar situation. If that primary jurisdiction decides to suspend, in a discriminatory fashion, the standards which it routinely applies to domestic awards, that is, awards of concern to it, should these "export model" awards be granted the same deference in secondary jurisdictions? Will they be granted such deference?

The scheme of Article 5 of the New York Convention represents a compact between two distinct groups, whose members shift constantly between each other in another sense. Arbitration may be viewed, from the perspective of business entities, as a convenient and comparatively economical method for resolving disputes. But from the perspective of national treasuries and exchequers, foreign arbitration taking place within the jurisdiction is a service and a form of invisible trade which may make a substantial contribution to the trade balance. If all states-parties to the New York Convention apply its control scheme in good faith, none of them enjoys a special benefit. As a result, the only factor that will lead potential litigants to select one or another jurisdiction will be those having to do with comparative advantage in a particular case. But if states-parties evade their obligations under the control system in an effort to make themselves more attractive fora for arbitrations, they deprive the other signatory states, in much the same way that trade-distorting legislation or subsidies in one state are unfair to other states under the rules of a free trade scheme. Evading primary responsibilities in arbitration may, of course, be to the liking of some litigants, just as dumping may be to the liking of some consumers. But that no more justifies evasion than it does dumping.

Unilateral evasions of responsibilities under the control scheme in order to gain advantages over other parties to the convention are akin to what economists call the "free-rider" problem. If other states, viewing themselves as comparatively deprived by the unilateral evasions of their cosignatories, themselves begin to reduce their responsibilities under the convention in corresponding fashion, two interrelated consequences ensue: first, possibilities of control over arbitration are reduced, and, second, there is a danger that the network of relationships which supports international commercial arbitration may begin to disintegrate.

Forms of Breakdown of Control

Obviously, the convention's control system breaks down if the national courts of states-parties do not fulfill their respective primary obligations. That would violate the compact between secondary and primary enforcers and could not but affect to some degree the secondary enforcer's willingness to lend its state power to effectuate an award which may not meet its minimum standards. It is this key strut of the control system of the New York Convention that is now in jeopardy. The danger derives not from national courts as such but from national legislatures. A certain number of instances of inadequate performance by courts in particular cases is inescapable in real life, for no control system can expect perfect effectiveness. It is less threatening precisely because it is episodic. Much more threatening are initiatives that have been taken by a variety of national legislatures, for if they are permitted to stand, their courts will thereafter be virtually hors de combat in all cases in which the New York Convention would have assigned them a primary jurisdictional role.

Episodic Judicial Nonperformance

On a number of occasions, national courts have refused to play by the convention rules. In 1977, for example, the Swiss Federal Tribunal refused to enforce an award which the Atlantic Richfield Company had secured against Libya. Switzerland was the primary jurisdiction, the venue in which the arbitration took place. It appeared that Switzerland was also the site of substantial Libyan assets which might have been withdrawn, as a measure at once protective for Libya and punitive for Switzerland, were it to appear probable that an award might be enforced against Libya. Whatever the reason, the Swiss Federal Tribunal, the highest court in Switzerland, refused to enforce the award, holding that there was an insufficient domestic relationship (*Binnenbeziehung*) between the plaintiff and Switzerland.[26] A parallel case, in a nonarbitral setting, arose in the United States, as a result of the reduction of the immunities available to foreign governments in U.S. courts in commercial actions. The Foreign Sovereign Immunities Act[27] expands the possibilities of suit against foreign governments, but does not, in explicit fashion, prohibit a foreign national from using U.S. courts as a forum of convenience to pursue such actions. In the Verlinden case,[28] a Dutch company sought to sue the Central Bank of Nigeria in New York. The ordinary jurisdictional contacts between the parties, the transaction, and the forum were quite insubstantial.

In cases like these, a national jurisdiction becomes sensitive to the fact that there may be real political costs for the government as a whole in exercising national jurisdiction against a foreign sovereign or its agent or instrumentality without explicit or constructive consent. The New York Convention represents a compact between the parties to it that each will bear those political costs when, in the ordinary course of things, they fall on it, with the corollary expectation that its coparties will also bear that cost in comparable circumstances. But if national jurisdictions refuse selectively to enforce awards which they have obliged themselves to effect under the convention because they decide that their governments might incur certain international political costs, the convention control regime breaks down.

The regime can also break down if secondary jurisdictions were to refuse to accept the universal consequences of a nullification by a primary jurisdiction. When this aspect of the control system operates according to its design, there is automatic deference by the secondary jurisdiction to the primary jurisdiction.

Consider one rather typical case. Contracts between a Dutch company and two French citizens contained an arbitration clause assigning key functions to the Court of First Instance of Paris. After the award was rendered against the company, the French citizens sought leave for enforcement from the Court of First Instance in Paris. Meanwhile, the company, the loser, appealed to the Court of Appeal of Paris against the lower decision. The French citizens sought enforcement of the award before a Dutch court, presumably as a step in securing the assets of the Dutch company. The Dutch court acceded to the request, but insisted that the French give the company security pending the decision of the French Court of Appeal. When the French Court of Appeal rejected the company's appeal, enforcement proceeded in the Netherlands.[29]

It is rather common for an award winner to seek enforcement in some secondary jurisdiction in which award debtor assets are to be found, while the loser challenges the award in the courts of the primary jurisdiction. Even when the court of secondary jurisdiction has ordered enforcement, as it is entitled to do in the absence of a nullification by the primary jurisdiction, the same court should quash its enforcement order if the primary jurisdiction subsequently nullifies the award.

In a very controversial series of decisions, generally known as the Norsolor cases, a nullification by a primary jurisdiction was almost ignored by a secondary jurisdiction which proceeded to order enforcement. The case arose from a contract of agency between a Turkish company, Pabalk Ticaret, and a French company, Norsolor. When difficulties erupted between the parties and the contract was unilaterally terminated, Pabalk initiated arbitration under the Rules of the International Chamber of Commerce. The ICC court fixed Vienna as the venue. Pabalk was partly successful in its claim. The tribunal, in an unusual initiative, rejected ordinary choice of law analysis which would have determined the applicable law as either the law of the place of performance or the proper law. The tribunal considered that: "[I]t was appropriate, given the international nature of the agreement, to leave aside any compelling reference to a specific legislation, be it Turkish or French, and to apply the international *lex mercatoria*."[30] *Lex mercatoria*, according to the tribunal, included the principle of good faith which "required conduct which can be linked to the general principle of responsibility."

Pabalk sought to enforce the award in France, but Norsolor challenged the award in Austria, alleging that the tribunal had effectively decided on the basis of equity rather than law, purporting to use a power which the parties had not assigned it. The French courts suspended the enforcement action, pending a decision by the Austrian courts.[31] The Austrian courts subsequently nullified part of the decision on the ground that the tribunal's inference of good faith from *lex mercatoria* was nothing more than a decision based on equity; the tribunal had purported to exercise a competence which the parties had not assigned to it.[32] Enforcement was still sought in France and appeared to have some possibility of success. The *cour de cassation* encouraged that effort in a decision in 1984.[33] This particular judicial initiative strikes me as inconsistent with the obligations of a secondary jurisdiction.

The allocation of responsibility under the two-tiered scheme of the New York Convention is also disturbed if national courts arrogate too much competence over an arbitration. This particular hazard is exemplified in the United States Supreme Court's decision in Mitsubishi Motors v. Soler.[34] The decision by the Supreme Court, which is considered an important one in international commercial arbitration, compelled an American party to arbitrate a dispute, in accordance with an arbitration clause, for which the venue was Japan. The key issue in the case in U.S. courts was the arbitrability of a claim sounding in antitrust law and not in a contractual matter. The court compelled the arbitration but, in a remarkable dictum, Justice Blackmun wrote: "The national courts of the United States will have the opportunity as the award enforcement state to ensure that the legitimate interest in the enforcement of anti-trust laws has been addressed . . . [and] to ascertain that the [arbitral] tribunal took cognisance of the anti-trust claims and actually decided them."[35]

Professor Park, the leading expert on ICC arbitration in the United States, has characterized this as the "Second Look" doctrine. He sees it as an erosion of an important part of the control system of international arbitration: "The 'Second Look' Doctrine is a problematic safety valve for ensuring that public law issues receive proper consideration. If it calls for review on the merits, it disrupts the arbitral process. But if it calls only for a mechanical examination of the face of the award, it may not provide an effective check on an arbitrator who mentions the Sherman Act before he proceeds to ignore it."[36] Professor Park also raises questions about the compatibility of this doctrine with the obligations under the New York Convention.[37]

Systemic Legislative Nonperformance

Episodic violations of judicial obligations under the New York Convention do not signal its breakdown. No legal system is 100 percent effective. As long as potential consumers of arbitration assume that there is a high probability of the effective operation of the convention, the system will continue to operate. But legislatively mandated changes in the obligations undertaken by parties to the New York Convention pose a much greater threat to its future operation. If states unilaterally begin to radically revise their conceptions and the scope of their responsibilities as primary jurisdictions within the meaning of the convention, the control system could break down. This development is no longer a theoretical possibility. It is a clear and present danger.

Until recently, national statutory regimes implementing the obligations of the convention covered a spectrum from intense and detailed judicial supervision of many phases of the arbitral process, both during the arbitration and after an award had been rendered, on through to selective legislatively directed abstinence by national courts. Though the spectrum seemed wide, there was actually a substantial common ground among the various fora participating in the New York Convention. The last decade has witnessed a variety of national and subnational legislative experiments about the proper role of primary jurisdictions.[38] Some have been animated primarily by a concern for what would be best for international commercial arbitration. Some have been concerned with updating legislation still reflecting obsolete conceptions. Some have been animated primarily by a concern for what would be best for the local bar and the national exchequer.

It is no secret that international commercial arbitration can mean attractive fees for that part of the bar that provides legal services to it and in the aggregate can constitute a significant invisible trade item. Hence, there has been an increasingly sharp competition by and among some jurisdictions to make themselves more attractive venues for international commercial arbitration. In some cases the result has been to reduce, even close to the vanishing point, any application of national standards of postaward control. By drastically limiting the supervisory role of domestic courts over international commercial arbitrations taking place within their jurisdiction, governments also reduce the efficiency, if not the entire operation, of the control scheme of the New York Convention.

The British model. The first major move in this direction was undertaken by the United Kingdom. It was widely acknowledged that arbitration law in the United Kingdom was anachronistically overcontrolled. The statutory regime existing prior to 1979 had incorporated English courts in the arbitration process to the point where little could be done without the approval of a court.[39] The 1979 statute[40] permitted parties drastically to reduce local court participation in their arbitrations by means of a so-called "exclusion agreement." Such an agreement must be in writing and, since 1983, it is a matter of judicial practice that reference to international institutional arbitration rules will be construed as an "exclusion agreement," if the rules in question incorporate waiver of a right of appeal.[41] But the British initiative in 1979 stopped short of a total withdrawal of national supervision by a court of a primary jurisdiction. Even with an exclusion agreement, an English court still has the competence to set aside an award for "misconduct" by the arbitrator. As Professor Park has put it, "English courts will continue to be able to insure the basic integrity of the arbitral process."[42]

States-parties to the New York Convention are certainly entitled to change their national policies about international arbitration. The convention did not impose a legislative freeze on them. Indeed, the extent of national judicial control in the U.K. over international arbitration prior to 1979 was probably too high. Experiments such as the 1979 act which sought to find an appropriate balance within the requirements of the convention's control system were in order. Until the 1980s they largely improved the international control system. Thereafter, national changes began to threaten it.

The French model. France, as well, has undertaken to adjust its domestic law with regard to international commercial arbitration to take account of contemporary realities. Article 1502 of the new Code of Civil Procedure provides

> A decision granting recognition or enforcement to an award is subject to appeal only in the following cases:

(1) If the arbitral tribunal ruled when there was no arbitration agreement or on the basis of an agreement which was null and void or expired;

(2) If the arbitral tribunal was irregularly formed or if the sole arbitrator was irregularly appointed;

(3) If the arbitral tribunal ruled without conforming itself to the terms of reference which was entrusted to it;

(4) When the principle of basic procedural justice has not been observed;

(5) If recognition or enforcement is contrary to French international public policy.[43]

Article 1504 provides

> An arbitral award rendered in France in matters of international arbitration can be challenged by an action to annul the award on the basis of the grounds provided for in Article 1502.
>
> The order granting enforceability to this award is not subject to any means of recourse. However, the action to annul an award entails as a matter of law, within the limit of the court's jurisdiction, recourse against the ruling of the judge for enforcement matters or his jurisdictional divestiture.[44]

The Netherlands has adopted a regime which is comparable to the French model.[45]

The French model represents a legislative instruction to national courts to perform control functions with regard to international commercial arbitration within the meaning of Article 5 of the New York Convention. Though national judicial control is carefully defined, it continues to operate.

The United States model. Section 10 of the Federal Arbitration Act provides

> In either of the following cases the United States court in and for the district wherein the award was made may make an order vacating the award upon the application of any party to the arbitration—
>
> (a) Where the award was procured by corruption, fraud or undue means.
>
> (b) Where there was evident partiality or corruption in the arbitrators, or either of them.
>
> (c) Where the arbitrators were guilty of misconduct in refusing to postpone the hearing, upon sufficient cause shown, or in refusing to hear evidence pertinent and material to the controversy; or of any other misbehavior by which the rights of any party have been prejudiced.

(d) Where the arbitrators exceeded their powers, or so imperfectly executed them that a mutual, final and definite award upon the subject matter submitted was not made.

(e) Where an award is vacated and the time within which the agreement required the award to be made has not expired the court may, in its discretion, direct a rehearing by the arbitrators.

Section 207 of the Federal Arbitration Act authorizes U.S. courts to refuse "confirmation" of an award on the grounds set forth in the New York Convention.

Thus, United States practice, like the British and French models, provides a role for national judicial control of international commercial arbitration whose venue is in the United States, but carefully limits the grounds on which that control is to be exercised in ways consistent with the control conception of the New York Convention.

The UNCITRAL Model Law. The United Nations Conference on Internaional Trade Law, commonly known by its acronym UNCITRAL, produced a set of rules for international commercial arbitration in 1976.[46] After the rules, UNCITRAL turned its attention to standardizing national legislation with regard to international commercial arbitration. The model law which resulted is particularly interesting, in this discussion, for it represents something of an international consensus on the appropriate role for national courts in performing control functions in international commercial arbitration.[47] Article 34(2) of the UNCITRAL Model Law provides

(2) An arbitral award may be set aside by the court specified in Article 6 only if:

(a) the party making the application furnishes proof that:

(i) a party to the arbitration agreement referred to in Article 7 was under some incapacity; or the said agreement is not valid under the law to which the parties have subjected it or, failing any indication thereon, under the law of this State; or

(ii) the party making the application was not given proper notice of the appointment of an arbitrator or of the arbitral proceedings or was otherwise unable to present his case; or

(iii) the award deals with a dispute not contemplated by or not falling within the terms of the submission to arbitration, or contains decisions on matters beyond the scope of the submission to arbitration, provided that, if the decisions on matters submitted to arbitration can be separated from those not so submitted, only that part of the award which contains decisions on matters not submitted to arbitration may be set aside; or

(iv) the composition of the arbitral tribunal or the arbitral procedure was not in accordance with the agreement of the parties, unless such agreement was in conflict with the provision of this Law from which the parties cannot derogate or, failing such agreement, was not in accordance with this Law; or

(b) the Court finds that:

(i) the subject-matter of the dispute is not capable of settlement by arbitration under the law of this State; or

(ii) the award is in conflict with the public policy of this State.

The UNCITRAL Model Law has been widely adopted. It represents a clear commitment to the national judicial role contemplated in the New York Convention.

In the competition for international arbitral business, it has been assumed, quite reasonably, that the lawyers and businessmen who will ultimately select one venue over another will select the venue that promises the most support for the arbitral process and the least judicial interference. Since parties contemplating arbitration appreciate that they require the support of the national courts of the venue for a variety of procedural orders, such as subpoenas, injunctions, and so on, the competition for international arbitral business has focused increasingly on reducing postaward scrutiny. In short, states which wish to become the heavy arbitration venues are competing with each other to reduce their commitments as primary jurisdictions under the control scheme of the New York Convention, while still benefiting from the convention thanks to which awards will continue to be enforceable elsewhere.

The motives of those initiating the changes have been expressed with remarkable frankness. In the debate in Parliament in the United Kingdom preceding the 1979 English Arbitration Act, Lord Cullen of Ashborne said that a new arbitration law might bring £500 million annually of "invisible exports" in the form of fees for arbitrators, lawyers, and expert witnesses.[48] Lord Lloyd of Kilgerran put it even more bluntly: "The main object of this Bill is to attract arbitration to London."[49]

The Belgian model. In 1985, in a much more far-reaching effort, Belgium legislated its courts out of *any* post-award control function for international commercial arbitrations taking place within its jurisdiction. The critical section of the law of March 27, 1985, which adds a new subparagraph to Article 1717 of the Belgian Code,[50] provides:

> The courts of Belgium may be seized of a request for annulment only if at least one of the parties to the dispute decided by the arbitral award is either a physical person having Belgian nationality or residence, or a

legal entity created in Belgium or having a branch or any other establishment in Belgium. Belgian courts cannot perform *any* post-award control function within the scheme of the New York Convention. They may assist the arbitration prior to award, but are paralyzed when the award is rendered, exactly the instant at which the control function under the New York Convention is needed.[51]

The Swiss model. Apparently motivated by similar considerations, the Swiss arbitral bar has lobbied for and succeeded in securing a comparable regime. The international arbitration statute in the new chapter 12 of the Swiss Law on Private International Law[52] is problematic from the standpoint of the control scheme in the New York Convention and, even more disquieting, with regard to basic fairness to the parties. Article 192, according to an unofficial translation, provides:

> 1. If neither party is domiciled, nor has its habitual residence or place of business in Switzerland, the parties may expressly agree in the arbitration agreement or in a subsequent written agreement, to waive their right to challenge an arbitral award before the Swiss courts; they may also waive their right only with respect to one or some of the grounds set forth at article 190(2).
>
> 2. When the parties have waived all recourse against the award and when its enforcement is sought in Switzerland, the New York Convention on the Recognition and Enforcement of Foreign Arbitral Awards of June 10, 1958, shall apply by analogy.[53]

The controls afforded by Article 5 of the New York Convention only operate if enforcement is sought in Switzerland and, then, only "by analogy." One would assume that most international arbitrations taking place in Switzerland will concern foreign assets. But the essential self-interest of the new Swiss regime is highlighted by Article 192(2). If an international award involves assets in Switzerland, the Swiss legislator says that, parties's wishes notwithstanding, Switzerland still merits a control system.

The contrast with the Belgian experiment is striking. Belgium's law is a take-it-or-leave-it offer. If parties choose Belgium as the venue of arbitration, they know that Belgian courts are statutorily excluded from performing the control function of a primary jurisdiction under the New York Convention.

But Switzerland poses an additional hazard. If the parties have agreed in the original arbitration clause to waive the jurisdiction of the Swiss courts, they simply surrender the international control function. But if they have not and one party presses for such a waiver after the dispute has arisen, the party that does not wish to surrender that control reassurance will find itself in an awkward and potentially damaging position. The party pressing for waiver will be implying complete confidence in the arbitrator or arbitrators; the party resisting waiver, however diplomatic it may be, will inevitably appear to be doing the opposite. The party pressing for waiver is also promising to ensure the arbitrator against the embarrassment of being criticized and reversed by a Swiss court. The party resisting waiver is withholding those important professional indulgences.

Lest one think that these are risks that can be avoided by deciding the waiver issue beforehand, bear in mind that even if the parties agree not to waive in the arbitration clause, either party may raise the issue again once the tribunal has been installed. And lest one think that these risks can be avoided by not selecting Switzerland as the venue, it is important to remember that this is not an option for the literally tens of thousands of arbitration clauses in extant commercial contracts which, in reliance on the older Swiss arbitral regime, have already designated Switzerland as the place of arbitration.

Some defenders of the Belgian and Swiss models have argued that, wholly aside from the self-interested motives of the states that initiated them, the laws themselves do no more than provide an option to consumers by offering them a product that each consumer can take or leave at his discretion. This strikes me as ingenuous and is akin, as I said, to arguing that dumpers are only providing an additional option to consumers to take or leave it. Markets, even those committed to maximum freedom, are regulated precisely when the urgent interests of all members of the market system could be undermined by certain types of uncontrolled private behavior. If country X wants to produce an export model automobile without antipollution devices and to sell it quite cheaply, it is not enough to say that as long as X openly states that the price differential is due to the absence of the expensive pollution control device, all X is doing is giving foreign consumers a choice. When X prohibits local sale of its export model, one wonders why it is denying its consumers the option? And if the protection of the environment is a common problem, should X be providing this "option" to foreign consumers? If protection of the environment has become a common international program, is it right for X to initiate this option for foreign consumers, supposedly in the name of freedom of choice?

Control implications. Several scholars have contended that the sort of unsupervised award contemplated by the Belgian law is not enforceable in secondary jurisdictions under the convention.[54] Others have insisted that it is. I would suggest that the question is not one of enforceability by a secondary jurisdiction, as such, but a decline in the degree of operational finality of foreign awards. Assume that an award which is the product of arbitral misconduct is issued by a tribunal sitting in Belgium (or, as the case may be, in Switzerland), and it is brought for enforcement to the United States. As the secondary enforcer under the New York Convention, the American court is still empowered to examine the allegations of the defendant in terms of Article 5 of the convention and to refuse enforcement if it finds that the facts sustain one of them. However, the U.S. judicial action will not constitute a nullification *erga omnes*, as would a comparable action in the primary jurisdiction.

The major difference that derives from the Belgian model is in the attitude of the secondary enforcement jurisdiction. Wholly apart from the New York Convention, which functions as a type of reciprocal judgment enforcement system, the courts of one state are more prone to give effect to the judgments of a sister state if a judicial process has taken place or, at least, was available and reasonably accessible to the parties. Will the same national court be as willing to grant a comparable degree of automatic enforcement to a putative legal act that emanates from a foreign jurisdiction but *could not* be reviewed by courts there? The point of emphasis here is on degree of operational finality of foreign awards. A United States court, in a secondary jurisdictional role, does not have an additional burden because of the statutorily mandated failure of the primary jurisdiction to fulfill its functions under the convention. After all, the defendant might elect not to seek nullification in the primary jurisdiction. Alternatively, the primary jurisdiction might refuse a request for nullification, in which case the award debtor could still raise claims before the secondary jurisdiction. But in the absence of even the possibility of an exercise of a primary jurisdiction, the degree of review in the secondary jurisdiction will probably (and, indeed, should) be greater.

Given the fact that decisions of secondary jurisdictions taken under Article 5 have no effect beyond their boundaries, the reduction in the degree of operational finality of foreign awards will be felt in each successive jurisdiction in which enforcement is sought. Thus, if the problem is not an increase in the burden of a single secondary jurisdiction, it is, in the aggregate, an increase in the burdens of all potential secondary jurisdictions, each of which may now be required to refuse enforcement for a defective award that could and should have been nullified in the primary jurisdiction.

In terms of the costs imposed on the parties, the major increase in burden due to the defection of a primary jurisdiction is imposed on the losing party in the arbitration, which no longer has the chance to stop a defective award once and for all in a single arena. If a United States corporation selects arbitration in Belgium, suffers a major adverse award, but has credible evidence of arbitral misconduct, it will have to defend against the award in any jurisdiction in which it may have assets. Given the geographical range of contemporary multinational activities, there may well be many such jurisdictions.

Remedies for the state which finds its burden under the treaty regime increased may not be readily available. While the failure of a state to fulfill treaty obligations with a resultant injury to a U.S. national would ordinarily permit the United States to espouse that national's injury on the international level against the treaty violator, such a claim might be barred by the fact that the U.S. national voluntarily selected Belgium and, arguably, waived its rights under the convention. But the United States could claim that such a waiver was not effective under the convention or under international public policy and that Belgium was not fulfilling obligations it had undertaken under the convention to the United States. On this basis the United States could insist upon compliance. As a matter of international law, the mere fact that Belgium had acted through its legislation would be no defense.

The burden of courts in secondary jurisdictions will increase due to the extra work required in examining awards emerging from arbitrations in venues that have adopted the Belgian model. The assumption in favor of validity that derives from the fact that nullification options were available in the venue can no longer operate. Hence a higher level of scrutiny, greater litigation costs for the parties, and a greater investment of the judicial resources of the secondary jurisdiction are required.

The "Free-Rider" Problem

As we have seen, the English and French adjustments[55] were well within the range of collaborative control requirements expected of parties to the New York Convention. In my view the Belgian and Swiss legislative experiments are not. As long as a very limited number of states follow the Belgian example, the aggregate consequences for the international arbitration system will be contained. The "Belgians," as it were, will take advantage of the more stringent jurisdictional practices of other jurisdictions to attract a quantity of arbitral business that would otherwise not have selected their venue. They are free riders, in the economic sense, benefiting from a general regime but refusing to pay their dues. They are, in this sense, engaging in an unfair trade practice by exploiting a noneconomic variable in order to make themselves more attractive to a class of potential consumers of services.

The problem will become aggravated if other jurisdictions observe that international commercial arbitral business is being diverted and, as a result, prescribe comparable legislation.[56] Like Belgium and Switzerland, they too will discover that they can reserve an appropriate degree of judicial control over arbitration that is of direct concern to them, while suspending their judicial control obligations with regard to the "export model" awards of foreign consumers. The most dramatic example of this, as we saw, was

Article 192(2) of the new Swiss law, which quickly reimposes a full control scheme if it develops that an "export model" award is going to be used in Switzerland. If more and more states begin to play this game, the net result will be a leveling of the effects they sought in their "free ride" and a disintegration of the 1958 control scheme. What will take its place?

Implications and Alternatives

The abdication of responsibility for providing some system of control over international commercial arbitration occurring within their jurisdiction by a number of major industrial states appears to have resulted from pressure from small segments of the bar anxious to attract more arbitral business. By some mysterious process of juridical transubstantiation, the interests of these small groups have been portrayed as the interests of the polity as a whole. What they are asking is the privilege of resolving disputes without any control over anything that may be done. For these advocates, local law is presented as atavistic and procedural or adjectival, as an anachronistic mortmain. But many of the procedural and substantive norms that have been prescribed in national communities represent fundamental value commitments and distilled organizational experience and should not be disposed of lightly.

The reasons given for the discharge of all control are the supposed danger to international arbitration posed by national courts intervening after an award has been rendered and substituting their views for those of the arbitrators. Too much national control is certainly undesirable. But international commercial arbitration specialists who brandish this threat continue to talk in the language of a half century ago, when the judges of many advanced industrial states were hostile to arbitration. Then there were compelling reasons for reducing national judicial controls over international arbitration. The contemporary judge in advanced industrial countries is familiar with international commercial arbitration, supportive of it, and sober and restrained when it comes to exercising a policing role over it. Moreover, the control system of the New York Convention offers a sound balance between arbitral autonomy and limited control by national institutions. To abolish such systems of control will ultimately harm the individuals who have sought arbitration. As they withdraw from a remarkable dispute resolution mechanism, their responses will hurt international business, the world community, individual nations, and international arbitration.

There are national exceptions: jurisdictions in which the judiciary is corrupt and national judicial control mechanisms are inoperative or ineffective. Some proponents of uncontrolled arbitration in the Belgian or Swiss format contend that in these circumstances, it is better to exclude all judicial tampering with arbitral awards. But this is no argument for the Belgian model. Practitioners are fully aware of the corrupted jurisdictions and have an ample number of jurisdictional alternatives.

Wholly apart from the risks posed to the parties by these legislative developments, the Belgian-Swiss trend poses dangers to the future of international commercial arbitration which are no less serious than those posed by systems of control which shift the critical decision competence in arbitrations to national courts. It is perilous to release all controls over an intensely adversarial process in which the stakes can be extremely large for the profit-maximizing entities and the governments involved. The danger is even greater in transcultural settings in which there are fewer common sets of cultural norms that can act as a standard for behavior and provide some restraint on deviations.

Arbitration awards that should be nullified, because of some serious pathology, will not be vacated if their primary jurisdiction has adopted a "hands-off" policy as a way of attracting arbitral business. If the pathological award is not nullified in the primary jurisdiction, the award creditor may pursue enforcement in any other secondary jurisdiction in which assets for satisfaction are available. Even if some of these jurisdictions refuse to enforce on the grounds available to secondary jurisdictions, the award creditor may still seek enforcement in other jurisdictions. The result will be to increase the nuisance value of a defective award which was not nullified in the primary jurisdiction, to provide the unscrupulous award creditor with multiple opportunities for harassment, and to increase the likelihood that the award debtor will settle, if not be obliged to pay, the face value of the award in some secondary jurisdiction. These "worst-case" possibilities expand when the primary jurisdiction adopts a policy of refusing to perform the functions assigned to it in the New York Convention's scheme.

The dangers presented here are more than particularized instances of injustice to one party in an arbitration. In a larger sense, the adoption by potential primary jurisdictions of "hands-off" policies as a way of attracting arbitral business increases the work load of already overtaxed courts in secondary jurisdictions. The jurisdiction that fails to perform its duty, like all economic externalizers, simply requires someone else to shoulder it. In this it threatens to erode the intricate but fragile network of reciprocation upon which jurisdiction in international law is ultimately based.

The point bears emphasis. One should remember that the allocation of international jurisdiction does not rest on an explicit "full-faith and credit" clause, policed by some international Supreme Court. It rests, instead, on an ongoing reciprocating process in which the responsible decision institutions of one territorial community give effect within their ambit of operation to the acts of decision institutions of other territories on the assumption that they have in fact behaved responsibly in discharging their own functions. As Max Huber long ago observed, the recognition of another's jurisdiction in international law is part of a compact, based on the expectation that that jurisdiction will be exercised in ways that protect the rights of others.[57] The "hands-off" policies of primary jurisdictions in international arbitration violate that compact and undermine the network of reciprocal expectations and trust that is the ultimate basis of international jurisdiction.

An Aggravating Factor: *Lex Mercatoria*

The emergence of a trend in which the judicial control system established by the New York Convention has begun to come apart is aggravated by another development which now intersects and synergizes with it. Parallel to the release from procedural discipline sought in the Belgian-Swiss schemes, a number of scholars and arbitrators have begun to espouse a theory of choice of substantive law discretion which, they have contended, should be viewed as inherent in an arbitration tribunal. Ordinarily, a tribunal would be obliged to apply the law the parties had designated or, in the absence of a party-designated law, to apply that law required by private international law principles. Only when arbitrators have been explicitly authorized by the parties to depart from the proper law and to decide according to their conception of equity, may they do so.

Under the leadership of Professor Berthold Goldman of Paris, a group of scholars and arbitrators have contended that the law which applies *eo ipso* to international commercial arbitrations is a supposed body of international law derived from the commercial usages of international merchants and businessmen and general practitioners of law.[58] It is referred to as *lex mercatoria*. The exact content of this body of prescriptions is not clear. But the need for such a body of prescriptions is. In many cases the national laws that would ordinarily be applied to an international transaction may be inappropriate. In some cases the level of development of the national law is inadequate. It is tempting to propose that just as the international business community has developed its own parallel system of agencies of application through arbitration, that it should also develop a parallel system of legislation, largely to be accomplished by arbitrators themselves and to be referred to as *lex mercatoria*.

Yet this idea encounters more than a few practical problems. The notion that international business is a truly coherent transnational culture and that its practices and usages are the same, whether the parties are from North

Africa, East Asia, or Western Europe, is appealing. But, considering the fact that law gives effect to key cultural values of different civilizations and that there are striking variations in legal arrangements in, let us say, contract law between countries as close as France and Germany or either of those countries and the United States, the proposition that there are specific common norms in international business remains to be established. Systematic comparative inquiry usually establishes remarkable differences between apparently similar legal approaches, even in systems that have common origins.

Proponents of *lex mercatoria* rarely engage in systematic empirical comparisons. Indeed, comments by some proponents lead one to believe that an entirely different function is being performed. Thus, Professor Glossner describes *lex mercatoria* as "the doctrine of generally existing rules accepted by the laws of all civilized nations which . . . seeks equitable solutions for transnational transactions, which otherwise remain insoluble if two or three national laws are applied."[59] The emphasis here appears to be on an equitable solution.

But *lex mercatoria* does not always import equitable decision. Often, some of its proponents seem to be calling for a resurrection of a type of early common law judicial method in which judges were authorized by the king to apply a limited number of general principles to specific cases. On the Continent the medieval revival of Roman law and the intermittent professorial jurisdictions in *Spruchcollegia* also purported to apply general principles from fragments of late Roman law to current disputes that were referred in the so-called *Aktenversendungen*. In terms of legal method, contemporary *lex mercatoria* evokes these old approaches. But there is a serious anachronism here. Modern law is increasingly a complex and nuanced social instrument designed to achieve a wide range of quite detailed social and economic objectives. It is changed frequently, for our period is marked by radical changes in context and goal and equally rapid adjustments in legal instruments. The older legal methods, refurbished as *lex mercatoria*, were cogent in their contexts but are not in this setting. If they are applied in a modern context, their effect will be simply to ignore and exclude prescribed national policies that would otherwise be relevant.

As long as an effective control system operates, unauthorized applications of *lex mercatoria* can be corrected at a later stage, for it is a classic *excès de pouvoir*. Indeed, the mere anticipation of such control would deter arbitrators, enchanted by the idea of forming a new body of law, from trying to do so without the parties' authorization. But the development of *lex mercatoria* coincides with the breakdown of the international control system.

There would be no problem, in terms of the control of arbitration, were parties to specify in their contract that it was to be governed by *lex mer-*

catoria, as determined by arbitrators. But, in the absence of such an instruction, an arbitral imposition of *lex mercatoria*, in place of the law designated by private international law or by the parties, would constitute a violation of their wishes and a usurpation of their power. In consequence, it would be little more than an equitable decision, rendered by a tribunal without authorization from the parties. There are also important national implications.

The notion that parties may select the law they wish to govern their transaction and to make it, by incorporation as it were, a part of their contract requires for its validity a more encompassing system of law which authorizes parties to make such choices. This other system of law, which makes choice of law possible, is generally referred to as the governing law. Governing law may authorize the parties to depart entirely from the precepts of a governing law. On the other hand, governing law may establish certain limitations which must be fulfilled before a purported choice of law is valid. Thus, for example, in a case in which New York law is the governing law and New York law prescribes a minimum of eighteen years of age for people to make certain types of contracts, parties may not choose a law which dispenses with that requirement as a way of evading this particular New York policy. Assuming, however, that both parties meet the eighteen-year requirement, their choice of law may then replace New York law for all other aspects of their contract. Governing law thus authorizes a choice of law and then recedes into the background. But it may reappear, especially if matters of important public policy would be compromised by the norms of a particular choice of law.

The governing law of a transaction is usually determined by principles of private international law. Since the implication of governing law is that the policies of a particular community should control a particular transaction, criteria such as contacts with the transaction, the effects of the transaction, the identity of the parties to the transaction, or the comparative interests of the different communities concerned will come into play in determining what the governing law is. Determinations as to what is the governing law in particular cases may be difficult.

Choice of law, whether in public or private international law, must be understood in the context of public international law. A basic postulate of public international law is that every territorial community may organize itself as a state and, within certain basic limits prescribed by international law, organize its social and economic affairs in ways consistent with its own national values. The Declaration on Principles of International Law Concerning Friendly Relations and Co-operation Among States in Accordance with the Charter of the United Nations[60] provides that "each State has the right freely to choose and develop its political, social, economic and cultural systems." Article 1 of the Charter of Economic Rights and Duties of States[61] provides that "every State has the sovereign and inalienable right to choose its economic system as well as its political, social and cultural systems in accordance with the will of its people, without outside interference, coercion or threat in any form whatsoever."

This public international law principle has a direct relation to private international choice of law. As an expression of and implementation of the basic right expressed in Friendly Relations, the *content* of the various legal codes of each state may be expected to vary, quite legitimately, reflecting the diversity of national political, economic, social, and cultural values which the international system permits and even encourages. As a reflection of those different values and social preferences, the various parts of the law of each community will vary with regard to the distribution of benefits and burdens in economic and social relationships and, in particular, in the allocation of risk. The point of emphasis here is that these variations are *internationally* lawful and are entitled to respect.

In transactions which are, factually, transnational and may be subject simultaneously or sequentially to the law of different states, parties frequently anticipate the dissonance (and economic risks) that may result from the uncertainty as to which law will be applied by explicitly selecting one particular law from the various competitors to govern their contractual relations. That choice by the parties will be honored by international law and most advanced municipal systems as a contractual option. In the Caltex case[62] the sole arbitrator, Professor Dupuy, posed the question of the availability of such choices to parties in international law: "Did the parties have the right to choose the law or system of law which was to govern this contract? . . . The answer to this first question is beyond any doubt: all legal systems, whatever they are, apply the principle of the autonomy of the will of the parties to international contracts."[63]

Where this option of choice of law obtains, it becomes a matter for negotiation between the parties, for it is appreciated that, precisely because legal systems are different, different legal systems are likely to benefit or prejudice one or the other party with regard to particular aspects of the transaction. Hence various concessions and trade-offs may be made in return for one party's acceding to the choice of law preference of the other. All of this is based on the recognition that the social and economic arrangements of that law may discriminate in favor of one party in regard to certain aspects or contingencies of the transaction.

Where such choices of law are made by the parties, third-party decision-makers are obliged, as an international legal matter, to give effect to the decision of the parties as to which set of norms or which legal system is to be incorporated within their contract. Respect for the contractual choice of law is no less mandatory than respect for any other term of the contract.

Lex mercatoria usurps parties' choice of law and the designation by private international law of some national law's system for governing that choice of law. It usurps the governing law and the controls that a particular national community deems necessary for commercial transactions occurring within its space.

Without ever making the issue explicit, *lex mercatoria* is, in effect, saying that such a usurpation is good. It is contending that in international transactions, parties may make their own law, for all purposes.

The proposal that international business should be completely internationalized and severed from any control by national communities is provocative. A detailed treatment of it cannot be addressed in this lecture. It seems to me to be axiomatic that communities may establish jurisdiction over matters of importance to them and prescribe policy for them. That is what a community is. The fact that a particular transaction takes place in more than one jurisdiction does not mean that its consequences may not be extremely significant for one or more of them. To say that because jurisdiction is shared, the private parties to the transaction over which that jurisdiction is shared are liberated from *any* of the restraints of *any* of the communities concerned seems to me to be, on its own terms, a curious notion of "shared jurisdiction" and, in terms of policy, a very questionable proposition. Yet that is what *lex mercatoria* seeks. At the same time, *lex mercatoria* seeks, as it must, to mobilize the enforcement capacities of the same states whose law has been ignored and to do it with less and less judicial control. I question the wisdom of this development as a matter of policy and doubt that its effects would actually help international arbitration.

At the core of the issue of *lex mercatoria* is the concept of jurisdiction. Communities must maintain their vital social and economic processes if they are to survive as communities. The fundamental function of law is to maintain and protect those social and economic processes that constitute the marrow of the community. Jurisdiction is a term to describe the claims that one community makes vis-à-vis other communities for the competence to make and apply law in order to maintain itself. So-called private international law is that part of international law that represents a common effort on the part of states and their institutions specialized to decide about the allocation of competence to make and to apply policy, through law, to people, events, and things that are subject to simultaneous or sequential control by them.

Lex mercatoria is a claim by certain members of the business community and arbitrators to break free of that process and to determine, for themselves and often on a case-by-case and sometimes ex post facto basis, what law and policy they will apply, without regard to the interests of the territorial communities which may thereby be affected. Given the potentially enormous impacts that international transactions may have on national economies, that is a very large claim indeed. Given the simultaneous decline of control systems, its scope could be even greater. Its consequences for democratic political values could be severe.

Conclusion

International commercial arbitration is a form of private international dispute resolution based on a network of public international agreements. It is neither self-sustaining nor autonomous nor is it driven by some sort of inherent logic which can persuade states to support it. Quite the contrary. In the absence of reciprocal commitments and effective controls, there is no reason why a government will allow its public powers to be used to seize the property of one of its nationals and to send it abroad, merely because a private and thoroughly nonofficial actor called an arbitrator has presumed to order it. That so-called arbitrator cannot even promise reciprocity for that state's nationals when they may have property claims against others, for arbitrators have no enforcement powers of their own. Without the assurance of enforcement by a national court in whose territory an award debtor's property is located, international commercial arbitration simply will not work.

International commercial arbitration has been able to operate because a large number of states, including all of the major economic powers, have agreed, as a primary matter, to police in a prescribed and controlled fashion and on a basis of reciprocity, arbitral processes that take place within their jurisdiction and, as a secondary matter, to give effect to the outcomes of such processes in all other jurisdictions. An allocation of competence, confirmed in the 1958 New York Convention but reflecting customary conceptions of arbitration and some of the continuing allocations of competence between states in private international law, has provided the basic structure for a control system for international commercial arbitration. The assurance of the execution of those competences in the appropriate cases by parallel state institutions has functioned as an indispensable control mechanism here, assuring secondary enforcers that an award ordering the transfer of wealth abroad has been appropriately policed in the primary jurisdiction where it was created.

While the implementation of the control role commitments in the New York Convention, like those of any treaty, necessarily allowed for a degree of national variation, recent developments in national practice have stretched that variation to the breaking point. Two states, in an effort to attract more arbitral business, have revised their legislation so that their courts may not or need not, as the case may be, discharge primary control functions prescribed by the convention.

In terms of narrow conceptions of self-interest, this is a clever move. It might bring more invisible trade, and it seems to have no downside costs, for the foreign arbitrations are of no concern to these states and they have been careful to reserve an adequate control system for arbitrations that do have national impacts. But the systemic implications of these changes are grave. If the Belgian and Swiss models prove able to attract more arbitral business, other jurisdictions may be expected to copy and even improve on them. Even if the mimesis is limited to a relatively small number of states, many other states will begin to ask themselves why they should be obliged to undertake the control costs that other states are shirking while those other states retain for themselves the advantages of the 1958 convention and take a larger share of international arbitral business.

If other control devices of international commercial arbitration were operating effectively, they might have been able to compensate for this particular breakdown. Unfortunately, the Belgian and Swiss initiatives coincide with the breakdown of another important control device: respect for and strict application of proper law. This breakdown is largely the result of arbitrator initiatives. While we saw that there are compelling reasons for these initiatives in terms of the progressive development of a contemporary transnational law which can facilitate and govern international transactions, there has been an insensitivity to the control function performed by choice of law. The threatened breakdown of primary jurisdictional control mechanisms means that the deterioration of choice of law discipline itself cannot be repaired by one of the fundamental control devices of the New York Convention.

The Belgian and Swiss initiatives can be reversed in a number of ways. States-parties to the New York Convention should protest to these governments over their policy of defection from obligations they have assumed under the convention. While a "clawback" type of legislative response[64] limiting secondary enforcement of awards to compliance by the primary forum with its obligations under the convention seems extreme, defections from the obligations of the 1958 regime will inevitably push other states-parties in this direction. States with bilateral treaty guarantees for their nationals might observe that the legislation discriminates in the degree of protection it affords nationals and non-nationals from arbitral abuse.

The major losers in this type of confrontation and indeed in any deterioration in the control mechanisms undergirding contemporary international commercial arbitration will be the international business community and the international bar. Until now, they have remained relatively neutral with regard to the Belgian and Swiss experiments, influenced by a residual (and, I believe, no longer justified) suspicion of national courts' relation to and effect on arbitration, curious about the extent to which the new models may help them but largely oblivious to their negative control implications. The international business community and the international market are the market here. If they speak with deeds, by avoiding jurisdictions that are evading their control obligations, they will rapidly change them. The Belgian and Swiss initiatives were not altruistic exercises in which two charitable states undertook, from the highest of disinterested motives and without concern for material gain, to provide international business with a broader range of choices. The Belgian and Swiss models were designed to attract more arbitration business to each of the states and to increase their share of this part of invisible world trade. In a word, they were done for money. If these legislative models have the opposite effect, you may be sure that they will be scrapped.

5 The System and Self: Changing, Repairing, and Reconstructing

Rien n'est possible sans les hommes,
rien n'est durable sans les institutions.
—Jean Monnet

The processes of breakdown of the various control systems which undergird the public and private dispute resolution mechanisms of the international economy are striking both for their variety and the commonality of the key problems. Common, too, is a virtual universal recognition of an increasingly interactive and interdependent world economy and, with that recognition, a sense of the need for reliable methods for resolving the disputes which appear inevitable in relationships that are, by their nature, both competitive and cooperative and whose incidence will increase as a function of economic activity. There is a common feeling that national decision institutions should be limited to a supporting role and that specialized transnational tribunals can make a special contribution. There is also a general perception that these transnational arrangements should be reinforced and extended. But for all this consensus, there has been a failing at the conceptual level with regard to the need and nature of control.

Discussions of control in political and legal arrangements frequently borrow metaphors from engineering, as indeed I did in the introduction to these lectures. Like all metaphors, they can highlight some striking similarities, but they sometimes obscure a major difference between physical and social engineering. Physical controls may be automatic and homeostatic. Legal controls, however they are designed, like all aspects of decision, at every level of social organization, must be effected by individual human beings, the ultimate actors in all social life. However well-designed a control mechanism may be, it is the quality of individual decision-makers' understanding of control functions and the quality of those decision-makers' self-understanding that will determine whether a control system will work as conceived, work better than conceived, for example, by surmounting a challenge that was not and perhaps could not have been anticipated by its designers, or break down.

Zen's insight into the integral relationship between the tool and the hand and the mind that wield it applies here with considerable force. Self-understanding and understanding control functions are intimately linked. Decision is an indispensable and inescapable part of organized community life. All decision involves making choices that influence the lives of others. All such choices are exercises of power. For many, such exercises of power can provide pleasures and gratifications and even ecstacies which run deep into the dynamics of the personality. But legal decision imports the exercise of that potentially pleasurable choice under restraints established by another, whether it be the prince, through his claim of sovereign power, or the democratic community, through the Rule of Law. The sum of those restraints for each job or task may be described as a "role," which is a specification of formal or informal authoritative guides on how a particular function is to be performed.

The person engaging in legal decision in our civilization is assigned and accepts a role, often ceremonializing acceptance by some ritual oath or traditional costume. The legal system as a whole is a series of interlocking roles: men and women participating in prescribing or lawmaking establish policies for various social and economic activities and men and women participating in tribunals make primary applications of those policies in ways they are expected and have committed themselves to do and men and women in implementation agencies then enforce those applications in ways they are expected and have committed themselves to do. The legal system can begin to break down when tribunals do not do what they are supposed to do or when the enforcers, for example, simply ignore the clear purport of the tribunals' decisions.

Fidelity in conforming to these legal role commitments[1] is a key strut of the legal control system in much the way that the fundamental fidelity of an actor to the playwright's conception is the basis of their collaboration. The role of the actor certainly calls and allows for brilliance and creativity in interpretation of the playwright's conception, but if at a certain point the actor ignores the instruction of the playwright and goes off on his own, without acknowledging that he is now writing his own play, the basis of their social collaboration is shattered. If the collaboration in question is between a builder and an architectural engineer, the detritus of their shattered collaboration may come raining down on many other people's heads.

Role fidelity is indispensable in the sorts of complex collaborative social arrangements on which our civilization has been reared, but role fidelity also blocks some of the promised ecstacies of power. A dishonest person knows this well and, commitments to others notwithstanding, gratifies his private wishes, and then simply conceals his defection by deceit: he "cons" us by using "the ubiquitous weapon of dishonesty."[2] Not every defection from a role commitment is necessarily a con job. For people who are not consciously dishonest but choose not to be reflective, it is easy to justify, sometimes at levels of consciousness so deep that one is unaware of them, departures from social and, particularly, legal role expectations. We are not talking about your garden-variety corruption. The payoffs here can be dizzying: deep narcissistic gratifications for the defecting actor or judge or arbitrator who would turn the pages of others into no more than a mirror for the self.

But if control systems ultimately depend on the systemic understanding and disciplined self-restraint of those authorized to decide, it is also clear that a simple ethic of following orders—"doing what you are told"—is also insufficient beyond the simplest discharge of basic clerical functions. Earlier, I referred to a builder ignoring the plans of his architectural engineer and, oblivious to the controls of his role, going off on his own. I said that the result might be the building raining down on our heads. The builder's initiative may also have corrected a mistake or oversight of the architectural engineer and saved us all.

Judging, too, is not simply obeying. As the very name of the activity imports, judging necessarily involves the exercise of judgment, the introduction of some choices by the decider himself. Some control systems may be genetically defective; the applier may have to complete them, as did Chief Justice Marshall. In advanced industrial- and science-based civilizations, in which things change rapidly, a control system which worked well in the past may prove obsolete under new conditions, and the applier who is to be controlled by it may have to supplement it. And in systems like the United States in which structural paralyses shift certain prescriptive competences to appliers, there may be latent authorizations to ignore certain controls in certain circumstances. Many of these conditions form a key part of the environment of the international arbitrator. The question is how to respond appropriately to them, to do a better job than was prescribed, but still to do the job that was prescribed.

I would emphasize that this is not a call for renascent Positivism. Decision covers a range of functions: the gathering of intelligence, the promotion of policy, its prescription, provisional characterizations of unlawful behavior and invocation of community response, application of prescriptions, termination of prescriptions, and appraisal of the aggregate performance of a decision process.[3] Roles in each of these decision functions import fidelity in the performance of the tasks assigned, but each role is different; some call for considerable "activism." I do not preach the passive virtues for all judges worldover. As I have said, American judges have been assigned a unique competence within their national constitutive process. What I do advocate is the fidelity of international judges and arbitrators to the manifest expectations of their roles, without which they will not be able to make a contribution to world order.

I submitted that in order to perform control functions properly it is necessary to understand control systems and one's own self-system and the relation between them. American legal education certainly teaches, in one form or another, the functions and mechanics of control systems. Perhaps we can address the subject in more efficient ways. Legal education has been less successful in dealing with the role of the self in decision. For complex reasons having to do with professional interests and legal theory, American legal thought, with the exception of the Legal Realists, has resisted acknowledging the role of the self in law. Only when we explicitly acknowledge that, can we begin to teach, as a part of professional education, effective ways for future decision-makers to engage in an ongoing self-scrutiny which will enable the decision-maker to become aware of deep impulses in the self that can distort perception and skew processes of choice.[4] But the perspectives which give rise to this problem may have formed at an earlier point and lie at an even deeper level.

The sense of honor and duty that presses men and women to try to do, honestly and to the best of their abilities and in each sector of their lives, what they have led others to expect them to do is, ultimately, not a result of professional education, but of character formation and civic acculturation. If it exists and operates, its roots will reach back to the earliest shaping of the personality in home and school, in religious institutions, and in the flood of myth, folklore, and miranda that gushes daily from the cables and pipes of the media network that ties the individual components of mass society together. Perhaps the ethical crises in so many professions and vocations in advanced industrial civilization have some common source.

Within the United States, our tradition of separation of power and checks and balances may provide controls that can surmount the difficulties caused by individual intellectual and moral frailties. Those structural controls do not obtain in international adjudication and arbitration. The healthy skepticism of our legal system about human nature and the limits on its perfectibility, born of the practice of our craft and our cumulative national political experience, continues to lead us to establish control mechanisms and, when necessary, to mend their fences carefully. Strange as it may seem, many American lawyers, who, thanks to the preeminent position of the United States in international politics and business, play a key role in the shaping and maintenance of the international legal system, seem prone to abandon their historic professional concern when they build internationally. But given the absence of structural checks and balances and the diversity of conceptions of professional ethics in the international bar, control mechanisms are needed even more urgently here than in domestic legal arrangements.

The failures of control mechanisms in three distinct international decision systems may be attributed less to venality and greed and, much more, to careless thinking and wishfulness. The skepticism about human nature that undergirds the American constitutional experience should apply a fortiori to international constitution building. The emergence of a true world public order of human dignity cannot be conceived without the necessary institutional underpinnings of all legal systems that seek to vouchsafe individual freedom: systems of control.

Notes

1 Introduction

1 Marbury v. Madison, 5 U.S. (1 Cranch) 137, 177–78 (1803) and discussion of judicial review. See also A. Bickel, The Least Dangerous Branch 1–33 (2d ed. 1986) (describing how "the institution of the judiciary needed to be summoned up out of the constitution of vapors, shaped and maintained"). In the Federal Republic of Germany, more explicit control mechanisms were conceived as an authentic part of the new constitutional order. See Karl-Ulrich Meyn, Kontrolle als Verfassungsprinzip (1982), and, for comparative but internal German purposes, see Georg Brunner, Kontrolle in Deutschland: Eine Untersuchung zur Verfassungsordnung in beiden Teilen Deutschlands (1972).

2 Declaration on the Establishment of a New International Economic Order, G.A. Res. 3201, U.N. GAOR Supp. (No. 1) at 3, U.N. Doc. A/9559 (1974).

3 Article 2(2)(c) of the Charter of Economic Rights and Duties of States specifies that each state has the right:

> To nationalize, expropriate or transfer ownership of foreign property, in which case appropriate compensation should be paid by the state adopting such measures, taking into account its relevant laws and regulations and all circumstances that the State considers pertinent. In any case where the question of compensation gives rise to a controversy, it shall be settled under the domestic law of the nationalizing state and by its tribunals, unless it is freely and mutually agreed by all states concerned that other peaceful means be sought on the basis of the sovereign equality of states and in accordance with the principle of free choice of means.

See G.A. Res. 3281, 29 U.N. GAOR Supp. (No. 31) at 50, U.N. Doc. A/9631 (1974).

4 The term appears to have been coined by Myres S. McDougal, but given its greatest currency by the late Judge Jessup in his Transnational Law. See P. Jessup, Transnational Law (1956). The term is useful for designating the norms and applicative systems for economic relationships that cross national political boundaries but do not engage, as direct parties, nation-states or their various agencies. In this respect, it can be a designative term to distinguish the law for commercial relationships which are not national but, strictly speaking, are not "international." But cf. for a more critical view, F.A. Mann, The Aminoil Arbitration 54 Brit. Y. B. Int'l. L. 213 (1983).

5 Digest of Justinian 4, 8–332–21.

6 The history of that search for a solution can be traced from 1874, when the Institut de Droit International undertook a study of the problem. See W.M. Reisman, Nullity and Revision: The Review and Enforcement of International Judgments and Awards, 31–34 (1971).

7 Treaty of General Arbitration, Jan. 11, 1894, United States-Great Britain, arts. 4, 5, reproduced in DeMartens, 28 Nouveau Recueil Général des Traités (2d ser.) (Fr.) No. 12, at 90, 92 (1902).

8 Grubel, "Risk, Uncertainty and Moral Hazard," 38 Journal of Risk and Insurance 99, 106 (1971).

9 In Nullity and Revision: The Review and Enforcement of International Judgments and Awards (1971), I explored this phenomenon in some detail, especially at chap. 7, 11, and 18. For an exposition of the term by its coiner, see Scelle, "Le Phenomene juridique du dédoublement fonctionnel," in Schätzel & Schlochauer, Rechtsfragen der Internationalen Organisation: Festschrift für Hans Wehberg 324 (1956). On Scelle, see generally the collection of essays in 1 European Journal of International Law 193–249 (1990).

2 The International Court

1 For a general discourse on the Iranian-U.S. Claims Tribunal, see R. Khan, The Iran-United States Claims Tribunal: Controversies, Cases and Contribution (1990).

2 Statute of the Permanent Court of International Justice, Adjoined to the Protocol of Signature of December 16, 1920, reprinted in 1 World Court Reports 17 (M. Hudson ed. 1934).

3 Id. at arts. 4–12.

4 Id. at art. 13.

5 Ambatielos Case (Greece v. U.K.), 1952 I.C.J. 28, 36 (Judgment of July 1).

6 For brief historical background and application history, see L. Goodrich, E. Hambro, & A.P. Simon, Charter of the United Nations (3d ed. 1969).

7 For an examination of the application of charter Article 94(2), see Reisman, Nullity and Revision: The Review and Enforcement of International Judgments and Awards (1971), chap. 18.

8 Judgment No. 2, Ser. A, No. 2.

9 Id. at 16.

10 Id. at 60.

11 Id. at 42.

12 1953 I.C.J. at 29.

13 See I. Shihata, The Power of the International Court to Determine its Own Jurisdiction: Compétence de la Compétence (1965).

14 U.N. GAOR Supp. (No. 9) at 7 (1952).

15 For a concise summary of the debate, see Shihata, supra note 13, at 11 n. 4.

16 See Commentary on the Draft Convention on Arbitral Procedure adopted by the International Law Commission at its Fifth Session, U.N. Doc. A/CN.4/92 at 105–10 (1955).

17 Id. at 105 (footnotes omitted).

18 Id. art. 30.

19 Id.

20 Concerning Rights of Nationals of the United States of America in Morocco (Fr. v. U.S.), 1952 I.C.J. 176 (Judgment of August 27).

21 Anglo-Iranian Oil Co. (U.K. v. Iran) (Jurisdiction), 1952 I.C.J. 93 (Judgment of July 22).

22 Certain Norwegian Loans (Fr. v. Nor.), 1957 I.C.J. 9 (Judgment of July 6).

23 Concerning the Aerial Incident of July 27, 1955 (Isr. v. Bulg.), 1959 I.C.J. 127 (Judgment of May 26).
24 Nottebohm Case (Second Phase) (Liecht. v. Guat.), 1955 I.C.J. 4 (Judgment of April 6).
25 Concerning Right of Passage Over Indian Territory (Port. v. India) (Merits), 1960 I.C.J. 6 (Judgment of April 12).
26 Concerning the Temple of Preah Vihear (Camb. v. Thail.) (Merits), 1962 I.C.J. 6 (Judgment of June 15).
27 Corfu Channel (U.K. v. Alb.) (Merits), 1949 I.C.J. 4 (Judgment of April 9).
28 1946–1947 U.N.Y.B. 392, U.N. Sales No. 1947.I.18.
29 Id. at 393.
30 Id. at 394.
31 Corfu Channel (U.K. v. Alb.) (Preliminary Objections), 1947–48 I.C.J. 15, 27 (Judgment of March 25).
32 See generally W.M. Reisman, Nullity and Revision, chap. 9 (1971).
33 Nuclear Tests (N.Z. v. Fr.) (Interim Protection), 1973 I.C.J. 135, 137–38 (Order of June 22).
34 See 1966–1967 I.C.J.Y.B. 52 (1967).
35 See supra note 33, at 138.
36 Nuclear Tests (N.Z. v. Fr.), 1974 I.C.J. 253, 270 para. 52, 272 para. 62 (Judgment of December 20).
37 Concerning Military and Paramilitary Activities in and Against Nicaragua (Nicar. v. U.S.) (Jurisdiction and Admissibility), 1984 I.C.J. 392, 396 para. 8 (Judgment of November 26).
38 Id. at 442, para. 113.
39 Id. at 427, para. 81.
40 Id. at 454, para. 12 (sep. op. Judge Ruda).
41 The late Judge Nagendra Singh was able to dispel for himself any lingering disquiet on this point by finding significance in the fact that "the jurisdictional clause of Article XXIV of the Treaty, does not specify the exclusion of Article XXI from the Court's jurisdiction." Id. at 446–48 (sep. op. Judge Nagendra Singh).
42 Id. at 442, para. 113.
43 Id. at 403–4, para. 25.
44 Concerning the Arbitral Award Made by the King of Spain on 23 December 1906 (Hond. v. Nicar.), 1960 I.C.J. 192 (Judgment of November 18).
45 Statute of the I.C.J.
46 Id. at 403–4, para. 25.
47 Id. at 405–8, paras. 29–35. For confirmation of its interpretation, the court relied on the "conduct" of international organizations. See id. para. 36. For examination of the problems of this approach and its implications, see Reisman (M.H. Arsanjani), "Dissemination of Information by International Organizations: Reflections on Law and Policy in the Light of Recent Developments," 17 Wellington Law Journal (Victoria University) 53 (1987).

All of the judges rejected the U.S. arguments of admissibility. In a fragile international political system which seeks to protect itself by insulating matters of vital interest to the major powers from review *even by the Security Council*, it is, of course, arguable that those very states which sought such insulation may still submit themselves to a decision entity which has no special mechanisms for protecting their interests. But surely, a prudent tribunal would look for a very high degree of clarity in the waiver of those very rights which international law has vouchsafed them. It is not the finding of admissibility of issues *in abstracto* which is puzzling in this case, but its finding of admissibility when all of the other grounds of jurisdiction are so tenuous and forced.

48 XIV Documents of the United Nations Conference on International Organization 289 (1945), cited in 1984 I.C.J. 571, para. 18 (diss. op. Judge Schwebel) and 1984 I.C.J. 536 (sep. op. Judge Jennings).

49 1984 I.C.J., supra note 37 at 421, para. 65.

50 Id. at 472 (sep. op. Judge Oda).

51 Concerning Military and Paramilitary Activities in and against Nicaragua (Nicar. v. U.S.) (Provisional Measures), 1984 I.C.J. 169 (Order of May 10).

Nor was this case free from some disquieting procedural pathologies. El Salvador, which had sought to intervene under Article 62 of the statute, was denied that option by the court. The decision itself tells us little. More significant is the fact that El Salvador was denied a hearing on the matter.

52 Treaty of Friendship, Commerce and Navigation, Jan. 21, 1956, entered into force May 25, 1958, Nicaragua-United States, 9 U.S.T. 449; T.I.A.S. 4024; 367 U.N.T.S. 3.

53 Reprinted in 1984 I.C.J., supra note 37, at 427.

54 Id. at 428, para. 83.

55 See id. at 635, para. 128 (diss. op. Judge Schwebel).

56 Id.

57 Id. at 428–29, para. 83.

58 Military and Paramilitary Activities in and Against Nicaragua (Nicar. v. U.S.) (Merits), 1986 I.C.J. 14 (Judgment of June 27).

59 1984 I.C.J., supra note 37, at 425.

60 See 1986 I.C.J., supra note 58, at 92–94, paras. 172–75.

61 Id. at 115, para. 221.

62 Id. at 116, para. 222.

63 Id. at 135, para. 271 et seq.

64 Id. at 136–37, para. 273, and 138, para. 275.

65 Id. at 23–24, para. 27.

66 Id. at 25.

67 1949 I.C.J., supra note 27, at 248, quoted in 1986 I.C.J. at 25. For further discussion of the Court's use of its own jurisprudence in this matter, see infra notes 85–86 and accompanying text.

68 Border and Transborder Armed Actions (Nicar. v. Hond.) (Jurisdiction and Admissibility), 1988 I.C.J. 69 (Judgment of December 20).

69 Id. at 108 (decl. Judge Lachs).

70 1984–1985 I.C.J.Y.B. 102–18 (1985). For a list of the FCN treaties, see Annex 51, List of Treaties of Friendship, Commerce and Navigation, in Pleadings, Oral Arguments, Documents, Case Concerning United States Diplomatic and Consular Staff in Tehran, 1979 I.C.J. Pleadings at 233–34.

71 1984–85 I.C.J.Y.B. 102–18 (1985).

72 Memorandum on Dispute Settlement Clause in Treaty of Friendship, Commerce and Navigation with China: Relationship of Article 27 of the Treaty between the United States and China, signed 4 November 1946, to Senate Resolution 196 of 2 August 1946, reproduced in Pleadings, Oral Arguments, Documents, supra note 70, at 234–36.

73 Department of State memorandum on Provisions in Commercial Treaties Relating to the International Court of Justice, reproduced in Pleadings, Oral Arguments, Documents, supra note 70, at 236–37.

74 1986 I.C.J. at 117, para. 224.

75 Id. at 138, para. 275.

76 Id. at 138, para. 276.
77 Reisman, "Private Armies in a Global War System," 14 Va. J. Int'l. L. 1 (1973), reprinted in Law and Civil War in the Modern World 252 (J.N. Moore ed. 1974) and in M. McDougal & W.M. Reisman, International Law Essays 142, 182 (1981).
78 For legislative history, practice, and comments on Article 53, see J. Elkind, Non-Appearance Before the International Court of Justice: Functional and Comparative Analysis (1984), especially at 79–102.
79 See supra note 58.
80 Id. at 24, para. 28.
81 Fisheries Jurisdiction (U.K. v. Iceland) (Merits), 1974 I.C.J. 3, at 9, para. 17 (Judgment of July 25).
82 1986 I.C.J., supra note 58, at 24, para. 29.
83 But cf. Frontier Dispute (Burkina Faso v. Mali), 1986 I.C.J. 554, 557 (Judgment of the Chamber, December 22).
84 1986 I.C.J., supra note 58, at 25, para. 30.
85 Id.
86 Corfu Channel (U.K. v. Alb.) (Assessment of Compensation), 1949 I.C.J. 244, 248 (Judgment of December 15).
87 Agreement Between the United Nations and the United States of America Regarding the Headquarters of the United Nations, June 26, 1947, 61 Stat. 756, T.I.A.S. No. 1676, 11 U.N.T.S. 11 (1947) [hereinafter Headquarters Agreement].
88 Id. § 21.
89 Joint Resolution of August 4, 1947, Pub. L. No. 80–357, 61 Stat. 756 (codified at 22 U.S.C. § 287 app. at 101 [1982]).
90 Id.
91 Headquarters Agreement, supra note 87, § 11. Section 11 provides in full:

> The federal, state or local authorities of the United States shall not impose any impediments to transit to or from the Headquarters District of (1) representatives of Members or officials of the United Nations or of specialized agencies as defined in Article 57, paragraph 2, of the Charter, or the families of such representatives or officials, (2) experts performing missions for the United Nations or for such specialized agencies, (3) representatives of the press, or of radio, film or other information agencies, who have been accredited by the United Nations (or by such a specialized agency) in its discretion after consultation with the United States, (4) representatives of non-governmental organizations recognized by the United Nations for the purpose of consultation under Article 71 of the Charter, or (5) other persons invited to the headquarters district by the United Nations or by such specialized agency on official business.

92 See, e.g., Observer Status for the South West Africa People's Organization, G.A. Res. 31/152, 31 U.N. GAOR Supp. (No. 39) at 136, U.N. Doc. A/31/39 (1976); Observer Status for the Islamic Conference at the United Nations, G.A. Res. 3369, 30 U.N. GAOR Supp. (No. 34) at 3, U.N. Doc. A/10034 (1975); Status of the Council for Mutual Economic Assistance in the General Assembly, G.A. Res. 3209, 29 U.N. GAOR Supp. (No. 31) at 2–3, U.N. Doc. A/9631 (1974); Co-operation between the United Nations and the Organization of African Unity, G.A. Res. 2011, 20 U.N. GAOR Supp. (No. 14) at 2, U.N. Doc. A/6014 (1965).
93 For a good history of observer status, see Suy, The Status of Observers in International Organizations, in 160 Recueil des Cours de l'Academie de Droit International 75 (1978).

94 Observer Status for the Palestine Liberation Organization, G.A. Res. 3237, 29 U.N. GAOR Supp. (No. 31) at 4, U.N. Doc. A/9631 (1974).

95 This is how the ICJ characterized the PLO in its recent case, Applicability of the Obligation to Arbitrate Under Section 21 of the United Nations Headquarters Agreement of 26 June 1947, 1988 I.C.J. 12, 15 (Advisory Opinion of Apr. 26, 1988) (quoting U.N. publications) [hereinafter ICJ Advisory Opinion].

96 The Anti-Defamation League (ADL) of B'nai B'rith is a civil rights association founded in 1913. The ADL was established "[t]o stop the defamation of Jewish people and to secure justice and fair treatment to all citizens alike." 1 Encyclopedia of Associations 1334 (1988).

97 Anti-Defamation League v. Kissinger, No. 74 Civ. 1545 (E.D.N.Y. Oct. 31, 1974), reprinted in part in 1974 Digest of United States Practice in International Law 27.

98 For descriptions of the Achille Lauro incident, see Gooding, Fighting Terrorism in the 1980's: The Interception of the Achille Lauro Hijackers, 12 Yale J. Int'l L. 158, 164–68 (1987); McGinley, The Achille Lauro Affair—Implications for International Law, 52 Tenn. L. Rev. 691 (1985).

99 Pub. L. No. 100–204, §§ 1001–5, 101 Stat. 1406 (codified at 22 U.S.C.A. §§ 5201–3 West Supp. 1988) [hereinafter Anti-Terrorism Act].

100 Id. § 1003 (codified at 22 U.S.C.A. § 5202 [West Supp. 1988]).

101 For the legislative history of the Anti-Terrorism Act, see 133 Cong. Rec. E1635–36 (daily ed. Apr. 29, 1987); 133 Cong. Rec. S6448–51 (daily ed. May 14, 1987); 133 Cong. Rec. H4047–48 (daily ed. May 28, 1987); 133 Cong. Rec. H4198 (daily ed. June 3, 1987).

102 See P.L.O. Backers Ordered to Close Capital Office, N.Y. Times, Sept. 16, 1987, at A1, col. 1; Washington Talk: State Department—Ousting the P.L.O., N.Y. Times, Sept. 24, 1988, at A24, col. 4; P.L.O. Given 6 More Weeks to Close Washington Office, N.Y. Times, Oct. 15, 1987, at A8, col. 1.

103 The Anti-Terrorism Act was added without hearings as a rider to the Foreign Relations Authorization Act for Fiscal Years 1988–89. See 133 Cong. Rec. S13, 851 (daily ed. Oct. 8, 1987). The Anti-Terrorism Act was briefly discussed during a joint conference on the Foreign Relations Authorization Act, during which the House conferees acceded to the Senate's version. See 133 Cong. Rec. S18, 193 (daily ed. Dec. 16, 1987).

104 See the articles cited at supra note 102.

105 ICJ Advisory Opinion, supra note 95, at 17–20.

106 Id. at 19–22.

107 G.A. Res. 229A, Resolutions and Decisions Adopted by General Assembly at its Forty-Second Session (29 February–2 March 1988), U.N. Doc. GA/7612/Add.1 (9 March 1988) at 1, reprinted in part in ICJ Advisory Opinion, supra.

108 G.A. Res. 229B, Resolutions and Decisions Adopted by General Assembly at its Forty-Second Session (29 February–2 March 1988), U.N. Doc. GA/7612/Add.1 (9 March 1988) at 3, reprinted in part in ICJ Advisory Opinion, supra.

109 Letter from U.S. Attorney General Meese to Chief of the PLO Observer Mission to the U.N. (Mar. 11, 1988), cited in United States v. Palestine Liberation Org., No. 88 Civ. 1962, slip. op. at 9 (S.D.N.Y. June 29, 1988).

110 ICJ Advisory Opinion, supra note 95, at 35.

111 United States v. Palestine Liberation Org., slip. op. at 35.

112 U.S. Will Allow P.L.O. to Maintain its Office at U.N., N.Y. Times, Aug. 30, 1988, at A1, col. 6.

113 Applicability of the Obligation to Arbitrate under Section 21 of the United Nations Headquarters Agreement of 26 June 1947, 1988 I.C.J. 12 (Advisory Opinion of 26 April 1988).

114 Agreement Between the United Nations and the United States of America Regarding the Headquarters of the United Nations, June 26, 1947, 61 Stat. 756, T.I.A.S. No. 1676, 11 U.N.T.S. 11 (1947) [hereinafter Headquarters Agreement].

115 Id. art. 21(a).

116 1988 I.C.J., supra note 113, at 29, para. 39. Despite the fact that the case was largely briefed and pleaded in English, the court designated French as the authentic language. Id. at 35, para. 58. The translation of this part of the judgment is not felicitous. The statement "we do not believe arbitration would be appropriate" is rendered in the authentic version as "nous pensons qu'un arbitrage ne serait pas opportun." Five lines later, the word "opportunité" in the important quotation from the 1930 Free Zones case (see, infra note 118) was rendered in English as "expediency." That is an accurate translation, but the translation of "appropriate" in the U.S. pleading as "opportun" viz. "expedient" in this setting does not capture the implication of the U.S. pleading. This interlinguistic adjustment does, however, make Free Zones quotable in this context.

117 1988 I.C.J., supra note 113, at 29, para. 40. Free Zones of Upper Savoy and the District of Gex, Order of 6 December 1930, P.C.I.J. (ser. A) No. 24, p. 15.

118 Free Zones of Upper Savoy and the District of Gex (Second Phase) (Fr. v. Switz.), 1930 P.C.I.J. (ser. A) No. 24, at 15 (Dec. 6) (emphasis added). The authentic language of the judgment was French and was as follows: "*Considérant . . . que si la Cour, étant une Cour de justice, ne peut faire abstraction de droits reconnus par elle pour se déterminer seulement par des considérations de pure opportunité, rien ne l'empêche, vu les avantages que pourrait présenter une solution de ce genre, d'offrir aux Parties, qui, seules, peuvent la réaliser, une nouvelle occasion d'atteindre ce but.*"

119 Elettronica Sicula S.p.A. (ELSI) case between the United States and Italy, 1989 I.C.J. Reports at p. 15, paragraph 126.

120 Id. at para. 124.

121 Id. at para. 128.

122 Id. at para. 123.

123 Id. at para. 124.

124 Id. at para. 128.

125 Asylum case, 1950 I.C.J. Reports at p. 284.

126 Resolution 337A(V); 5 U.N.GAOR, Supp. 20 at 10–12 (A/1775) (1950).

127 Frontier Dispute (Burkina Faso v. Mali), 1986 I.C.J. 554, 557 (Judgment of the Chamber, December 22).

128 Letter of Termination by Secretary of State Schultz to Secretary-General Perez de Cuellar, October 7, 1985, Department of State Bulletin, January, 1986.

3 The ICSID Experiment

1 See generally, 2 Convention on the Settlement of Investment Disputes between States and Nationals of Other States (documents concerning the origin and foundation of the convention).

2 10 League of Nations O.J. 1125, 1126 (1929) (memorandum submitted to the Committee of Jurists by M. Rundstein, member of the committee).

3 See generally, Recueil des Decisions des Tribunaux Arbitraux Mixtes (Fr.) (1922–30).

4 Proposal of the Government of Finland to Confer on the Permanent Court of International Justice Jurisdiction as a Tribunal of Appeal in Respect of Arbitral Tribunals Established by States, Annex 6, League of Nations O.J., Spec. Supp. 76, at 82.

5 Report of the Committee Appointed by the Council, League of Nations Doc. C.338 M.138 1930V (1930).

6 Resolutions Votèes par L'Institut au cours de la XXXVI Session, Annuaire de L'Institut de Droit International (1929) Vol. 2, at 304 (translation by the author).

7 September 25, 1929, cited in Report of the Committee of Jurists, League of Nations Annex 122 para., 338.

8 Id.

9 Commentary on the Draft Convention on Arbitral Procedure adopted by the International Law Commission at its Fifth Session, prepared by the Secretariat, U.N. Doc. A/C.N./9.

10 Arbitral procedure, Report of Int'l L. Comm'n, 7 U.N. GAOR, Supp. No. 9, ch. II, U.N. Doc. A/C.N.4/109 (1957).

11 Model Rules on Arbitral Procedure, adopted by the International Law Commission, Report of the International Law Commission Covering the Work of Its Tenth Session Apr. 28–July 4, 1958. U.N. GAOR 13th Sess. Supp. No. 9 (A/3859) [hereinafter ICSID Model Rules].

12 Convention on the Settlement of Investment Disputes Between States and Nationals of Other States, done at Washington, March 18, 1965, art. 52(1), reprinted in 575 U.N.T.S. 160 (1966) [hereinafter ICSID Convention].

13 Id. art. 52(3).

14 Id. art. 52(4).

15 Id. art. 52(5).

16 On this aspect of ICSID, see generally M. Feldman, The Annulment Proceedings and the Finality of ICSID Arbitral Awards, 2 ICSID Review of Foreign Investment 85 (1987); P. Khan, Le Coutrôle des sentences arbitrales rendues par un Tribunal CIRDI, in La Juridiction Internationale Permanente 363 (1987); Lattanzi, Convenzione di Washington Sulle Controversie Relative ad Investimenti e Invalidata delle Sentenze Arbitrali, 70 Revistadi Diritto Internazionale 521 (1987); Pirrwitz, Annulment of Arbitral Awards under Article 52 of the Washington Convention on the Settlement of Investment Disputes Between States and Nationals of Other States, 23 Texas International Law Journal 74 (1988); Seidl-Hohenveldern, Die Aufhebung von ICSID Schiedsprüchen, 1989 Jahrbuch für die Praxis der Schiedsgerichtbarkeit 100 (1989); Thibaut, L'article 52 de la Convention de Washington du 18 mars 1965 et les premiers enseignements de sa pratique, Revue de l'Arbitrage 95 (1988).

17 Klöckner GmbH v. United Republic of Cameroon (ICSID Case No. ARB/81/2) [hereinafter Klöckner Award]. Excerpts from the original French text of the award are published in 111 Journal de Droit International 409 (1984). The full text of the award in English translation is annexed to J. Paulsson, Third World Participation in International Commercial Arbitration (1984). Subsequent references to the award will be to Paulsson, "The ICSID Klöckner v. Cameroon Award: The Duties of Partners in North-South Economic Development Agreements," 1 J. Int'l. Arb. 145 (1984). The award is also examined in 1 "News from ICSID" No. 2 at 5 (1984). An English translation of the portion of the award dealing with the issue of jurisdiction is reprinted in "Arbitral Award of Oct. 21, 1983," 10 Y.B. Com. Arb. 71–78 (1985). Substantial parts of the Dissenting Opinion appear in Niggemann, "The ICSID Klöckner v. Cameroon Award: The Dissenting Opinion," 1 J. Int'l. Arb. 331 (1984).

18 Paulsson, supra note 16, at 154.

19 Id. at 149–52.

20 Id. at 153.
21 Id. at 157.
22 Id. at 157–58.
23 Id. at 158–61.
24 Id. at 162–63.
25 Niggemann, supra note 16, at 348.
26 The decision of the ad hoc committee was published in the ICSID Review—Foreign Investment Law Journal, from which all citations are taken. See "Klöckner v. Cameroun: Decision of the Ad Hoc Committee," 1 ICSID Review—Foreign Investment L.J. 89 (1986) [hereinafter Klöckner Decision.] For commentary on the decision, see Thompson, "The Klöckner v. Cameroon Appeal—A Note on Jurisdiction," 3 J. Int'l. Arb. 93 (1986); Feldman, "The Annulment Proceedings and the Finality of ICSID Arbitral Awards," 2 ICSID Review—Foreign Investment L.J. 85 (1987).
27 Klöckner Decision, supra note 26, at para. 151.
28 Id. at para. 82.
29 Id. at para. 96.
30 Id. at para. 107.
31 Id. at paras. 113, 119–20.
32 Id. at para. 179.
33 Id.
34 Id.
35 Id. at paras. 58–59.
36 Id. at para. 58.
37 Id. at para. 52.
38 Id.
39 Id. at para. 151.
40 Id. at para. 82.
41 Id. at para. 52(b).
42 Id.
43 Id. at para. 66.
44 Sidarma Società Italiana di Armamento S.p.A. v. Holt Marine Indus., 515 F. Supp. 1308–9 (S.D.N.Y. 1981).
45 Klöckner Decision, supra note 26, at para. 67.
46 Id.
47 Id.
48 Id.
49 Id. at para. 68.
50 Id.
51 Id. at para. 75.
52 Id. at para. 79.
53 Id. at para. 81; see also para. 179 ("The contested arbitral Award must therefore be annulled . . . in its entirety").
54 K. Llewellyn, The Common Law Tradition: Deciding Appeals 402 (1960).
55 Klöckner Decision, supra note 26, at paras. 68–79.
56 The interpretation of ICSID Article 42 presents complex problems. In my view the most plausible interpretation is offered by Broches, The Convention on the Settlement of Investment Disputes Between States and the Nationals of Other States: Applicable Law and Default Procedure in International Arbitration (Sanders ed.) at 12, 16--17.

57 See infra pp. 66–78.

58 AMCO Asia Gvp. (Delaware, U.S.A.), Pan American Devpt., Ltd. (Hong Kong), and P.T. AMCO (Indonesia) v. Republic of Indonesia, Case ICSID (ARB/81/1) [hereinafter AMCO Award]. The full text of the award is published in 1 Int'l. Arb. Rep. 601 (1986); excerpts are reprinted in 24 I.L.M. 1022 (1985). For the text of an interlocutory decision see 10 Y.B. Com. Arb. 61 (1985), reprinted in 23 I.L.M. 351 (1984). For doctrinal notes see Curtis, 83 Am. J. Int'l L. 106 (1989); Branson, "Another ICSID Arbitral Award Annulled," 18 Corporate Counsel's Int'l Adviser 9 (1986); Redfern, ICSID—Losing Its Appeal? 3 Arbitration International 98 (1987); Schatz, The Effect of the Annulment Decisions in "AMCO v. Indonesia" and "Klöckner v. Cameroon" on the Future of the International Centre for the Settlement of Investment Disputes, 3 AJILP 481 (1988).

59 AMCO Award, at para. 155.

60 Id. at para. 156.

61 Id. at para. 159.

62 Id. at para. 160.

63 Id. at para. 172 ("[A] State has a duty to protect aliens and their investment against unlawful acts committed by some of its citizens. . . . If such acts are committed with the active assistance of state-organs, a breach of International Law occurs").

64 Id. at paras. 172–73 ("[A]n internationally wrongful act was committed; . . . this act is attributable to the Government of Indonesia which therefore is internationally responsible. . . . [T]he takeover of the hotel . . . was an act of illegal self-help").

65 Id. at para. 176 ("[J]udgements [of the Indonesian Supreme Court] of January 12, 1982 and November 28, 1983, on the merits . . . do not purport to legitimize the unilateral acts").

66 Id. at para. 188.

67 Id. at para. 189 ("[A] State may terminate such a relationship either for reasons of public interest and welfare—which is inconceivable in the case of a private law contract—or for reasons of non-fulfillment by the foreign applicant of its obligations").

68 Id. at para. 192 ("[T]o be lawful, the withdrawal of an administrative act which terminates a bilateral relationship between a State and a private party, which relationship has created reciprocal legal obligations on both sides, has to satisfy two requisites: '[P]rocedural ones, as set up by the applicable law and which are to be in accord with the fundamental principle of due process' and 'the substantial requirement that the revocation be based on grounds that justify it legally.' ")

69 Id. at para. 242 ("[I]ndependently from this examination and its conclusions, the mere lack of due process would have been an insuperable obstacle, to the lawfulness of the revocation"). Id. at para. 244 ("The withdrawal of the investment authorization, decided without due process being granted to the investor, and for reasons which did not justify it in substance, permits the liability of the Republic of Indonesia under Indonesian as well as under international law, that is to say under the two systems of law applicable in the instant case").

70 Id. at para. 199 ("[I]nfringement of the due process principle is met again when examining the manner in which the revocation was prepared"); id. at para. 201 ("[T]he revocation of the approval of the investment application was unlawfully and therefore wrongfully decided, whatever the reasons on which it was based, and even if, as a matter of substance, said reasons could have justified it").

71 Id. at paras. 194, 198 ("[T]he State's right to withdraw the approval where the recipient does not fulfill its obligations (provided . . . the failure is material) derives from the very

nature of the legal relationship established by the application and the approval [*sic*] thereof. [T]he warning (or warnings) are an element of due process . . . established by Indonesian law to protect the investor, in particular where a sanction as heavy—and indeed, irremediable—as a revocation is envisaged against him. In the instant case, this protection was not made available to the Claimants, who were thus deprived of due process, contrary to Indonesian law as well as contrary to general principles of law").

72 Id. at para. 205 ("Thus, the other grounds for a suggested "review" of the authorization put forward in Mr. Usman's Summary (namely: the failure to report to Bank Indonesia concerning transfers abroad; the failure to report to BKPM concerning the realization of AMCO's capital investment; alleged tax manipulation; assets owned by the hotel allegedly given in guarantee for obtaining a loan, without the approval of the owner, P.T. Wisma Kartika: see above, paras. 118–123) are not mentioned in the Decision of July 9, 1980, in spite of said grounds having been, in essence, repeated in Mr. Harun's Memorandum of May 10, 1980 (Resp. Exh. to C.M. Vol. 4, No. 89; see above, para. 14) and in the Request for Guidance presented on May 12, 1980 by the chairman of BKPM to the president of the Republic (Resp. Exh. to C.M., No. 90; see above para. 126").

73 Id. ("Accordingly, the tribunal does not have to consider these grounds, since they have not been relied upon in the legal act which pronounced the revocation.

"It might be that the chairman of BKPM considered that it was not necessary to refer to them, because he may have thought that the two grounds ultimately invoked (i.e., the transfer of the management to AEROPACIFIC and the nonfulfillment of the obligation to invest in the amount promised) were sufficient to justify the revocation. However, it might also be that the chairman considered that in the circumstances of the case, the other grievances would not have justified the revocation.

"Be that as it may, it is not for the tribunal to build hypotheses nor to try to guess thoughts which the author of the revocation did not express. The tribunal has to evaluate the lawfulness of a legal decision and the tribunal can do so by evaluating it as it is, and as it has been drafted by the Indonesian authority that issued it; the tribunal has not to supplement the decision in question by adding to it grounds which it does not contain, although they were invoked in the preparatory documents of the decision.

"Accordingly, the tribunal will consider only the two grounds of revocation on which the decision is expressly based.")

74 Id. at para. 287.

75 Id. at para. 241. For a discussion on the insufficiency of the investment see id. at paras. 220–43.

76 The chairman was Professor Ignaz Seidl-Hohenveldern. The other members of the tribunal were Judge Florentino P. Feliciano and Professor Andrea Giardina.

77 It has been published in full in 1 Int'l. Arb. Rep. 649 (1986) [hereinafter AMCO Decision]. For commentary on the decision, see Pirrwitz, "Annulment of Arbitral Awards under Article 52 of the Washington Convention on the Settlement of Investment Disputes Between States and Nationals of Other States," 23 Texas Int'l. L.J. 73 (1988); Feldman, "The Annulment Proceedings and the Finality of ICSID Arbitral Awards," 2 ICSID Review—Foreign Inv. L.J. 85 (1987); Branson, "Annulments of 'Final' ICSID Awards Raise Questions About the Process, Nat'l L.J., Aug. 4, 1986, at 25, col. 1.

78 AMCO Decision, supra note 77, at para. 97.

79 See Klöckner Decision, supra note 26, at para. 179.

80 See AMCO Decision, supra note 77, at para. 104. See also id. paras. 114, 118, and 120.

81 Id. at para. 58. See also id. para. 75 ("The Tribunal . . . held in effect that P.T. Amco was

denied a fair and adequate hearing in the course of BKPM's revocation procedure, a denial which the Tribunal held to be contrary "to the general and fundamental principle of due process"); id. para. 78 ("The general standards which Indonesian counsel affirms are part of Indonesian administrative law and which an Indonesia court would apply in resolving a challenge to the validity of an act of an administrative agency by a private person agreived [*sic*] thereby, involve the purpose and tenor of the relevant statute[s] as well as the concepts of reasonableness, proportionality, lack of arbitrariness and conformity with community notions of substantial justice. It appears to the ad hoc Committee that these general standards of Indonesian law are not qualitatively different from, and seem equivalent in a functional sense to, what the Tribunal appears to have had in mind in referring to "the general and fundamental principle of due process"); id. para. 79 ("For these reasons, the ad hoc Committee holds that this portion of the Award is not vitiated by a failure to apply the applicable law amounting to a manifest excess of power on the part of the Tribunal, nor by failure to state reasons").

82 AMCO Award, supra note 57, at paras. 220–43.

83 AMCO Decision, supra note 77, at para. 98.

84 AMCO Award, supra note 57, at para. 212.

85 Id. at para. 213.

86 Id. at para. 218.

87 Id. at para. 230.

88 Id. at para. 232.

89 Id. at paras. 240–41 ("[T]he investment amount which the Tribunal finds the Claimants have produced sufficient evidence of is US $2,472,490. . . . It is thus established that the Claimants did not realize an investment of U.S. $3,000,000 in the framework of Law No. 1/1967. . . . [T]he insufficiency was of slightly more than 1/6th of the amount Claimants had undertaken to invest. . . . [T]his insufficiency is not material enough to justify the revocation of the license").

90 AMCO Decision, supra note 77, at para. 93.

91 Id. at para. 94.

92 Id. at para. 95.

93 Id. at para. 97.

94 Id. at para. 98.

95 Id. at para. 103 ("Because the ad hoc Committee has annulled the conclusions of the Tribunal on the calculation . . . and on the amount of P.T. Amco's investment . . . it follows that the Tribunal's ruling on the non-materiality of the shortfall of P.T. Amco's investment must also fall").

96 Id. at para. 105 ("For the reasons set out above paras. 95 and 103, the conclusion of the Tribunal [Award para. 241] that BKPM was not justified in revoking Amco's licence on account of the shortfall of the investment, which the Tribunal calculated without regard to the applicable law and held immaterial, has to be annulled").

97 Id. at para. 81.

98 Id. at para. 106 ("However, if BKPM was not unjustified in revoking the licence on substantive grounds, then, according to the findings of the Award itself [supra para. 74], no compensation was due for the lack of three warnings and for other procedural defects of the revocation order. Therefore, the part of the Award granting P.T. Amco damages on this account has to be annulled").

99 Id. at para. 107 ("As the withdrawal of the investment licence cannot be considered unjustified, the resulting effect of such withdrawal cannot be considered unjustified either,

i.e. P.T. Amco's inability to exercise its right to manage the Kartika Plaza Hotel as of the day of issuance of the revocation order, [July 9, 1980], whatever would have been the outcome of the litigation begun by P.T. Wisma against P.T. Amco before the Jakarta Courts").

100 Id. at para. 109 ("The damage caused to P.T. Amco by the action of Army and Police personnel came to an end on the day of the revocation of P.T. Amco's license, i.e. on July 9, 1980. Consequently, the ad hoc Committee annuls the grant of damages to P.T. Amco . . . for the period beyond July 9, 1980").

101 Id. at para. 71 ("Indonesia argued . . . that a series of letters from the Bank of Indonesia . . . to P.T. Amco over the years repeatedly reminding the latter of the registration, or lack thereof, of the investment made or claimed to have been made by P.T. Amco . . . should be regarded as substantially equivalent to the warnings contemplated in BKPM decree 01/1977. The Tribunal . . . refused to regard the letters . . . as substantial compliance. . . . Whatever one may think as to the necessity or propriety of the literalness with which the Tribunal interpreted . . . the BKPM decree, . . . the ad hoc Committee does not believe itself justified in annulling this portion of the Award for failure to apply the applicable law").

102 Id. at para. 106 ("[I]f BKPM was not unjustified in revoking the license on substantive grounds, then, according to the findings of the Award itself . . . no compensation was due for the lack of three warnings and for other procedural defects of the revocation order. Therefore, the part of the Award granting P.T. Amco damages on this account has to be annulled").

103 Id. at unnumbered para. 126 (X-Award).

104 On doctrinal consideration of this problem, see Curtis, International Investment Disputes—*Res Judicata* Effect of Partially Annulled ICSID Awards, 83 AJIL 106 (1989); Ramband, La compétence du tribunal CIRDI saisi après une décision d'annulation, 34 Annuaire Français de Droit International 209 (1988).

105 27 I.L.M. 1281 (1988). See also AMCO v. Republic of Indonesia: Resubmitted Case—Decision, 3 ICSID Review—Foreign Inv. L.J. 166 (1988); 14 Y.B. Commercial Arbitration 92(1989).

106 AMCO Award, supra note 57, at para. 44.

107 AMCO Award II.

108 Id. at para. 75. In the critical paragraph 75 of its award, the tribunal says

> The Tribunal believes that the relevant issue is not whether (as Amco contends) procedural irregularities generate compensation, even if the substantive decision might be lawful; nor whether (as Indonesia contends) compensation is only due for procedural violations if these are themselves the cause of an unlawful substantive decision. Rather, the issue that must be determined is whether there exists a generally tainted background that necessarily renders a decision unlawful, even if substantive grounds may exist for such a decision. This background includes, but is not limited to, the question of procedural irregularities.

109 To date, there has been relatively little doctrinal review of this phase of the MINE case. But see Niggemann, Die Dritte Annullierung eines ICSID—Schiedspruches—Die Entscheidung in Sachen Mine v. Guinea, 11 IPRAX 77 (1991).

110 Mine Ad Hoc Committee Decision, paragraph 6.06 to be published in ICSID Review. Hereinafter MINE Decision.

111 MINE Award at p. 33.

112 Id.

113 MINE Decision para. 4.11.
114 Id., supra note 110, at para. 4.12.
115 Id. at para. 4.06.
116 Id. at para. 4.09.
117 Id. at para. 4.10.
118 Id. at para. 4.07.
119 Id. at para. 5.03.
120 Id.
121 Id. at para. 5.04.
122 Id. at para. 5.05.
123 Id. at para. 5.06.
124 Id. at para. 5.07.
125 Id. at para. 5.08.
126 Id. at para. 5.09.
127 Id.
128 Id. at para. 6.83, recapitulating, in slightly different terms, para. 5.13.
129 Id. at para. 6.38.
130 Id. at para. 6.36.
131 Id. at para. 6.4.
132 MINE Award at p. 29.
133 Id. at pp. 38–39.
134 MINE Decision, supra note 110, at para. 6.46.
135 Id. at para. 6.48.
136 Id. at para. 6.50.
137 Id. at para. 6.51.
138 Id. at para. 6.53.
139 Id. at para. 6.79.
140 MINE Award at p. 38.
141 Ibid.
142 Id. at 39–40.
143 MINE Decision, supra note 110, at para. 6.101.
144 5 U.S. (1 Cranch) 137 (1803).
145 Klöckner Decision, supra note 26, at para. 58.
146 Article 44 of the ICSID Convention provides: "Any arbitration proceeding shall be conducted in accordance with the provisions of this Section and, except as the parties otherwise agree, in accordance with the Arbitration Rules in effect on the date in which the parties consented to arbitration. If any question of procedure arises which is not covered by this section or the Arbitration Rules or any rules agreed by the parties, the Tribunal shall decide the question."
147 K. Carlston, The Process of International Arbitration 53 (1946).
148 W.M. Reisman, Nullity and Revision: The Review and Enforcement of International Judgments and Awards 618 (1971).
149 1960 I.C.J. 192 (Nov. 18, 1960).
150 Arbitral Award Made by H.M. Alfonso III, King of Spain, in the Border Dispute Between the Republics of Honduras and Nicaragua, on 23 December 1906, Pleadings, Oral Arguments, Documents, vol. I, annex 2, at 18–26.
151 1960 I.C.J. at 216.
152 Carlston, supra note 44 at 53.

153 Bucher, Le nouvel arbitrage international en Suisse 126 (1988).
154 Poudret in Lalive, Poudret & Reymond, Le droit de l'arbitrage interne et international en Suisse 431 (1989) and see also id. at 212 for other Swiss authorities in accord.
155 Blessing, The New International Arbitration Law in Switzerland: A Significant Step Toward Liberalism, 5 Journal of International Arbitration 71 (1988).
156 Pious Funds Case (Mex. v. U.S.), Hague Ct. Rep. (Scott) 1 (Perm. Ct. Arb. 1902).
157 1 Convention on the Settlement of Investment Disputes Between States and Nationals of Other States (documents concerning the origin and foundation of the convention) 219.
158 ICSID Convention Article, supra note 12, 52(6).
159 Klöckner Decision, supra note 26, at para. 82.
160 See supra footnotes 36–39 and accompanying text.
161 Orinco S.S. Co. Case (U.S. v. Venez.), Hague Ct. Rep. (Scott) 226 (Perm. Ct. Arb. 1902).
162 Id. at 231.
163 Ralston and Doyle, Report of French-Venezuelan Mixed Claims Commission of 1902, at 355.
164 See supra note 153, at 429.
165 Interpretation of Judgments Nos. 7 & 8 Concerning the Case of the Factory at Chorzow, 1927 P.C.I.J. (ser. A) No. 11, at 24 (Dec. 16, 1927) (Diss. op. of Judge Anzilotti).
166 1925 P.C.I.J. (ser. B) No. 11, at 31; see also J.J. Simpson & H. Fox, International Arbitration: Law and Practice 231 (1959).
167 U.N. Doc. A/CONF./39/27, (1969), reprinted in 63 Am. J. Int'l. L. 875 (1969).
168 ICSID Model Rule 55(3).
169 Id. Rule 55 note D.
170 ICSID, Administrative Council, 1988 Annual Meeting, Berlin, Federal Republic of Germany, December, 1988 at page 3 (copy available from author).
171 The Arbitration Act 1979, 18 I.L.M. 1249 (1979).
172 For the text, see Poncet & Gaillard, Introductory Note and Translation of the New Swiss Law in International Arbitration, 27 I.L.M. 37 (1988). See also Blessing, "The New International Arbitration Law in Switzerland," 5 J. Int'l. Arb. 9 (June 1988).
173 Law of March 27, 1985, enacting Code Judiciare, Article 1717.
174 1960 I.C.J. 192 (Nov. 18, 1960).

4 Non-Institutional International Commercial Arbitration

1 The ICC was founded in 1919; in 1922 an ICC Court of Arbitration was created to promote arbitration of all types of international commercial disputes. Although referred to as a "court," it is not an arbitral body and does not actually arbitrate cases; it serves as an administrative council within the general structure of the ICC. See Sacerdot, "The New Arbitration Rules of ICC and UNCITRAL," 11 J. World Trade L. 248, 250 (1977). The literature on the history, functions, and procedures of the ICC Court of Arbitration is very extensive. See, e.g., W. Craig, W. Park, & J. Paulsson, International Chamber of Commerce Arbitration (2d ed. 1990); Kassis, "The Questionable Validity of Arbitration and Awards under the Rules of the International Chamber of Commerce," 6 J. Int'l Arb. 79 (1989); Comment, "A Survey of Arbitral Forums: Their Significance and Procedure," 5 N.C.J. Int'l L. & Comm. Reg. 219 (1980); Jarvin, "The Enforcement of ICC Arbitral Awards," Rev. Dr. Aff. Int'l 241 (1988).
2 The AAA was founded in 1926 through the merger of two prior organizations, the Arbitra-

tion Society of America and the Arbitration Foundation. It has its headquarters at 140 West 51st Street in New York, with twenty-six other regional offices throughout the United States. It has a panel of arbitrators comprising of persons qualified in many domestic and international law fields. Discussions on the AAA are provided in International Commercial Arbitration in New York (J. McClendon & R. Goodman eds. 1986); Comment, supra note 1, at 220–26.

3 The London Court of International Arbitration is one of the oldest arbitration bodies in the world. It deals with all types of commercial disputes. L. Kos-Rabcewicz-Zubkowski & P. Davidson, Commercial Arbitration Institutions 66 (1986). Its aim is "to provide rules, services, and facilities for the settlement of arbitration of any dispute, commercial or otherwise and wherever occurring, which may properly be submitted to arbitration." Id.

4 The Arbitration Institute of the Stockholm Chamber of Commerce (SCC Institute) evolved from a committee created in 1917 by the Stockholm Chamber of Commerce to settle commercial disputes. See Arbitration in Sweden 5 (2d rev'd. ed. SCC, 1984). The SCC Institute is now recognized as a major international arbitration institute. See Wetter, "East Meets West in Sweden," 13 Int'l Law 261 (1979). The SCC Institute acts in accordance with its own rules as well as any other rules connected with arbitration. In particular, it is willing to act as appointing authority under the UNCITRAL Arbitration Rules. Arbitration in Sweden, id. For more detailed discussions, see generally Alley, "International Arbitration: The Alternative of the Stockholm Chamber of Commerce," 22 Int'l Law 837 (1988); Comment, supra note 1, at 235–37.

5 U.N. Comm'n on Int'l Trade Law, Arbitration Rules (1976), reprinted in 15 I.L.M. 701 (1976). The UNCITRAL rules were adopted by the UN General Assembly in December 1976. See UNCITRAL Report, 31 U.N. GAOR Supp. (No. 17) at 34, U.N. Doc. A/31/17 (1976). The rules can be used in both ad hoc and institutional arbitration if the parties so agree. McLaughlin, "Arbitration and Developing Countries," 13 Int'l Law 211, 228 (1979); I. Dore, Arbitration and Conciliation Under the UNCITRAL Rules: A Textual Analysis (1986).

6 See, e.g., Arbitration (Foreign Awards and Agreements) Act 1974 (An Act to approve Accession by Australia to a Convention on the Recognition and Enforcement of Foreign Arbitral Awards, to give effect to that Convention, and for related purposes), reprinted in Int'l Handbook on Comm. Arb. Supp. 8 (ICCA, Dec. 1987); The Commercial Arbitration Rules of the Korean Commercial Arbitration Board (As approved by the Supreme Court on 21 May 1981 and 11 May 1983), reprinted in Int'l Handbook on Comm. Arb. Supp. 6 (ICCA, Nov. 1986); International Arbitration Convention (Concordat), 27 August 1969, and chap. 12 of the Swiss Private International Law Act of 18 December 1987, reprinted in Int'l Handbook on Comm. Arb. Supp. 9 (ICCA, Sept. 1988).

7 See supra discussion in the Introduction.

8 See supra chapter 2.

9 See supra chapter 2, fns. 12–15 and accompanying text. For a discussion of the ICC's internal "court," see generally W. Craig, W. Park, & J. Paulsson, International Chamber of Commerce Arbitration (2d ed. 1990).

10 Convention on the Recognition and Enforcement of Foreign Arbitral Awards, 21 U.S.T. 2517, T.I.A.S. No. 6997, 330 U.N.T.S. 38 [hereinafter New York Convention].

For details of the New York Convention and relevant implementing legislation, see Aksen, "American Arbitration Accession Arrives in the Age of Aquarius: United States Implements United Nations Convention on the Recognition and Enforcement of Foreign Arbitral Awards," 3 Sw. U.L. Rev. 1 (1971).

11 As of January 1991 the following states were parties: Algeria, Antigua; Argentina; Aus-

tralia; Austria; Bahrain; Belgium; Benin; Botswana; Bulgaria; Burkina Faso; Byelorussian Soviet Socialist Rep.; Cambodia; Cameroon; Canada; Central African Rep.; Chile; China; Colombia; Costa Rica; Cuba; Cyprus; Czechoslovakia; Denmark; Djibouti; Dominica; Ecuador; Egypt; Finland; France; German, Fed. Rep.; Ghana; Greece; Guatemala; Guinea; Haiti; Holy See; Hungary; India; Indonesia; Ireland; Israel; Italy; Ivory Coast; Japan; Jordan; Kenya; Korea; Kuwait; Lesotho; Luxembourg; Madagascar; Malaysia; Mexico; Monaco; Morocco; Netherlands; New Zealand; Niger; Nigeria; Norway; Panama; Peru; Philippines; Poland; Romania; San Marino; Singapore; South Africa; Spain; Sri Lanka; Sweden; Switzerland; Syrian Arab Rep.; Tanzania; Thailand; Trinidad & Tobago; Tunisia; Ukrainian Soviet Socialist Rep.; Union of Soviet Socialist Reps.; United Kingdom; United States; Uruguay; Yugoslavia. See Treaties in Force (U.S. Dept. State, 1989); see also 9 USCA § 201, at 197) (West Supp. 1989). Argentina ratified the convention on March 14, 1989. See 29 I.L.M. 212 (1990).

12 Article 5(2) of the New York Convention provides:

> 2. Recognition and enforcement of an arbitral award may also be refused if the competent authority in the country where recognition and enforcement is sought finds that:
> (a) The subject matter of the difference is not capable of settlement by arbitration under the law of that country; or
> (b) The recognition or enforcement of the award would be contrary to the public policy of that country.

13 Article 4 states:

> 1. To obtain the recognition and enforcement mentioned in the preceding article, the party applying for recognition and enforcement shall, at the time of the application, supply:
> (a) The duly authenticated original award or a duly certified copy thereof;
> (b) The original agreement referred to in Article II or a duly certified copy thereof.
> 2. If the said award or agreement is not made in an official language of the country in which the award is relied upon, the party applying for recognition and enforcement of the award shall produce a translation of these documents into such language. The translation shall be certified by an official or sworn translator or by a diplomatic or consular agent.

14 See Van den Berg, infra note 23.

15 International Standard Electric Corporation v. Bridas Sociedad Anonima Petrolera, Industrial y Comercial 745 F. Supp. 172 (S.D.N.Y. 1990) at 178.

16 Id. at 177.

17 The relevant part of the French text states: "1. *La reconnaissance et l'éxecution de la sentence ne seront refusées, sur requête de la partie contre laquelle elle est invoquée, que si cette partie fournit a l'autorité competente du pays où la reconnaissance et l'execution sont demandées la preuve.*"

18 The relevant part of the Spanish text provides: "*Solo se podrá denegar el reconocimiento y la ejecución de la sentencia, a instancia de la parte contra la cual es invocada, si esta parte prueba ante la autoridad competente del pais en que se pide el reconocimiento y la ejecución.*"

19 See Vienna Convention on the Law of Treaties, adopted May 22, 1969, U.N. Doc. A/CONF./39/27 (1969), reprinted in 63 Am. J. Int'l L. 875 (1969).

20 Article 31 of the Vienna Convention provides:

> 1. A treaty shall be interpreted in good faith in accordance with the ordinary meaning to be given to the terms of the treaty in their context and in the light of its object and purpose.
> 2. The context for the purpose of the interpretation of a treaty shall comprise, in addition to the text, including its preamble and annexes:
> (a) any agreement relating to the treaty which was made between all the parties in connexion with the conclusion of the treaty;
> (b) any instrument which was made by one or more parties in connexion with the conclusion of the treaty and accepted by the other parties as an instrument related to the treaty.
> 3. There shall be taken into account, together with the context:
> (a) any subsequent agreement between the parties regarding the interpretation of the treaty or the application of its provisions;
> (b) any subsequent practice in the application of the treaty which establishes the agreement of the parties regarding its interpretation;
> (c) any relevant rules of international law applicable in the relations between the parties.
> 4. A special meaning shall be given to a term if it is established that the parties so intended.

21 See supra pp. 70–71.

22 See especially, Paulsson, "Arbitration Unbound: An Award Detached From the Law of its Country of Origin," 30 Int'l. & Comp. L. Q. 358 (1981); Paulsson "Delocalization of International Commercial Arbitration," 32 Int'l. & Comp. L. Q. 53 (1983). Paulsson is the most cogent of the exponents of this view.

23 Van den Berg, The New York Arbitration Convention of 1958: Toward a Uniform Judicial Interpretation 355 (1981).

24 Restatement (Third) of the Foreign Relations Law of the United States (1987), chap. 8, "Foreign Judgments and Awards."

25 13 U.L.A. 263.

26 Libya v. Libyan American Oil Co. (LIAMCO) (S. Crt., Switz), reprinted in 20 I.L.M. 151 (1981).

27 Foreign Sovereign Immunities Act, 90 Stat. 2891, 28 U.S.C. §§ 1330, 1332(a)(2)(3)(4), 1391(f), 1441(d), 1602–11, reprinted in 15 I.L.M. 1388 (1976). For recent amendments to the act, see "United States: Amendments to the Foreign Sovereign Immunities Act," 28 I.L.M. 396 (1989).

28 Verlinden B.V. v. Central Bank of Nigeria, 647 F.2d 320 (2d Cir. 1981).

29 Maatschappij voor Industriele Research en Ontwikkeling B. V. v. M. Liebremont et autre (Cour de Cassation, 1st Civ. Ch, May 25, 1983), reprinted in 12 Y.B. Comm. Arb. (1987); Henri Liebremont and Adolphe Cominassi v. Maatschappij voor Industriele Research en Ontwikkeling B.V. (President Rechtbank, Zutphen, Dec. 9, 1981), reprinted in 12 Y.B. Comm. Arb. (1987).

30 Norsolor S.A. v. Pabalk Ticaret Ltd. (Austrian S. Crt, Nov. 1982), reprinted in part in 9 Y.B. Comm. Arb. 159, 162–63 (1984).

31 The decision by the French Court of Appeal to adjourn the enforcement action pending a decision on Pablak's appeal is discussed in 8 Y.B. Comm. Arb. 364 (1983).

32 Id. at 365.

33 Reprinted in 11 Y.B. Comm. Arb. 484 (1986) (Cour de Cassation, First Civil Chamber, 9 Oct. 1984).

34 473 U.S. 614 (1985).

35 Id. at 638.

36 Park, "National Law and Commercial Justice: Safeguarding Procedural Integrity in International Arbitration," 63 Tul. L. Rev. 647 (1989).

37 Id. at 670.

38 See, e.g., The Netherlands Arbitration Act CCP Book IV, 1 December 1986, reprinted in Int'l Handbook on Comm. Arb. Supp. 7 (ICCA, April 1987)(1986 Arbitration Act replacing Dutch arbitration law contained in the Code of Civil Procedure of 1838); Decree No. 81.500, May 12, 1981, reprinted in Int'l Handbook on Comm. Arb. Supp. 1, annex 1 (ICCA, May 1984) (new French law completely reorganizing the French legal system concerning arbitration); Judicial Code, sixth part; Arbitration (adopted 4 July 1972 and amended 27 March 1985), reprinted in Int'l Handbook on Comm. Arb. Supp. 8, annex 1 (ICCA, Dec. 1987) (Amendment to Article 1717 of the Judicial Code stating that the Belgian Court "can take cognizance of an application to set aside only if at least one of the parties to the dispute decided in the arbitral award is either a physical person having Belgian nationality or residing in Belgium, or a legal person formed in Belgium or having a branch [*une succursale*] or some seat of operation [un siege quelconque d'operation] there."); see also UN Model Law on International Commercial Arbitration, 1985, annex 1 to U.N. Doc. A/40/17. As Redfern and Hunter explain, although the Model Law was prepared with the understanding that it would apply to "international commercial arbitration," there is nothing to stop national legislatures from giving it to a more extensive application. See A. Redfern & M. Hunter, International Commercial Arbitration 389 (1986).

39 See generally, Arbitration Act, 1950, 14 Geo. 6, c. 27. See also Park, "Judicial Supervision of Transnational Commercial Arbitration: The English Arbitration Act of 1979," 21 Harv. Int'l L.J. 87 (1980).

40 Arbitration Act, 1979, chap. 42. For a general discussion on the act, see Comment, "England and Wales: Arbitration Act of 1979," 13 J. World Trade L. 463 (1979).

41 Arab African Energy Corp. v. Olieprodukten Nederland B.V., [1983] Lloyd's Rep. 419 (Q.B.).

42 Park, supra note 36, at 693. For a more expansive view of the role of courts in cases of alleged arbitral misconduct, see Mustil & Boyd, The Law and Practice of Commercial Arbitration in England 646–48 (2d ed., 1989).

43 Nouveau Code de Procédure Civile.

44 Id.

45 Article 1065, Burgerlijke Rechtsvordering, reprinted in 12 New Book of Commercial Arbitration 370, 383 (1987).

46 See footnote 47 infra, for references to the Rules and scholarly discussion of them.

47 See Broches, "1985 UNCITRAL Model Law on International Commercial Arbitration: An Exercise in International Legislation," 18 Neth. Y.B. Int'l L. 3 (1987); Ungar, "The Enforcement of Arbitral Awards under UNCITRAL's Model Law on International Commercial Arbitration," 25 Columb. J. Transnat'l L. 717 (1987).

48 See 392 Parl. Deb., H.L. (5th ser.) 99 (1978), discussed in Park, supra note 36, at 96.

49 See Park, id.

50 Code Judiciare, Article 1717.

51 Id. For an enthusiastic support of the law, see Paulsson, supra note 22.

52 Loi Federale sur le Droit International Privé, Article 192.

53 For authentic texts and doctrinal comment see Lalive, Poudret, & Reymond, Le Droit de l'arbitrage interne et international en Suisse (1989).

54 See Park, supra note 36.

55 See supra note 40.

56 It is, one should add, far from certain that prudent rational actors will elect Belgian-type jurisdictions. To date it appears that there has not been a stampede to Belgium.

57 Island of Palmas Case, 2 U.N. Rep. Int'l Arb. Awards 829 (1928).

58 For two representative pieces on Goldman's views, see Goldman, "L'arbitrage, les conflicts de lois et la lex mercatoria," in L'arbitrage Commercial International 103 (1984); Goldman, "The Applicable Law: General Principles of Law—The Lex Mercatoria," in Contemporary Problems in International Arbitration 113 (J. Lew ed. 1987). See also Lando, "The Lex Mercatoria in International Commercial Arbitration," 34 Int'l & Comp. L. Q. 747 (1985).

59 O. Glossner, The Influence of the International Chamber of Commerce on Modern Arbitration in 60 Years of ICC Arbitration: A Look at the Future 399, 403 (1984).

60 G.A. Res. 2625 (XXII) October 24, 1970.

61 G.A. Res. 3281, 29 U.N. GAOR Supp. (No. 31) at 50, U.N. Doc. A/9631 (1974).

62 Texaco Overseas Petroleum Co. and California Asiatic Co. v. Libyan Arab Republic, 17 I.L.M. 1 (1978).

63 Id. at para. 25.

64 See, for example, The Protection of Trading Interests Act, 1980, expressing the British response to U.S. claims.

5 The System and Self

1 For a discussion of the implications of role fidelity in law, see W.M. Reisman, Folded Lies: Bribery, Crusades and Reforms 132–37 (1979).

2 Weisburd, Wheeler, Waring & Bode, Crimes of the Middle Classes 184 (1991).

3 For elaboration, see McDougal, Lasswell & Reisman, "The World Constitutive Process of Authoritative Decision," in 1 Black & Falk eds., The Future of the International Legal Order 73 (1969). Also published in 19 J. Legal Ed. 253, 403 (1967) and reprinted in M. McDougal & W.M. Reisman, International Law Essays 191 (1981).

4 These themes are explored in Reisman, "The Tormented Conscience: Applying and Appraising Unauthorized Coercion," 32 Emory L.J. 499 (1983), especially at 530–37.

Table of Cases: Arbitration

Index

W. Michael Reisman, Wesley Newcomb Hohfield Professor of Jurisprudence at Yale Law School, is the author of numerous books, including *Folded Lies: Bribery, Crusades and Reforms* and *Nullity and Revision: The Review and Enforcement of International Judgments and Awards.*

Library of Congress Cataloging-in-Publication Data
Reisman, W. Michael (William Michael), 1939–
Systems of control in international adjudication and arbitration : breakdown and repair / W. Michael Reisman.
Includes bibliographical references (p.) and index.
ISBN 0-8223-1202-6 (cl.: alk. paper)
1. Arbitration and award, International. 2. Arbitration, International. 3. International courts. I. Title.
K2400.R45 1992
341.5'22—dc20 91-33033 CIP